football!

Then strip lads, and to it, though sharp be the weather,
And if, by mischance, you should happen to fall,
There are worse things in life than a tumble on heather,
And life is itself but a game of foot-ball!
Sir Walter Scott, 1815

Some people think football is a matter of life and death.
I don't like that attitude. I can assure them it is much
more serious than that.

Bill Shankly
Manager of Liverpool Football Club, 1973

the story
of all the world's
football games

FOOTBALL!

NICHOLAS MASON

TEMPLE SMITH · LONDON

First published in Great Britain 1974 by
Maurice Temple Smith Ltd
37 Great Russell Street, London WC1

© 1974 Nicholas Mason
ISBN 0 8511 7063 3

Type set at Western Printing Services Ltd, Bristol
Printed by Clarke, Doble & Brendon Ltd, Plymouth

contents

illustrations

between pages 160 and 161

Front endpapers: Association Football in the 1880s *Football Association*
Back endpapers: The Yale–Princeton game, 1898 *Culver Pictures Inc.*

TO JANE
and the children

acknowledgements

The original idea for this book was suggested to me by Godfrey Smith, perennial host at the finest hamper lunches to be found in Twickenham's East Car Park on international-match Saturdays. The initial impetus he gave to the book, and his subsequent interest in its development, did much to ensure its eventual completion.

Football, in all its forms, is rich in its historians, its evangelists, its statisticians and its devoted commentators, and my debt to their work can be gauged from the bibliography on page 234. But it would be unfair to deny two books a special mention here: Percy Young's *A History of British Football* is an incomparable study of the origin and early years of Soccer, and any orderly impressions of football's evolution in Britain that might emerge from my early chapters are in large part due to the lucidity of Dr Young's scholarly and thoroughly readable account. Similarly, any examination of the early, frenetic years of American College Football would have proved very difficult without *Oh, How They Played the Game*, a remarkable collection of articles and interviews edited with wit and authority by Allison Danzig. To the student of football's past, both books are essential reading.

More immediate assistance has been generously given. Norman Harris and Dudley Doust both cast expert eyes over large sections of the manuscript, and the authoritative advice offered by Brendan MacLua and Bruce Andrew respectively on the Gaelic and Australian codes was invaluable. To all of them I am extremely grateful, as I am to Sheila McNeil, who typed the manuscript; to Philip Norman, Peter Gillman and Gilvrie Misstear for their contributions to my American research; to Ken Lewis for the diagrams in the Appendix; to Colin Jacobson for his help in accumulating the illustrations; and to my wife Jane, not only for her work on the index once the book was finished, but primarily for her incalculable patience and support while it was being written.

introduction

'So you're writing a book about football', he said, in the unmistakable accents of Merseyside, telegraphing in his good-natured belligerence an uncomfortable half-hour's ear-bending about The Greatest Team in the World. I mentally tossed a coin—heads it's Everton, tails it's Liverpool—and called heads. Wrong again! 'You've got to have a chapter about Bill Shankly, you know. You can't write a book about football without a chapter on Bill Shankly. He's only created the greatest team in the world, that's what he's done . . . only the greatest bloody team in the world.'

I mumbled something about Bill Shankly being a remarkable manager, about Liverpool being a very good team at the moment, about my book being planned on a rather wider scale, about the need to cover all sorts of other football codes, like Rugby and American and Gaelic Football, as well as almost a century of Soccer before Bill Shankly even joined Liverpool.

In any case, I said, sensing hostility and back-pedalling furiously, dozens of people had written chapters and hundreds more had written articles about Bill Shankly and his beloved Liverpool, and of course no one could hope to survey the contemporary English Soccer scene without whole sections devoted to Bill Shankly. It was just that mine wasn't quite that sort of book . . .

'It's about football, isn't it?'

'Well, yes, but . . .'

'You *can't* write a book about football without a chapter on Bill Shankly.'

And you can't, I have begun to fear, write a book about football without a chapter on Vince Lombardi or Collingwood Football Club or the mighty Kerry teams in the 1920s or the Washington Redskins or Helenio Herrera or Carwyn James and the goalposts at Llanelli. For football is an intensely personal game, a game arousing loyalties and passions of an uncompromising, blinkered parochialism. To the supporter of Liverpool, football is a game that every Englishman worth his salt watches on a Saturday afternoon from behind the Kop goal at Anfield. He has never heard of Vince Lombardi; he has never heard of the Green Bay Packers, whom Lombardi nursed back to glory in the 1960s like another Shankly; he has probably

never seen, not even on his world-shrinking television, the game that the
Packers play, with their vast squads of players and their shoulder-pads,
their knee-breeches and their crash-helmets.

Yet the Packers play football, just as Liverpool play football, and as the
Rugby men of Wanganui play football and dream of an All Black shirt,
and as the men of Cork and Galway play their own football, and as the
bronzed young giants of the Melbourne suburbs play football on their
vast oval fields, and as the boys of Eton College, on a muddy pitch six
yards wide along the side of an ancient wall, also play football.

It is this game, this whole family of games, so different in detail and so
closely related in their background, that forms the subject of this book.
One hundred and fifty years ago football was virtually non-existent
outside the British Isles, and even here it was a formless throwback, a piece
of traditional rough-house to warm the feet on Boxing Day, or on Shrove
Tuesday to hold at bay the gloomy prospect of Lent. Adapted as a convenient form of winter recreation by the British public schools and universities, a free-ranging, unpretentious form of football was embraced by
a newly leisure-conscious Victorian society with the sort of passion
generally reserved by Englishmen for non-conformist religious movements or abuse of the French.

The game's evolution might easily have been halted there and then,
dictated by the idealistic young men feverishly attempting to standardise
the rules. Cricket, England's other great game, had evolved to something
like its present state of development by the start of the 19th century, and
has remained much the same ever since: no internal squabbles leading to
seven-man cricket on a triangular pitch; no hybrid American breakaway
played in a maze of concentric boundaries. But cricket had, by some
miracle, evolved as a game of both town and countryside, of the farm and
the manor. Football, by contrast, was a diverse, parochial ritual with
fierce local loyalties.

Between 1850 and 1875 five distinct, separate and incompatible football
games, each jealously guarding its young traditions, had sprung from the
same fertile root. All these branches are flourishing still, and several more
have joined them.

They have made football an international language and a universal
preoccupation. In the British Isles four types of the game—Gaelic and
Association Football, Rugby Union and Rugby League—regularly pull
in crowds of 50,000. In South America Soccer has assumed a deep national
importance ('You *can't* write a book about football without having a
chapter on Pele'). In the United States their characteristic brand is
spectacular big business. In Australia, their very own creation, the biggest

and most spectacular of all football games, draws blanket television coverage every week and crowds of 100,000 to an important game.

This book is an attempt to examine the family of Football as a whole—to establish, if possible, why there should be a dozen codes rather than just one; how these developed from common beginnings; how they faced the disturbing transition from a friendly weekend pastime to a furiously contested, mass spectator sport; how the games formed their differing attitudes to the insidious approaches of professionalism; how they have coped with the demands for more and more competition; how they have spawned heroes to be idolised, to be imitated and to hawk detergents on television; how the attitudes of their theorists and their administrators have, with subtle tactics or bulldozing legislation, all perceptibly widened the gulfs that separate the members of the family.

On the formation of the Football Association in 1863, every possible attempt was made to legislate for a universal game, a football code that would satisfy both Rugby men and 'dribbling' men and eventually, one would imagine, the Irish and the Australians and the Americans as well. As there is now a rich variety of football where there might have been only a single specimen, we must be grateful that these efforts failed; but in another sense football *has* become the one great universal game. The emotions aroused by a goal in São Paolo or a touchdown in Kansas City or a try in Cardiff or a high mark in Melbourne are identical—a ritual release of tension, recognised instantly in a Soccer crowd or a Rugby crowd or an American Football crowd. The members of football's family may all have matured in isolation—the rule-makers of one code acting quite without reference to those of another, the stars of one code provoking extravagant headlines if they presume to transfer their skills to another—but the essential excitement of the game remains constant. That is why the supporters of Liverpool Football Club, though they may admit the existence of no other game but Soccer, can by their very appreciation of Soccer's intricacies warm to the skills of Rugby's Barry John or American Football's Don Maynard.

I have tried to show that it is one game, albeit in a variety of disguises, rather than a dozen different games, that has stirred the emotions of the world; that there is no essential difference between the thrill a veteran Rugby follower feels at the recollection of George Nepia and that felt by his American counterpart at the memory of Red Grange. The adulation of the football fan for his hero may be partisan, sectarian, selfish, jingoistic; but it is a partisanship shared and understood throughout the game. Harry Vassall caused hearts to beat faster at Oxford, just as Steve Bloomer did at Derby and Pudge Heffelfinger did at Yale. The men who roared for

Ronnie Poulton at Twickenham shared a common excitement with those who roared for Jim Sullivan at Wigan or for Polly Farmer at Perth or Ferenc Puskas in Budapest or Mick O'Connell in Killarney. And the inspiration of Amos Alonzo Stagg, goading generation after generation of Chicago students into match-winning combinations, has been echoed in its tactical genius and masterly man-management across the whole spectrum of the game—by Herbert Chapman at Arsenal, by Knute Rockne at Notre Dame, by Vittorio Pozzo at Turin, by Danie Craven at Johannesburg, by Paul Brown at Cleveland. And, of course, by Bill Shankly at Liverpool.

By tinkering with the rules, men have created a whole kaleidoscope of football games; but they have been unable to tinker with the triumphs and the disappointments, the week-by-week compulsiveness, the sheer excitement of speed and skill and courage. However far the members of the family of football may seem to drift apart, these will always be there to hold it together.

1

the founding fathers

Early Football: the Dark Ages to 1863

Football was first banned in Britain, so far as we can tell, in the year 1314, when that least prepossessing of Plantagenet kings, Edward II, objected to a 'great noise in the city caused by bustling over large balls'. Football was by then a popular and universal town game, with a long if not particularly honourable history. It was a rough game, too; the British sense of fair play in the 14th century fell a long way short of the public school ideals of the 19th. Some thirty years even before Edward's peevish complaint, a certain Henry of Ellington was unfortunate enough to run into one of the opposing defenders during a game of football at Ulgham, in Northumberland; this defender, David le Keu, was wearing a knife at the time (whether as part of his football kit, or merely workaday apparel which he had omitted to take off, is not revealed). Henry died of his wounds. And in the earliest years of the 14th century Adam of Salisbury met the same fate while playing football in the High Street at Oxford. Today anyone playing football in the High Street at Oxford would be killed by a bus; Adam was killed by an enraged team of Irish students.

The game, even allowing for daggers and Irish students, was clearly an extremely robust one at this stage in its development. In the course of the next 150 years the bans were posted thick and fast. Edward III, a considerably sterner monarch than his father, commanded the sheriffs of London to suppress 'games, football being an example', on the grounds that bowmanship was being neglected. (This was in 1349, and a slightly churlish backhander for the archers who had so humbled the French at Crécy only three years before: rather as if the Government had banned football in 1948 because not enough young men were training with the Territorial Army.) In 1389 Richard II placed a ban on all 'playing at tennis, football and other games'. His deposer Henry IV re-enacted the same ban, and in 1410 sought to raise a little extra money by imposing a 20s. fine on mayors who allowed the game to be played within their jurisdiction. Not only the monarchy was distressed by this rowdy British pastime. The town of Halifax fined people 1s. in the 1450s if they were caught playing dice, bowls or football. Soon afterwards, the game was prohibited in Leicester.

The clergy, to their credit, customarily turned a benevolent eye towards football—indeed, they anticipated professionalism by some 450 years by paying local players 'gifts to the value of 4*d*.' to play the game on the feast of St Catherine in the grounds of Bicester Priory, but even they had been publicly warned against the game by the Synod of Ely in 1364. Chester, a stronghold of the game for years, where the shoemakers of the city had provided a three-and-fourpenny leather ball every year for the annual set-to, thought the better of its own irresponsibility in 1539 and instead offered 'six darts of silver' as prizes in an annual running race. In the same century Londoners faced prison for playing football in the City. Early in the next century Manchester, beset, so the records say, by 'lewd and disordered persons' breaking windows, imposed a twelve-penny fine on footballers.

If England appears to have been less than encouraging to the spiritual ancestors of Bloomer and Dean and Matthews and Charlton, Scotland certainly provided no haven. James I of Scotland, having spent 19 years in prison in England, passed an Act of Parliament on his return, forbidding football on pain of a fine of a staggering 50*s*. James II followed suit. So did James III and James IV. James V, who was only one year old when he came to Scotland's throne, and may thus be excused for failing in family solidarity, apparently forgot to ban football (though there is no evidence that he actually played it) but James VI restored the balance on becoming James I of England, by expressly forbidding his son Henry from 'rough and violent exercises at football'.

This melancholy list of official repression against innocent public pleasure (or, from the opposite point of view, this honourable roll of administrative courage in combatting riotous hooliganism) did not coincide with the start of football in Britain, nor, in any context of martyrdom or glamorous outlawry, could it be considered the making of football. The bans lasted for roughly 300 years, from Edward II's order in 1314 to the municipal by-law passed against footballers by Manchester in 1608. The one thing that emerged virtually unchanged from this period of official disapproval was football itself. It may or may not have been feasible to ban football in the streets and yards of Edinburgh and London and Glasgow, but it was virtually impossible to ban it from every town and village in the British Isles. The British—Celts as well as Anglo-Saxons—wanted to play football, and it had proved impossible to stop them.

Football's nature is a curious one. It is a war-game and at the same time a game of the most delicate finesse. Throughout its long history it has had to walk the tightrope between skill and violence. Its ancestors—indeed, certain of its offshoots—had in some cases opted for one element and abandoned the other. In China, under the Han Dynasty, which ended in A.D. 220, 'footballers' with the skill of jugglers rather than those of mid-field ball-winners played *Tsu-Chu* ('kickball') on the Emperor's birthday, contriving to kick a ball through holes in silk curtains. In Ancient Mexico delicacy rather than drive was needed to prosper in the ceremonial game in which balls were hit with the feet, shoulders and heads through rings set high in the temple wall. In Thailand even today they play a strange, juggling game with a wickerwork ball, with heads, shoulders, thighs and legs, with no goals and no points, only admiration for skill, artistry and, one feels, patience.

If ball skills were old, violence was equally well established. In Classical Greek times ball games involving free use of the hands were an integral part of the ceremonial athletic festivals. The Roman legions developed, probably from the Greek games, the game of *harpastum*, a war-game with a ball that came three-quarters of the way to modern football. They needed a rectangle of land, which was easy to come by, a ball and two teams. Team A tried to force the ball, by whatever means possible, across the line defended by Team B, and vice versa. Save for a few refinements, the addition of some of the ancient skills, and the re-allocation of certain roles to certain players, there is very little difference between this and American Football, or Rugby League; and though the means have been modified, the ends are identical.

For centuries after the Romans had abandoned their camps and cities in Britain and France, their game was imitated and adapted and accepted into local customs. Some say that the Shrove Tuesday game at Derby goes back to A.D. 217, when a British team beat a team of Roman legion-aries in the town. (Or does it, as some believe, commemorate a much later skirmish between Danes and Saxons?) At any rate, it developed over the years into a parish battle, with All Saints defending the waterwheel at Nun's Mill against St Peter's, whose goal was a prominent gate about a mile from town. On Shrove Tuesday, too, the massed villagers of Ash-bourne, in Derbyshire, would cross and recross the village stream, defending and attacking in turn the church gates at one end and Ash-bourne Hall gates at the other (the scorer of a goal used to get 10*s*.).

In Workington, Cumberland, the Colliers (the Uppies) had to force the ball over the gates of Curwen's Hall while the Sailors (the Downies) had to hit the harbour capstan. In Cornwall, the mass game across open country was called 'hurling'; in Normandy *Choule*; in Brittany *La Soule*. In all cases a soldiers' rowdy battle, half-earnest and half-fun, had become

folk custom, a way of letting off steam, of proving strength, perhaps of
settling old scores. But a way, too, of chasing a ball across a meadow just
for the joy of it.

Within a century of the Norman Conquest football had also established
itself in the life of London. By 1175 football was readily accepted by the
clergy and the aldermen alike as part of an annual festival; students
played apprentices—probably at Smithfield—and the City Fathers came
on horseback to watch and cheer.

It does not sound from this like a game that was heading for trouble.
But in the century following, football must somehow have tilted out of
balance. True, there is not a lot of evidence of skill and artistry tempering
the sheer muscular endeavour of apprentice and scholar. But there was
enough entertainment, enough *excitement*, in the game to attract spectators
and to establish it as a regular spectacle. In the coming years the entertainment must have dwindled, the rivalries intensified, the methods
become more and more direct, and football became a fight. The men who
banned football were not religious bigots, nor well-known killjoys, nor
specially noted for deliberately taking steps to displease their subjects,
unless they had a new tax in mind. Football in the 14th, 15th and 16th
centuries had become anti-social, and as such had to be curbed. (It was to
suffer the same strictures, but for a far shorter period of time, in America
in the late 1890s. The laws of American College Football at that time were
so ill-regulated that the death-rate of young American undergratudates
was leaping every autumn. Both the services colleges, West Point and
Annapolis, as well as a number of smaller colleges, cancelled their fixtures,
and in 1905 Theodore Roosevelt threatened to outlaw football altogether
unless there was a change in the laws. He won his point and the American
game survived, but the parallel is striking.)

Today, such various forms of football as survive have written rules that,
drawn up and amended over a whole century, keep football, in the main,
on the acceptable side of the line dividing expertise from sheer power.
At times both American Football and Rugby Union have had to alter their
rules to keep the games on the right side of that line; Gaelic and Australian
Football, their critics might say, stray all too often on to the wrong side
without offending any written law; but on the whole the balance is
amicably kept, and the baying of blood-roused spectators is rarely echoed
in the actions of the players.

Despite James I's personal ban on his son playing football, the Elizabethan
Age in Britain had seen a much readier acceptance of the game by the
authorities. Either the bans had had their effect or, more likely, the 300

years of evolution since Edward II's day had allowed the game to mature
in entertainment value and grow out of its more objectionably violent
habits. By 1613 King James and Queen Anne were not only entertained
by music and a football match while travelling in Wiltshire, but actually
appointed the man who organised the game, the Rev. George Ferebe,
to a King's Chaplaincy. As all folk customs, however deeply rooted in
violence and vulgarity, achieve a respectability with time, so football was
becoming respectable. The puritan voice was still against it—the celebrated words of Philip Stubbs, attributing the imminent end of the world
to 'football playing and other devilishe pastimes', were written in 1583—
but nobody else was. Already Richard Mulcaster, Headmaster of Merchant Taylors' School and later High Master of St Paul's, was anticipating
Victorian attitudes in his theories of educating the whole man: in the
classics, of course, but in music, drama and athletics as well. And football,
said Mulcaster, 'strengtheneth and brawneth the whole body'. By the
1580s, too, the game was tolerated within the colleges at Cambridge,
though there were strict rules against playing in the public streets.

The game that had been too rough for whole towns to tolerate was now
practised everywhere; forty-two separate communities in the British Isles
celebrated Shrove Tuesday with a football match. Married men played
single men to provide the village with a whole year's chatter; masters
played with their servants; Oliver Cromwell played it at Sydney Sussex
College, and during his Commonwealth watched a hundred and fifty
Cornishmen demonstrate their version of the game in London. Pepys
knew about football and Charles II watched his servants playing it.

While this vogue was at its height in Britain, such English intellectuals
who were looking to the continent for cultural satisfaction were offered,
by the city of Florence, a subtler, more skilful form of football than they
had ever seen at home. This was *Calcio*, a game maintaining strong links
with medieval Italian chivalry. In its purest forms it must have been a
delicate blend of speed, toughness and artistry; by the 17th century it
had absorbed a lot of the robustness of town football, and the twenty-
seven-a-side matches played on stone city squares can hardly have appealed
to the effete. But *Calcio* had a touch of class, a game with enough romantic
association for men to write stories about it. Boccalini's *I Ragguagli di
Parnasso* (*Advertisements for Parnassus*), which was translated into English
in 1656, tells of a 'Spruce Foreign Courtier' arriving in Florence and,
virtually, challenging the Florentines at *Calcio*. True to all that is best in
schoolboy fiction, the Foreign Courtier made mincemeat of the opposition:
'whereas the Florentines, who were masters of the sport, thought to have
thrown him down, they were thrown down themselves ... And the

Courtier having overcome all that withstood him, threw the ball over the lists and won the Prize.'

This is the stuff of Robin Hood or King Arthur or Wyatt Earp; football was, even then, a game for heroes. By the end of the century Britain was receiving similar literary attention from abroad: Henri Mission de Valbourg, writing in France about his travels in England, said that in winter 'football is a useful and charming exercise . . . A leather ball is propelled by the feet through the streets by anyone who can get hold of it; there is nothing else to it.' No rowdiness? No violence? No bloody noses? The game for ruffians had become a 'useful and charming exercise'. Who knows, one day people might even pay to watch it played!

In Wales and Ireland, as in England, they were playing the game with vigour and with purpose. In some parts of the Celtic fringe the hurling tradition was maintained (not yet, as in modern Ireland, with staves to propel the ball; Cornish hurling in the 17th century was far closer to the Gaelic Football of today, with 'fifteen, twenty or thirty' players per side, and a strong tradition of man-to-man marking). But football in a more basic tradition—parish versus parish—was common too, and Christmas Day matches in Cardiganshire (between Llandryssul and Llanwenog) and in County Meath (between the Boyne men and the Nanny men) are described with relish by contemporary writers, particularly in the latter match, where some feeling was aroused by the Boyne men taunting the Nanny men about their tendency to adopt the habits of their English settlers. There were supporters, too. The old men and the women and children came to watch and cheer and tend to the wounded. Christmas Day in Llandryssul had all the hallmarks of New Year's Day in Glasgow: a holiday atmosphere, a football match to watch, a fierce local rivalry, a team with which to identify. It was no longer necessary to take part in the cross-country ball-hunts to enjoy football; it had become a spectator sport.

It seems strange, therefore, that by the beginning of the 19th century, the century in which football was to achieve a status and a popularity no mere game had ever before commanded, that both in England and Scotland writers were bewailing its decline, almost composing its obituary. One of them was Joseph Strutt, antiquary, engraver and novelist, who in 1801 published his *Pastimes of the People of England*. Strutt gives a fascinating description of how football was played—a game that would be perfectly familiar, in general terms, to anyone watching it today:

When a match at football is made an equal number of competitors take the field and stand between two goals placed at a distance of eighty or an hundred yards one from the other. The goal is usually made with two sticks driven into the ground about two or three feet apart. The ball, which is commonly made of a blown bladder and cased with leather, is delivered in the midst of the ground, and the object of each party is to drive it through the goal of their antagonists, which being achieved the game is won. The abilities of the performers are best displayed in attacking and defending the goals; and hence the pastime was more frequently called a goal at football than a game at football. When the exercise becomes exceedingly violent the players kick each others' shins without the least ceremony, and some of them are overthrown at the hazard of their limbs.

Not a bad game to watch, certainly. Skill was now clearly at a premium; attack and defence had already taken on their own specialist characteristics; violence may have been part of the programme, but it seems to have been given and received without rancour. The pitch, too, had been conveniently reduced to a mere 80 or 100 yards (modern dimensions, in fact) which made things far easier for spectators, who would have needed a sound-winded horse to follow the tides of attack and defence in the old inter-village games. The goals were very narrow; what 'driving' the ball through the opposing lines means is not explained (though both hands and feet were almost certainly employed). And the habit of ending the game once a goal had been scored, strange though it sounds, did not mean that everyone packed up and went home after the first score; a 'game' of football was won like a set at tennis. The winner got a point, the teams changed round, and the match continued. The habit of teams changing ends after a score survived late into the 19th century, and was part of the first set of rules drawn up by the Football Association in 1863.

Familiar though these conventions sound, they were not familiar, in any firsthand sense, to Joseph Strutt. He almost certainly wrote this account from hearsay, and he himself asserts that football, which was 'formerly much in vogue among the common people . . . of late years . . . seems to have fallen into disrepute and is but little practised'. The Industrial Revolution, the lure of the new working-class towns and the long, cruel hours of work necessary to earn a living there, had left football on one side; free time was short and the spirit, released for three or four public holidays in the year, was not willing. Not until the Factory Acts of the mid 19th century, when leisure was once again grudgingly granted to working men, women and children, did the town- and city-dwellers of industrial Britain feel the inclination to play and watch football again.

In Scotland, too, historians noted a decline in the game. Sir Walter Scott himself lamented what he saw as the passing of football, regretting that by now (this was 1815 or thereabouts) it was not always safe to have even the games between villagers as 'the old clannish spirit is too apt to break out'. The same old clannish spirit, presumably, that had caused so many Scottish King Jameses to pronounce their edicts against the game. It was not, however, so fearsome a spirit as to deter Sir Walter. One of the most celebrated occasions in Sport's Dark Ages was a football match between the men of Selkirk and the men of Yarrow on 5 December 1815. Not only did Scott, in his capacity as Keeper of the Forest, back the Selkirk team (the opposition were backed by the then Lord Home), he also wrote a ballad to commemorate the occasion, which was printed on broadsheets and handed to the spectators. Of these there were a reported 2,000—a crowd which would delight today's managers of Scottish Second Division clubs on most Saturdays of the season—and they were treated to a keenly contested double-header. The Selkirk men, distinguished by their 'slips of fir', won the first 90-minute game. The Yarrow team, in their 'sprigs of heath', took the second game, to make a decider necessary. But the banquet was already laid out on the tables. The teams were tired and thirsty. Sir Walter and Lord Home were content to call off their bets and the game was abandoned as a draw. Football may have been ailing in England and Scotland; but with games like this to punctuate the depressed years, it was hardly conceivable that it could die out.

The new momentum that was to bring the game back to England, Scotland and the rest of the world before the century was over, came not from the workers massed in the new, smoky cities nor from the villagers whose ancestors had played the game for so long. It came from the schools, the fast-expanding breeding-grounds of the professions, where a new class of Briton was being moulded.

   The public schools had been founded, in general, as charitable institutions, where a few poor but bright boys could receive the education they could otherwise never hope to pay for. From early in the 19th century, their role began to change. Thomas Arnold, headmaster of Rugby from 1827 to 1841, established a system of education which, it was firmly believed by both parents and Arnold's imitators, equipped young men for leadership. The basis of this leadership was corporate living and, to some extent, corporate teaching, with a well-defined line of command from headmaster to junior master to senior boys and finally to junior boys. With corporate living, inevitably, came corporate leisure. In the claustrophobic atmosphere of a boarding school, however well endowed, the sons of the landed gentry and the new rich merchant classes had little time and less opportunity to indulge in the shooting and fishing and riding and hunting that their home estates afforded; these, in any case, were individualist activities, and not part of the Arnold 'plan'. What they could play,

in the squares or the cloisters or the quadrangles or the surrounding fields
of their schools, were the games which they had seen, or which their
fathers and grandfathers had seen, at village festivals year after year:
football, a game that could be played anywhere, with any number in a
team, for as long as the players liked.

Dr Arnold was not a football enthusiast; it had been played at Rugby
to a pattern very close to the old village traditions for a long time before
he arrived there. What he did was merely to tolerate it. His disciples did
the rest; with the Arnoldian principles of education, they adopted, almost
as part of a 'package deal', a benevolent acceptance of football: old-estab-
lished schools like Eton, Charterhouse, Westminster, Harrow, Shrewsbury; new ones like Cheltenham, Marlborough, Uppingham, Wellington;
they became the stereotyped ideals of top people's education, and they all
played football with official blessing.

What is more, they each played it in different ways. The dogmatic
attitudes of the 1860s and 1870s by which football was irretrievably split
into two separate codes—handling and dribbling—were fostered, not by
deeply held principles of sporting ethics, but by the species of game allowed
at the various public schools in the first half of the century. And the
games evolved at the schools in direct relation to that part of the school
grounds where football was traditionally played. Thus Rugby, with the
whole spacious Close at its disposal, was able to develop a game with big
teams, long, high kicks, tall goals and concerted forward rushes. At Winchester the game was played in a long, narrow field without goals (a ball
kicked over the opposing 27-yard goal line counted as a score) and to keep
the scoring within practical limits dribbling was allowed among the
twenty-two players on each side—first-time kicking, as opposed to dribbling, being the customary way of gaining ground—and no kicking the
ball above shoulder height. At Harrow, where the game was played in a
generally muddy field at the foot of the famous Hill, football appears to
have been a far slower affair, with only eleven players (two backs and nine
forwards), a big, heavy ball to force through the mire, and restriction on
rough play.

The most famous, and understandably the least imitated, of all those
games whose form has been dictated by environment is the Eton Wall
Game. The Wall against which it was, and is, played was built in 1717,
and the game was well established by the start of the 19th century. It
occupied a pitch 120 yards long, with the Wall at one side and a line
parallel to it, just six yards away, as the touchline. The goals (as opposed
to the goal-lines, which were at either end of the Wall) were both some
distance from the pitch, one of them a small garden door, the other a tree

trunk. It was played with eighteen or twenty on a side, and took the form
of a long and heated rugger scrum, attempting for long periods at a time
to kick the ball through the opposing pack. After a particularly ferocious
fight in 1827 it was banned for ten years, and by the 1840s the Field
Game, a much more open game, played with eleven-a-side and without
the use of hands except to touch down for a score over the opposing line,
was being actively encouraged by the masters.

The Wall Game, where goals are scored with inspiring regularity
roughly once every twenty-five years, has atrophied into a little-appreciated
parody of itself over the last century and a half; the skills of Eton's Field
Game, however, where dribbling by packs of forwards was at a premium,
and where for some reason passing to one side or another was forbidden,
must have done much to contribute to the Soccer success of the Old
Etonians in the early years of the Football Association.

It was the restrictions of city buildings, however, that gave the dribbling
game its most important early exponents. At both Westminster and
Charterhouse (the latter school was housed in the City of London until
1872), the only space for the boys' outdoor recreation were the cloisters
and quadrangles of the old school buildings. At Charterhouse the game
that developed was a ferocious twenty-a-side affair down the length of a
long, brick cloister, open at one end and blocked in by a wall at the other.
No long kicks were allowed, no handling the ball, no passing forward;
dribbling the ball was the only way to make ground, and the natural sense
of preservation dissuaded players from too much falling or diving on the
stone floor. Thus, the charging packs of forwards adopted an upright
rather than a crouching stance—another characteristic of the early
Soccer, which received much of its impetus from the old boys of London's
public schools.

The conventions of these various school games were not, for many
years, given the formality of written rules. Football codes in the early
19th century were based on tradition, just as the old village and town
festival games had been. Senior boys taught junior boys what was expected
of them in the scrimmage: where they were supposed to stand, whether
or not they were allowed to pick the ball up in their hands, whether or not
they were allowed to advance ahead of the ball. But this informality could
not be allowed to last. Closed societies have always felt an urge to commit
their rituals to paper for the guidance of posterity; the young gentlemen
who every year reached the top echelons of the public schools, and thereby
achieved a measure of power in the school sphere which they could hardly
expect to wield in the outside world for another twenty years, were no
exception.

In retrospect it looks slightly ridiculous that all over Britain self-elected committees of 17-year-old sons of the landed gentry were solemnly writing down rules to govern what for years had been regarded as little more than a traditional school riot. Nevertheless, it is their persistence that gave football its first clear guidelines for future development. The busiest years of rule-making came between 1840 and 1860; the two most important sets of rules—partly because they are extant, partly because both contributed a lot to modern football codes—were those of Rugby and Harrow.

At Rugby the traditional football game was in an uncharacteristic state of uncertainty. Until the 1820s the customs had been well established and faithfully upheld, particularly the convention by which any player could catch the ball with his hands provided that he then kicked it back towards the opposition; running while carrying the ball was taboo. In 1823, however, as every Rugby player reverently tells his grandchildren, William Webb Ellis picked up the ball during a game on the Close, and ran with it. In many ways it was a curious action, not because a boy, frustrated with the school game, suddenly decided that the most efficient way to deposit the ball behind the opposing goal was to put it there himself, but because it actually attracted attention.

Had Rugby by then written down its rules, Webb Ellis would merely have been pulled up for unfair play and have conceded a free kick, and everyone would have forgotten about it. No Rugby player today is going to revolutionise the game by deciding in a flash of brilliant intuition that he can split defences more readily by passing forwards to his threequarters rather than backwards; that sort of inventiveness has been curbed by codification. And even in 1823 it is hard to imagine that Webb Ellis, in no way a school hero or a particularly notable figure at Rugby, was received with rapture after his piece of improvisation. If public schools at that time received flamboyant individualism with the same mistrust as they do today, Webb Ellis was probably kicked by his seniors, ignored by his contemporaries and giggled at behind his back by the juniors. But clearly he had given Rugby something to think about. The concept of 'running in'—the term adopted at Rugby to describe what Ellis did, the equivalent of scoring a try by carrying the ball across the line—was a step back towards the old and unsubtle village football of bullocking charges by hefty men forced forward by their colleagues; on the other hand, it made for spectacular and courageous action on the part of both attackers and defenders, and it took twenty years for the pros and the antis to sort out a satisfactory agreement.

Thomas Hughes, whose *Tom Brown's Schooldays* contains the famous account of a football match at Rugby, was himself at the School from the year 1834. In the 1880s a committee of Old Rugbeians, looking into the origins of Rugby Football, received a letter from Hughes saying that in 1834 'running with the ball to get a try by touching down within goal was not absolutely forbidden, but a jury of Rugby boys would almost certainly have found a verdict of "justifiable homicide" if a boy had been killed running in. The practice grew, and indeed became rather popular in 1838–9 from the prowess of Jem Mackie, the greater "runner in".'

By 1841, apparently, the rule-makers at Rugby had given in to the popularity of 'running in'. No longer was it ungentlemanly or bad form; so long as the ball was caught 'on the bound', running in was legal. (So influential were the rules of the schoolboys at Rugby that it was not until 1874, three years after the formation of the Rugby Union and the first England–Scotland international, that a player could pick up the ball at any time, not merely when it was 'on the bound'.)

The first surviving code of written rules we have for any football game was written at Rugby slightly later than this—in 1846. It contains such oddities as one stipulation against standing on the crossbar to stop a goal, and another that if a match was level after 1 p.m. it would be continued the next day and so on, with a limit of three days for a goalless draw or five days if goals had been scored. But the rules also laid down important precedents for the future: they set specific bounds for the game by forbidding players to take the ball off the Close. They defined a fair tackle (a player in possession could be held with one arm but not with two) and they legalised 'hacking' (i.e. the stopping of an opponent with the foot), allowing, in effect, a deliberate kick on his ankle or shin, but prohibiting a kick to the knee, thigh or groin. The margin for error must have been small, and the effects correspondingly painful.

At Harrow there was no such heresy as that committed by William Webb Ellis at Rugby, which, conversely, is why Harrow Football is not played round the world and why no Harrovian has had plaques raised to his memory, glorifying his 'fine disregard for the rules'. But the rigid conventions of Harrow's muddy game, well established by 1815 and certainly codified by 1830, were equally influential. It was played, with a fine disregard for laundry bills, in white ducks and black gaiters, over two days, with a ball of an 'irregular oval' shape and a rather meagre seven minutes each way for extra time in the event of a draw. Harrow, too, allowed a free kick if the ball were caught, but it could be carried only three paces in any direction. In no other circumstances could it be handled, a clear pointer to the Soccer tradition, particularly as in most of the kicking games of the time players were allowed to 'steady' the ball with their hand at any time. Charging, presumably with the shoulder, was allowed, but not holding, tripping, 'shinning' (Harrovian for 'hacking'), or pushing. Goal-kicks and throw-ins were defined (the latter executed with one hand, not two), and the principle of off-side was established, by which no one between the ball and the opposing goal could interfere with play.

Such rules as these—and there were many different codes drawn up by individual schools in the early years of Victoria's reign—were perfectly adequate so long as the games were confined within the schools themselves. Inter-school matches were not encouraged, so far as records show, until the 1850s, and regular fixtures under agreed rules were not common until Westminster and Charterhouse began a series of matches, under the rules of the 'dribbling' game they had regularised together in the early 1860s. But long before this, the future leaders of the nation, having taken their first steps on the ladder of command at their public school, had begun to meet the products of other public schools at Oxford and Cambridge and had begun to play football with them—a futile exercise without a common set of rules. To some undergraduates the football of others was understandably incomprehensible: 'My brother tells me,' wrote J. Venn in his *Early Collegiate Life* in 1913, 'that he remembers a friend coming into Hall and relating that he had seen a number of Rugby men, mostly freshmen, playing a new game: that "they made a circle round a ball and butted each other".' Any game of football at Oxford or Cambridge had necessarily to be preceded by a long wrangle between the two captains about the numbers of men per team, the rules about handling, about running with the ball, about hacking, about throw-ins, about off-side and like matters. All too often such communications were indecisive, leading to bad feeling on the pitch. The consequence was that football once again split up into public school factions, with Rugbeians preferring to play the game they knew with other Rugbeians, and so on.

Around 1840, however, it was clear that an attempt had to be made to work out common laws, and a former Shrewsbury schoolboy later wrote of drawing up a set of rules 'to be fair to all the schools' when he and others formed a football club at Cambridge some time between 1837 and 1842. Football had been strong at Shrewsbury (where it was called dowling, after the Greek word for 'slave'), and in the mid 1840s a number of Old Salopians and Old Etonians formed a Cambridge University team. In 1848 a workmanlike fourteen-man committee of both public school and non-public school men endured a seven-hour rule-making session to draw up the 'Cambridge Rules', many of which were incorporated in a further Cambridge set of Rules in the mid 1850s now surviving in the Shrewsbury School Library. These laws are once again a strong pointer towards the game of Soccer rather than to any game of man-to-man contact. No holding, tripping, or pushing was permitted, a goal was scored by kicking it 'through the flagposts and under the string', handling was allowed only to stop the ball or to catch and then kick; and the rules included one refinement that was to survive, and form the basis of Soccer tactics for the next seventy years: even if the ball was passed forward to him, a player was allowed to play it so long as three members of the opposing side were between him and the opposing goal line.

In these laws, carrying the ball is strictly forbidden, and there is no talk of a touchdown behind the opposing line, two points that are all the more significant for the fact that the committee who signed them included a representative of Rugby School where running-in, tackling and try-scoring were the game's major attractions. In the cause of uniformity a lot of concessions were being made; without spirited rearguard action in the next few years, Rugby Football could have faded away into insignificance as meekly as Harrow Football and Winchester Football and the Eton Field Game.

The impression left by these frenzied bouts of rule-making at Cambridge and the public schools, rules that enabled inter-college and inter-university football to establish themselves by the late 1850s, is that the whole football dynamic was centred on the two great universities, the sons of rich southern families, and the well-heeled clubs of university graduates and public school Old Boys springing up in the more respectable suburbs of London. This is misleading; football in the city street and the village green had largely died out by the middle of the 19th century, but the new middle class had carried it far beyond the traditional seats of privilege.

The game was attracting interest in several of the northern towns and cities, as young men of the professional classes in the provinces were leaving their northern public schools or their endowed grammar schools with a taste for organised sport. The major centre of football growth in the provinces was Sheffield, where the game was developed with such enthusiasm in the 1850s that, in the event, it was only by chance that London rather than Sheffield played the major part in organising football on a countrywide basis. In the days of street football, back in 1793, a famous match had been played in the city between Sheffield (six men in red) and Norton (six men in green), that went on for three days during which whole crowds of spectators joined in on the Sheffield side, forcing Norton to send press-gangs out into the Peak District for reinforcements: 'There were many slightly injured, but none killed . . . the hostile feeling continued so that for several years afterward the people of Norton felt a dread to come to Sheffield, even about their necessary business.'

This sort of escapade was long in the past. Football was now respectable, and it was no sort of anomaly that Sheffield's most influential football club was formed in the genteel atmosphere of Sheffield Cricket Club. In 1855 the cricketers had inaugurated their new ground at Bramall Lane and one of them, William Prest, together with some of his friends from the Collegiate school in the city, were given the use of the ground and formed the Sheffield Football Club.

From this base they laid the foundations of the competitive football—both amateur and, later, professional—that has characterised the North of England ever since. Within a couple of years the Sheffield Club, quite independently of the law-makers still active at Cambridge and in the public schools, had written a constitution and published a set of rules. Apart from the sensible provision that all members should have one dark blue flannel cap and one red one to distinguish the teams when they played among themselves, their rules were not unlike the Cambridge ones. They too were happy to allow a free kick after a fair catch; they too outlawed hacking and tripping. But in Sheffield a player could push another with his hands, and could also push or hit the ball forwards with his hand (a convention that has died out in all forms of football now played in Britain, but which is still allowed, with certain reservations, in both Gaelic Football and Australian Rules). Goals, however, had to be kicked.

Within five years of these rules being written, there were fifteen clubs in the Sheffield area, including the celebrated Hallam, the Sheffield Club's greatest rival. These two met in a spectacular match in 1861 at Bramall Lane in a charity game in aid of a local hospital, attracting 600 spectators to see Sheffield win 2–0. (Seventy-five years later, at that same Bramall Lane, Sheffield United were to cram 68,000 spectators into the ground for a cup tie against Leeds United.) A return game the following year was marked by a memorable fracas in which Sheffield's Major Nathaniel Creswick was illegally held by two Hallam men, one of whom, named Waterfall, he punched. Waterfall took off his waistcoat and retaliated, precipitating a general mêlée that was stopped only by the intervention of spectators. Mr Waterfall took the blame, it is reported, and was sent back to keep goal.

In the south, the rule-makers were still engaged in furious activity that was to come to its momentous climax in 1863. At Uppingham School in Rutland, where one of the great innovators of Victorian education, Edward Thring, had been Head since 1853, the rules for 'The Simplest Game' were published. They had been drawn up in 1862 by the

Headmaster's younger brother, J. C. Thring, and provided for a very straight-forward game which, incidentally, Thring proposed should last for ninety minutes; no sort of violence, no kicking the ball while it was in the air (it could, instead, be caught, placed on the ground, and then kicked), no player allowed in front of the ball. The rules were not particularly exciting, but they did, indeed, simplify the game and a number of other schools agreed to adopt them.

The same year, at Cambridge, the rules for a match arranged by Cambridge Old Etonians and Cambridge Old Harrovians specified 11 players per side, an umpire for each side as well as a referee, goals 12 ft across and up to 20 ft high, the 3-man off-side rule and an hour-and-a-quarter's play only. The rules were said to have worked well. In the following year they formed the basis of the revised Cambridge Rules and, not long afterwards, many of them were adopted by the young Football Association. (The chief exception was the goals themselves; 12 ft wide by 20 ft high is a very odd shape, not all that different from a present day Soccer goal stood on its end. Twelve feet is far too narrow for goals to be scored with any regularity *past* the goalkeeper, whereas the 20 ft height means a huge expanse of goal where not even the tallest and most agile keeper could hope to touch the ball. This tall, narrow shape was never adopted again.)

In October 1863 Cambridge University issued another set of revised rules, but their painstaking work as law-makers and football administrators was virtually at an end. By the end of the year, control of the game passed from the scholars to the football clubs, and there it has remained ever since.

Cambridge's intention had always been to give football a set of common rules that would serve the game in any part of the country; their support was naturally not drawn only from Cambridge, and both their rules and their aims were adopted by a number of clubs—not necessarily of university graduates—in and around London. One of these, the Forest Club, was founded among Old Harrovians living and working in London and played at Snaresbrook in Epping Forest. Two of its most prominent members were C. W. and J. F. Alcock, keen footballers with the Harrow Old Boys side as well as with Forest and another North London club, Kilburn No Names. J. F. Alcock was to be one of the more important members of the founding committee of the Football Association; C. W. Alcock, its most influential secretary, was to found the F.A. Cup, win a Cup-winner's medal and an international cap, and see Soccer through the trials of early professionalism. The Alcocks' contribution to the history of football while with the Forest Club was to adopt the Cambridge Rules, to amend them slightly so as to place the goalposts 8 yards apart (as they

1 Throwback: by the end of the 19th century, the
idiosyncrasies of public school football had largely been
abandoned in favour of Rugby or Association rules. But the
Eton Wall Game has survived—lumbering and indecisive,
with constricting laws and a ludicrous pitch—a ritual for
ritual's sake. *Syndication International*

2 Saturday scene: in sixteenth-century England football had become so barbaric that it had been summarily banned by successive monarchs. In the Italian states, however, more than one form flourished; this familiar touchline scene preceded a game of *Pallo*. *Radio Times Hulton Picture Library*

3 Latin grace: the best known Italian version, *Calcio*, was played in the piazzas of Florence. The courtliness and discipline shown in the painting were certainly part of the tradition, but *Calcio* was also a game of furious rivalries and considerable violence.

Mansell Collection

4 Free for all: at Ashbourne, in Derbyshire, the uncomplicated football of the medieval English villages has been played through streets and stream every Shrove Tuesday for centuries; the cruel winter of 1947 was no exception. *Derby Photo Service*

Eleven of the Forest Football Club, October 1863

R.E..... C.Biglam, J.F.Alcock, C.W.Alcock, C.D.Jackson, C.M.Tebbut, W.B.Standidge, A.M.Tebbut A.T.C

5 Founding fathers: the Forest Club, photographed during English football's fateful year of 1863. Within twelve months, two of its members, the brothers J. F. and C. W. Alcock, were leading lights in the new Football Association, and the club itself had changed its name to Wanderers and embarked on a glorious era of southern amateur supremacy. *Football Association*

6 The first Soccer international: Scotland *v.* England, Glasgow 1872, a goalless draw recorded by an unusually whimsical illustrator and played, it seems, with a distinctly melon-shaped ball. *Radio Times Hulton Picture Library*

7 The thirty-first F.A. Cup Final: Sheffield United *v.* Southampton, Crystal Palace, 1902. With press photography as yet a cumbersome business, magazines still relied on their artists to capture the highlights. *Radio Times Hulton Picture Library*

8a, 8b The fathers of Australian Football: Tom Wills (right, photographed on leaving Rugby in 1856) and his cousin Henry Harrison. *Mitchell Library, Sydney*

8c The biggest game of all: Australian Football as played at its nursery, Melbourne Cricket Ground, in 1881.   *Mitchell Library, Sydney*

9 The universal lure of a Cup Final: a match for the Premiership, Melbourne, 1891. *Mitchell Library, Sydney*

10 First flowering: Oxford University, 1882—perhaps the greatest Rugby team of the nineteenth century. Captained by the huge Harry Vassall (centre), pivoting on its half-backs Grant Asher (by Vassall's left knee) and Alan Rotherham (farthest left of the capped players), they were powerful, fast, revolutionary and unbeatable.

11 Grass roots: Rugby football at Rugby School in the 1840s, where running with the ball had by now been accepted, where hacking an opponent on the shin was all part of the fun, and where most of the game was spent in heaving, steaming mauls like this. *Illustrated London News*

12 The inventor: Walter C. Camp in his student days at Yale— athlete, swimmer, baseball player, gymnast, football half-back and captain. Within a decade, virtually unaided, he has turned the rules of Rugby inside out and created American Football.

13 The weapon: Yale's Flying Wedge of the 1890s was designed to thrust man and ball through the opposing defence at maximum speed with maximum thrust; the only way to stop it was to hurl oneself at its legs. Injuries were frequent, deaths occasional. *Culver Pictures Inc.*

14 Inter-college rivalry provided the main drama in American Football's first fifty years. The most keenly fought games of all were between West Point Army cadets and their Navy counterparts at Annapolis. This was the first, at West Point in 1890. Navy won 24–0. *U.S. Naval Academy*

15 Professional rivalry brought the biggest crowds to the Soccer stadiums in Britain. The F.A. Cup made its annual headlines, but the hard weekly struggles by top-class teams—such as this between the reigning League champions Sunderland and top-of-the table Aston Villa, in 1893—established the pattern of the twentieth-century urban weekend. *Football Association*

16 International rivalry, from the start, gave Rugby much of its impetus. Scotland was England's oldest opponent, but by the turn of the century Wales was her fiercest. Between 1900 and 1910 Wales played 36 internationals and won 29 of them, including this 22–0 thrashing of England at Swansea in 1907.
Radio Times Hulton Picture Library

stand today) and to fine members half-a-crown for infringing any of their laws.

In the autumn of 1863, a series of keenly argued and sometimes acrimonious meetings took two vital steps in the formation of modern football. It formed a Football Association which has since controlled, or passed on the control of, the entire administration of football's most popular offspring. And at the same time it alienated irreparably the adherents of the 'carrying game'; it became certain that there could never be one definitive game of football in Britain, and the Rugby Football Union, though still some years away, became inevitable.

The drama began on 26 October 1863, when delegates from a number of football clubs met in the Freemason's Tavern in Great Queen Street, London. The meeting was by no means representative of the whole footballing spectrum of the day. Though many of the delegates were themselves public school Old Boys, not one public school as such was represented (Charterhouse sent an observer); Cambridge University had not been consulted, though, again, many of the delegates were in favour of the Cambridge Rules, and there appears to have been no attempt to canvas the views of Sheffield or any of the other provincial footballing centres. The consequence was that though the delegates succeeded, eventually, in agreeing on a formula for their Association, it was to be some years before they could be said to represent football nation-wide.

At the first delegates' meeting, the majority were clearly in favour of adopting football rules based firmly on those advocated both by Cambridge and by the Sheffield Club—rules that they felt were rightly doing away with the more objectionable aspects of a less scrupulous era. But at the meeting there was a strong Rugby element: the Blackheath Club, which had been founded by Old Rugbeians a few years earlier, had two delegates, and two Blackheath schools, who played football under the influence of the clubs, were also represented. These men would in no way agree to the voluntary eclipse of their own rules.

The meeting was adjourned. At a subsequent sequence of gatherings various draft rules were considered, some of them proposed and amended by delegates, others sent in by letters from outside interests. As a magnanimous gesture to the minority, and to provide a basis for negotiation, the delegates even considered a proposition to adopt the Rugby rules, with a Harrow-style, crossbar-less goal. But always the stumbling block to any agreement were draft rules 9 and 10. They were:

9 A player may be entitled to run with the ball towards his adversaries' goal if he makes a fair catch, or catches the ball on the first bound;

but in the case of a fair catch, if he makes his mark he shall not
run.

10 If any player shall run with the ball towards his adversaries' goal, any
player on the opposite side shall be at liberty to charge, hold, trip or
hack him, or wrest the ball from him, but no player shall be held and
hacked at the same time.

The Rugby adherents stood by these rules adamantly; the 'dribbling'
supporters were for excluding them both.

The matter came to a head at the decisive meeting of 1 December.
Mr E. C. Morley, captain of Barnes Football Club and the first honorary
secretary of the Football Association, said that if hacking were allowed,
'men of business, to whom it is of importance to take care of themselves',
would be unwilling to play football. The champion of the Rugby cause
was F. W. Campbell of Blackheath, who claimed that hacking was nothing
like so lethal today as it had been in the past, and that a rule to prohibit it
'savoured far more of the feelings of those who liked their pipes or grog
or Schnapps more than the manly game of football'.

'I think,' he went on 'the reason they object to hacking is because too
many of the members of clubs began late in life and were too old for that
spirit of the game that was so fully entered into at the public schools and
by public school men in after life.'

This last remark stung Morley, who had not been to a public school,
and the argument degenerated somewhat; Campbell became even less
tactful, taunting the anti-hackers by saying that he could bring a crew of
Frenchmen across the Channel to beat them at football within a week.
He then demanded an adjournment to canvas opinion in the schools. He
was defeated soundly on the vote, and both hacking and running with the
ball were outlawed.

The first rules of the Football Association did more than settle a few
arguments between a small band of English football players. They comprise a set of conventions in which can be seen the rudiments of all the
games that have subsequently stemmed from the football of the 1860s;
no game today is played exactly to these rules, but without them, and the
men who drafted them, no modern game of football would be the same.
They are, in summary:

1 Ground: maximum 200 yards by 100 yards. The goal two uprights
8 yards apart without tape or bar.

2 Toss for choice of goals, the side losing the toss kicking off from the
centre; the other side shall not approach within 10 yards until the
kick-off.

3 After a goal is won, losing side shall kick off; the two sides shall change goals.

4 A goal shall be won when the ball passes between the posts or over the space between the posts, at any height, not being thrown, knocked on or carried.

5 When the ball is in touch, the first player who touches it shall throw it from a point on the boundary line where it left the ground in a direction at right angles with the boundary line; the ball shall not be in play until it has touched the ground.

6 When a player has kicked the ball any one of the same side who is nearer the opponents' line is out of play, and may not touch the ball himself; no player is out of play when the ball is kicked off from behind the goal line.

7 In case the ball goes behind the goal line if a player on the side to whom the goal belongs first touches the ball, one of his side shall be entitled to a free kick from the goal line. If a player of the opposite side first touches the ball one of his side shall be entitled to a kick at the goal only from a point 15 yards outside the goal line opposite the place where the ball is touched.

8 If a player makes a fair catch, he shall be entitled to a free kick, provided he claims it by making a mark with his heel at once.

9 No player shall run with the ball.

10 Neither tripping nor hacking shall be allowed, and no player shall use his hands to hold or push an adversary.

11 A player shall not be allowed to throw the ball or pass it to another with his hands.

12 No player shall be allowed to take the ball from the ground with his hands under any pretext whatsoever while it is in play.

13 No player shall be allowed to wear projecting nails, iron plates or gutta percha on the soles or heels of his boots.

That these rules were the basis of Association Football will be ironic to any devotee of Rugby Football who studies them. Rules 1–8 are Rugby rules, and have largely survived as such to this day. Rules 4–8, on the other hand, were soon to be drastically altered by the Association; indeed, some of Soccer's most distinctive modern features are forbidden by these laws: the role of the goalkeeper, for example, the forward passing, the crossbar, the corner-kick, the throw-in.

Nevertheless, the Rugby faction felt they had suffered a defeat. A week after the acrimonious argument over the rules, the Football Association met again formally to adopt the new laws. As the delegates patted themselves on the back, arranged for Mr John Lillywhite to print copies of the laws and proposed an inaugural match under their jurisdiction, Campbell of Blackheath rose. The laws as adopted, he said, entirely destroyed the game and took away all interest in it. As the laws stood, they made the difference between baseball and football, and Blackheath therefore wished their names to be withdrawn from the list of the Association's members.

The aim had been one universal game of football. Now, it seemed, there were to be two. In time there were to be many more.

2

a game for the people

Association Football: 1863 to 1900

The Rugby men who walked out of the Football Association over the hacking and carrying laws were not the only football enthusiasts to question the somewhat high-handed methods of the Association. Its aims had been commendable enough; the members of the Association were young men, footballers all, unencumbered by the combination of advanced age and extreme conservatism that were later to be the hallmark of powerful sports committees; all they wanted was to buckle down to their weekly game of football knowing that the other side was going to turn up with the same number of men as they did, expecting to play in front of goal posts of the same shape. They had, however, forced through a compromise set of laws in a bare two months; it was not surprising that the clubs now springing up fast across the country were not all prepared to bend their rules to the F.A.'s whim.

The main centre of opposition to the F.A. was Sheffield. The Sheffield Club, to do them justice, had no wish to be disruptive—indeed, they had expressed the politest interest in the F.A.'s birth—but the Sheffield rules were now the basis of dozens of small football clubs recently formed in Yorkshire. Other clubs, many of them hardly able to follow the intricacies of rule changes in the 1850s and 1860s, played just what their secretary or captain said they would play, a factor which once again depended on what school had taught the captain his football. So at Clapham in South London the Rovers, resplendent in their cerise and French grey, sponsored both Association and Rugby football; Kettering F.C. played to rules laid down by the Derbyshire F.A.; Norwich modified both the F.A. rules and the Cambridge University code.

The situation was becoming serious. Not only was club playing club, but city was being matched against city. Representative football had become a major crowd-puller, and still the F.A. and the other associations had not been able to agree on a common set of laws. It says much for the diplomatic talents of both Sheffield and the Football Association that no harm came of these early differences. Both parties agreed to modify their rules for a single representative game between London and Sheffield in Battersea Park in 1865 (the Londoners won by 2 goals and 4 touchdowns to nil), and the success of the match initiated a succession of representative games in the South of England to match the popularity of those in the North.

In 1868, too, the severities of the off-side law, which had at the F.A.'s formation reverted to the Rugby convention of keeping all men behind the ball, were relaxed so that the rules of Charterhouse and Westminster—and, incidentally, those in the early Cambridge Rules of the 1850s—were adopted: a player was on-side so long as three members of the opposition were between him and the opposing goal-line. Now the ball could be kicked forward to a member of one's own team and the 'pass', though still rarely used as a relief from individual dribbling, was at least a possibility; football was opening out tactically as well as administratively. In the same year the F.A. showed a keen diplomatic sense in widening the F.A. Committee to include three members from Yorkshire, in an attempt, as C. W. Alcock wrote later, to 'still further remove the barriers which prevent the accomplishment of one universal game'. In this aim he was winning. He would never see the Rugby men back in the Association, but by 1876 even Sheffield found themselves so far out on a limb that they voluntarily agreed to fall in with the F.A.'s laws.

The 1860s had seen the Football Association, by good sense and patient management, establish itself firmly in control of the dribbling game; the 1870s were to see the Association set the pattern for the mass spectator sport of today. Already there had been significant changes in the laws. In 1866 the privilege of a free kick at goal after making a 'fair catch' had been abolished, though not yet the free kick at goal after a touchdown; the tape across the top of the goalposts had been restored, too, and only shots passing beneath it counted as goals (the tape was replaced by a crossbar in 1875). In 1870 Association Football took the one decisive step which today distinguishes it from all other major games called football—it abolished handling: 'no player shall carry or knock-on the ball'. Football, said the F.A., was to be 'foot ball'; the feet and their skills were to be tested by the game, not the respective strengths of two packs of heaving forwards carrying the ball towards the opposing touchline, nor by men patting the bouncing ball down to make it easier to kick. Only one member of the side was to have the privilege of using his hands in open play—the goalkeeper (and here, again, Soccer distinguished itself from all other football games by binding one member of the team with an entirely separate code of rules from his colleagues).

This piece of legislation was a master-stroke. By some strange fluke it achieved a balance of power between attack and defence that has endured for more than a century without ever looking likely to break down. As the skills of the shooting forwards have improved, so has the expertise of the goalkeepers; in top-class Soccer throughout the world, the size of the goals, the abilities of the goalkeepers and the prowess of the attackers have remained so remarkably constant in relation to one another that goals are frequent enough to be expected at almost every match, yet rare enough to be supremely exciting when they occur, and at the same time a remarkably fair indication of one team's superiority over another. Occasionally a goalkeeper is 'too good'—his skills are such that the opposition's abilities are disproportionately reduced; but this is rare. The goalkeeper, with the tremendous advantages near his own goal of hands and consequently height, is an essential regulator of the game, and as such a lonely, commanding figure to the spectators, a hero in a hostile environment, subject to triumphs and downfalls at almost any moment of a match. No other football game can boast a figure with the stature of Soccer's goalkeeper—not an American Football quarterback, nor a Rugby Union scrum-half, nor even an Australian full-forward; the isolation accorded the goalkeeper by the law amendments of 1870 set him above all these. Without this refinement Soccer could never have become the game that it is.

Despite these major improvements, Association Football was still not the Soccer we know today. The sides still changed ends when a goal was scored, and the event of a ball going into touch frequently precipitated a free fight for the privilege of taking the throw-in—it was still awarded to the first man to secure the ball after it left the pitch; and the throw-in itself, still hurled with one arm, was tantamount to a free kick. The game was still, too, a game played for pleasure: from the start no substitutions were to be allowed for any player injured or 'otherwise prevented', and even now no dispute was settled without the two captains being called together for their views by the referee and the two umpires (the referee had little real power at that stage; he was not given a whistle till the late 1870s, and not until 1895 could he make a major decision without conferring with the umpires).

It was against this background that Association Football began its advances of the 1870s and 1880s. It was guided through these momentous years by the dedication and foresight of a man whose tact and quiet efficiency were such that, paradoxically, in any popular history of Soccer he is apt to be forgotten. No one could ignore the flamboyant, red-bearded extrovert Lord Kinnaird, in his Old Etonian colours and his long, white trousers—football's equivalent, if it ever had one, of cricket's W. G. Grace —and every gentleman could aspire to the integrity and incorruptibility of Major Marindin, founder and chief architect of the great Royal Engineers side of the 1870s, and later the most famous referee in the country, but the role of Charles W. Alcock tends to be relegated to the footnotes. Yet without Charles Alcock football might never have achieved the popular following that the hitherto middle-class code was soon to attract; and without his guidance in the troubled years of the 1880s, the smooth evolution into professional football might have proved far more painful.

Alcock, as we have already seen, was a footballer, an accomplished centre-forward with, by all accounts, a fearsome shoulder charge that was well known among the goalkeepers of the London clubs. When the Football Association was founded in 1863, with his elder brother J. F. Alcock on the original committee, he was only twenty-one, a keen member of the Forest Club, and a passionate believer in the importance of spreading the game to as many people as could be persuaded to play. With this aim in mind, he persuaded the committee of Forest to open its membership to players other than Old Harrovians, and to abandon the ground in Epping Forest in order to tour round London playing matches wherever the opposition could accommodate them. It was not an entirely popular move —some of the members openly opposed 'an organisation of ex-public schoolboys wandering from place to place' (the 19th-century equivalent, it seems, of 'hanging around street corners'), but Alcock was equal to their complaints, and made a virtue of the team's rootlessness by renaming it The Wanderers—one of the most celebrated names in the history of the game. Two years later, already becoming known as a regular member of F.A. representative teams, Alcock was elected to the Committee in place of his brother, and in 1870, at the age of only twenty-eight, he became its Honorary Secretary. It was in the two following seasons that the F.A., in both cases at Alcock's prompting, launched their two most exciting and most enduring competitions: the F.A. Challenge Cup and the England–Scotland internationals.

The Scottish connection was forged first. The game north of the Border owed less to middle-class fervour than it did in the south of England. Though a number of the Lowland academies had taken to the Rugby game with their adoption of the Arnoldian principles of education, it was not the public schools' Old Boys but the young artisans and professional men of the towns and cities who recognised football for the simple, energetic pastime it was. In Glasgow, the keenest players eventually gravitated to one of the City's three public parks—Queen's Park. On 9 July 1867, together with members of the local Y.M.C.A. and a handful of exiled Highlanders who used the park for caber-tossing practice, they formed the Queen's Park Football Club, officially establishing the game in Scotland and founding a tradition in Glasgow which, for single-minded fanaticism, would be difficult to parallel anywhere outside Rio de Janeiro.

Queen's Park's early success was legendary. Between their formation in 1867 and 1872 not a single goal was scored against them. They actually remained unbeaten until February 1876—nearly nine years after their first fixture—when they went down to The Wanderers, and only in December of that year, by which time Scottish competition had become much fiercer, did they lose at home. Not only did they win all their matches, they laid down all the rules (based generally on F.A. lines) for Scottish football, rules that were obediently followed by early local opponents such as Thistle, Hamilton Academicals and Airdrie, all of whom, incidentally, played their football in the summer months, a time when men in a less heathen land might have been expected to give way to the cricket season.

In 1870 Queen's Park assured national recognition for Scottish football. Charles Alcock, recently elected as Secretary of the F.A., wrote a provocatively-worded letter to the *Glasgow Herald* announcing that teams of English and Scottish players were to meet at Kennington Oval. He invited nominations from Scotland with a stirring call to arms: 'In Scotland, once essentially the land of football, there should still be a spark left of the old fire and I confidently appeal to Scotsmen . . . ' etc., etc. No one, certainly not a gentleman footballer with Scots blood in his veins, could resist a challenge like that. Queen's Park nominated Robert Smith, a founder member of the Club now living and working in London, as their player, and the teams met at the Oval on 19 November 1870. The English won 1–0.

This was not international football, by any means. The Scottish team was composed largely of well-heeled young men who owed their names and their backgrounds to Scotland (one, it was rumoured, based his participation on the fact that he had once travelled into Scotland to shoot grouse) but all of whom lived in or near London, and all of whom had time on their hands to play football. One of their number, G. F. Congreve, was an Old Rugbeian, who had presumably learnt to play football in quite a different style; another, W. H. Gladstone, was the son of the Prime Minister and was himself a Member of Parliament; a third was Quintin Hogg, founder of the Polytechnic movement, and both father and grandfather to Lord Chancellors of Great Britain; and there, too, was the Hon. Arthur Fitzgerald Kinnaird, fiery red beard and all, the most famous footballer of his day and later to be a successful banker, a peer, Lord High

Commissioner of the Church of Scotland, and for thirty-three years President of the Football Association. As an exhibition match the game was counted a success, and three more similar games followed, 'England' winning two of them and the other being drawn 1–1.

In 1871, however, the Football Association received a blow to its pride that ensured that there would no more such 'friendly' encounters arranged cosily from among club colleagues in the London suburbs. In March 1871 at Raeburn Place in Edinburgh, Scotland had played England in an international football match—at Rugby, the wrong football, whose principles had been successfully barred from the Football Association. To the football fanatic Alcock and the Scottish patrician Kinnaird, this must have been particularly galling, particularly after the F.A.'s prevarication in the face of Queen's Park's repeated proposals for just such a match. But at the start of the next season, on 30 November 1872, England travelled North to teach the Scots, they supposed, how to play football. Alcock, though selected for the match, was hurt and could not play (injuries deprived him of all but one international cap: he played against Scotland only in his final playing season, in 1874–5); but his sense of occasion might possibly have ensured that the two teams, as the Rugby sides had been, were photographed for posterity. In the event the players would not guarantee to buy prints, so the photographer went off in a huff without exposing any plates; at the return match at Kennington Oval the following year the photographer took his pictures, but the England players had insisted on pulling faces and no frames were developed.

The first international, played at the West of Scotland Cricket Ground at Partick, was not a spectacular game; it ended in a goalless draw, a stalemate that was to be repeated only twice in the next hundred years, and the fact that every one of Scotland's team played, or had played, for Queen's Park meant that their understanding more than recompensed for any superiority in skill the English might have had. But 4,000 people turned up to watch, 'including many ladies', and Queen's Park were spurred to look for a bigger ground in which to hold future matches. The Corporation agreed to lend them Hampden Park, Mount Florida, a ground whose site had changed twice since the 1870s, but whose name and whose roar has remained a symbol of Scottish football ever since.

Alcock now had two successes on his hands. His policy of encouraging representative games had reached the first of many peaks with the establishment of the England–Scotland international; his other innovation, a knock-out cup competition, was going to prove even more of a crowd-puller. The idea was not new; several schools used this 'sudden-death' arrangement for deciding house matches, and Alcock remembered the excitement of such tournaments from his days at Harrow. In 1871 he suggested that this idea be transferred to the member clubs of the Association, and proposed that 'It is desirable that a Challenge Cup should be established in connection with the association for which all clubs should be invited to compete.' The F.A. Committee was enthusiastic—they were, after all, predominantly public school men, and shared the same sort of memories as Alcock; they bought a cup for £20, and invited entries.

The first-ever major football knock-out competition, the F.A. Cup of 1871–2, makes strange reading; the 15 teams on the entry list are names with a ghostly, alien air about them, names hardly credible when considered in association with the illustrious roll-call of Cup giants in the succeeding hundred years: Donington School (from Lincolnshire) entered; so did Barnes and the Civil Service, Clapham Rovers and Maidenhead, Harrow Chequers (a team of old Harrovians) and Reigate Priory, Royal Engineers and Crystal Palace (an older and unrelated version of the present club of that name), Great Marlow and The Wanderers, Hitchin, Hampstead Heathens, and Upton Park; and the barely known Queen's Park from Glasgow, who had made the magnificent gesture of sending a guinea—a sixth of their annual income—towards the purchase of the trophy.

If the names seem strange, the results were even stranger. Four different teams scratched at various stages of the competition; Queen's Park had a bye into round two, were given a walkover by Donington School (who had exams) into round three, and then another bye into the semi-final. Crystal Palace and Wanderers, who drew their quarter-final tie, were *both* given a place in the semi-finals. In the semi-finals Queen's Park made their first, celebrated appearance in London, described at the time as 'the most remarkable event in modern football'; Wanderers dribbled with customary dash, Queen's Park passed the ball with their feet with great accuracy; no one scored, and Queen's Park had to go home before any decider could be played.

Their departure left Wanderers to face Royal Engineers in the first F.A. Cup final, on 16 March 1872, at Kennington Oval. The Engineers started at odds of 7–4 on, so the bookmakers presumably had a good day. Wanderers won by a single goal scored by a pseudonymous A. H. Chequer (standing for A Harrow Chequer; it was, in fact, an Old Harrovian called M. P. Betts); in the true tradition of the Royal Engineers a Lieutenant Cresswell played throughout the game after breaking his collar-bone in the first ten minutes, and the occasion attracted a modest crowd of 2,000. It would have been bigger, *Bell's Life* said, but for the fact that a shilling per head was charged for admission. The F.A. had nothing to reproach themselves with; ninety years later, in 1961, with a nation of fanatics primed by the press, the Football League attracted a derisory 12,000 for the first leg of the first League Cup Final.

The Cup, anyway, was an immediate success. The following year, when, for the only time in its history, the holders upheld their right to play only in the Final, Wanderers met Oxford University. The crowd was fifty per cent up on the previous year's, Wanderers won again, primarily through a superb dribbled goal by A. F. Kinnaird, and Oxford had the additional frustration of wandering down to the Thames in the afternoon and seeing their fellow Blues lose to Cambridge in the Boat Race. Such were the priorities in 1873 that the Cup Final had to be held in the morning so that the players (and, one assumes, the crowd) could get to the really important business of the day after lunch.

The steady spread of the game in the 1870s and the early 1880s was founded on the success of the Cup (in 1873-4 the newly formed Scottish Football Association started their own knock-out tournament—it was duly won by Queen's Park for the first three years) and of the England–Scotland internationals. These inspired a subsidiary rash of provincial games, too, that brought representative football even further into corners of the country that London's clubs might never penetrate, but into which Charles Alcock was ever keen to spread the light.

'What was ten or fifteen years ago the recreation of a few has now become the pursuit of thousands,' wrote Alcock in the 1878 *Football Annual*, 'an athletic exercise carried on under a strict system and, in many cases, by an enforced term of training, almost magnified into a profession.' Almost magnified into a profession . . . even if no one else saw it coming Charles Alcock would not be caught unawares when the dam finally broke.

It was not to break, however, for a while. The problems of tackling powerful, hungry teams from the mill-towns of Lancashire or the factories of the Midlands were in the future. Football in London was still a game for the leisured classes, and the gentlemen of The Wanderers were showing everyone else the way; in the first seven years of the F.A. Cup they played in five finals and won them all.

The gentlemen from Chatham, too, were making a considerable name for themselves. Though no one in the Guards or a cavalry regiment would dare have whispered it, the Royal Engineers were the new élite of the Army; a commission was won—not bought—against the stiffest opposition, and in both mental and physical prowess the Royal School of Military Engineering was turning out an impressive new breed of soldier. Their feats at cricket were already celebrated; now Major Francis Marindin constructed a football team to beat all comers. He did it by picking his teams carefully from the huge store of talent he had available at Chatham: 'the centres were selected for weight, strength and charging powers as well as their talent as dribblers, the game being perhaps a bit strenuous and many goals got for the R.E. by hustling goalkeepers through their own goal all ends up.' And he developed teamwork to make best use of the individuality with such effect that, Cup Finals apart, the Royal Engineers had by far the best results of any English club in the mid 1870s. Their great season was 1874–5, when they did, just once, take the Cup back to the officers' mess at Chatham at the expense of Old Etonians. There is a legend that Major Marindin, an Old Etonian himself and a gentleman to his boots, bowed out of the final rather than make a decision as to which side he should play for. This would have been characteristic, but was in fact decided for him as he had been posted away from Chatham earlier in the season. Thereafter Marindin played little football, though he holds the record of having refereed eight Cup Finals. He later became Inspector of Railways for England and was given responsibility for setting up London's electric lighting system.

With the Cup crowds in England growing modestly and Cup entries growing fast (by 1879 fifty-four clubs entered for the first round), football in Scotland was advancing at breakneck speed. On 7 March 1874, 7,000 spectators saw the Scots beat England for the first time. The 'beautiful and scientific play' of the victors was a joy to watch; the Scots played as a team (seven of them were from Queen's Park) splitting England's defence again and again with accurate passing, and their hero in the 2–1 victory, the midfield player Harry McNeil, was carried shoulder high from the pitch; it was a fitting climax to the Scottish F.A.'s first season. In the following few years they made an embarrassing habit of repeating this football lesson. In 1875 the two countries drew; in 1876 Scotland won 3–0; in 1877 they beat England for the first time in England; in 1878 they overwhelmed them 7–2 at Hampden Park. Of the first eleven matches from 1872 to 1882, Scotland won seven, England only two. On four occasions the Scots scored five or more goals: they had taken England on at their own game and succeeded in making them look foolish.

It was the 'passing game' that made the difference between the two countries as pronounced as it was. There is still doubt as to whether Marindin's Royal Engineers or the men of Queen's Park first saw the advantage of tempering the public school dribbling skills with tactical passing, but though the Engineers were an accomplished club, their influence on the Football Association's teams was limited. Queen's Park, on the other hand, virtually ran Scottish Football, and their well-thought-out, beautifully executed methods of play were both attractive and devastating. They increased the scope of the game, they doubled the speed of the attacks, they produced far more goals. It was hardly surprising that by 1880 they were attracting 12,000 people to watch internationals at Hampden.

As the game grew in both skill and popularity in Scotland, with young footballers flocking to the new clubs—long-forgotten names like Renton and Oxford Glasgow, still familiar ones like Kilmarnock and Dumbarton—subtle, barely perceptible changes were appearing in the structure of the English game that were soon to explode in both countries.

First, almost as an aside to the main drama, The Wanderers had disappeared. One season they were there, as talented, apparently, as ever; the next they were gone. It was a sad end to an illustrious club, barely twenty years from its formation as Forest, and winner, in that short time, of as many F.A. Cups as, at the time of writing, Burnley, Leeds United, Chelsea, West Ham and Huddersfield Town combined. In 1878 they won the Cup for the third year in succession, graciously giving it back to the F.A. on the condition that no one was ever to win it outright again. (Characteristically, too, they won their last Cup Final with their goalkeeper nursing a broken arm, a common hazard in the days when charging the goalkeeper, with or without the ball, was all part of the fun.)

Throughout the 1870s, however—like so many of the best clubs in London, Pall Mall and St. James's not excepted—they had been heavily infiltrated by Old Etonians. Towards the end of the decade, the Old Etonians themselves became a formidable football team, and loyalties within The Wanderers became strained. In 1876 five former Wanderers, including the formidable Kinnaird, played for the Old Etonian side that lost to the Engineers in the final. Kinnaird was back with The Wanderers the following season, but the drift to the closed fellowship of the Old Boys' clubs was not stemmed. In September 1878, after that last Cup triumph, Kinnaird and other senior Wanderers resigned to play for the Old Etonians. In the following season, as the fates would have it, the two clubs drew each other in the first round of the Cup, and the Etonians won by a crushing seven goals to two.

The shock of being out of the competition was too much for the ailing Wanderers; they tried to rally some of the fast-waning enthusiasm by arranging a floodlit game against Clapham Rovers (the first such game in London, though a month before a floodlit evening match had been played at Sheffield); the lights, alas, were not adequate, and the game was abandoned early. The rest of the season was disheartening; the drain on their

best players had been bad enough, but on top of that the old concepts of
Association Football were being overtaken, and The Wanderers were not
moving with the times. Alcock and his fellow veterans were still committed
to the individual dribbling that had made football at school so exciting;
the younger men did not have the drive or the status to introduce the new
skills of 'passing on' to the team.

In 1879 they made a final effort to regain their feet. In the first round
they were confronted with an Old Boys team with even more sophistication
and promise than the Old Etonians—the Old Carthusians, who were to win
the Cup in 1881—and exhibited some of the old fire by beating them 1–0.
Then, such was their luck, they faced the Old Etonians in the second
round, lost by three goals to one, and never played a cup tie again. The
next season, humiliated by their two disastrous years and further depleted
by player-desertion, the once-proud Wanderers had to scratch from the
Cup, and quietly faded into oblivion.

'Passing on' could no longer be ignored, now that refusal to adopt it was
a guarantee of failure; and it was not only the frequently humbled England
team who had come to realise that the best exponents of the passing game
were the Scots. Scotland, who had borrowed a ready-made game from
England in the 1860s, were now, in the 1880s, setting their own stamp on
it. First, in 1880 they established the new rule about throw-ins. In England
it had been the practice to hurl balls from the touchline with one arm;
the Scots were in favour of a less powerful throw, taken from behind the
head with both hands; the dispute came to a climax in the 1880 international when the referee agreed before the game to allow the English
throw but, once it had started, insisted on the more difficult Scottish
version; by 1882 the dispute had been settled in favour of Scotland, and
the two-handed throw, permitted in any direction, has been a feature of
Soccer—alone of all football codes—ever since.

But the Scottish throw was a minor matter when set against the 'Scottish
professors'. Their arrival in England's industrial North coincided almost
exactly—and perhaps appropriately—with the Wanderers leaving the
serene playing fields of the South. The sensation of the 1879 Cup competition was the Lancashire mill town of Darwen, composed not of public
school Old Boys or young professional men, but of working lads from the
local factories, and in the fourth round they were drawn to play the Old
Etonians, the very antithesis of mill-town working lads, at the Oval.
Local subscription paid their fares to London; they were overwhelmed
by the occasion, overrun in the first three-quarters of the match; with
quarter of an hour still to go they were losing 5–1. It is conceivable that
someone then remarked—not for the first time and, oh so tediously, not

for the last—that football was a funny game and nothing was over till the final whistle. At any rate, Darwen scored four times in fifteen minutes, and so astounded their illustrious opponents, Kinnaird and all, that the Etonians did not feel up to playing extra time.

Replays in those days were played at the same ground as the first game, so Darwen had to take round the hat once again; the F.A. gave them £10, the Old Etonians themselves £5, the necessary £175 was raised and back they came to London to draw 2–2. Another anxious week of fund-raising for the Committee, another nervous week in the mills for the players, and only after a third wearying train ride to London did Darwen finally succumb. Their feat was the first, unheralded hint that the North was one day to present a footballing threat to the men of the South; the other hint, even less readily perceptible, was of footballers playing the game for more than the fun of it.

In Darwen's gallant team of 1879 were James Love and Fergus Suter, two Scotsmen from Partick, Glasgow. There is no evidence at all that they were paid to play for Darwen (a side that could not afford a rail fare was not the sort of club to be paying its footballers). Nevertheless, it is pretty certain that they were not living in Darwen by accident, that they had found jobs vacant at the local mill at such a convenient time, or that they, as total newcomers, were available to play football for a small-town club at the height of its fortunes. The practice may have been unfamiliar to the strict amateurs of London and the South-East; in Lancashire the resident Scotsman was already a reality; in a year or so he would be a commonplace.

It was not only for the mill and factory and pit welfare clubs that these men were being recruited. The celebrated Blackburn Rovers was very much a public school club at its foundation. Three members of the team that reached the 1882 Cup Final had learned their game at Malvern College, and a notable player in their formative years was A. N. Hornby, a Harrovian, an England opening batsman and a major force in Lancashire cricket in the last quarter of the 19th century; he was in the Rovers team that played a match against Partick Thistle in 1878, and both he and the rest of the team were struck by the play of the Partick full-back—Fergus Suter. A year later Suter was with Darwen; by 1882 he was a member of the Blackburn Rovers team, as were Hugh McIntyre, another Glaswegian, and two other Scotsmen.

Football was not the sole lure. The industrial boom of the 1870s was felt throughout the industrial areas of the North and Midlands, and there were vacancies for any man who wanted work. Irish and Welsh, as well as Scots, headed for the unlovely cities; advertisements in the Glasgow newspapers drew attention to jobs waiting in Darwen and Accrington, Preston and Blackburn and so on, and it did not take much reading between the lines to see them as advertisements for football talent. And the English clubs over-ordered ludicrously. No Lancashire team was content with its own, talented Scotsman—it had to have five or six; one club had ten Scottish professors, with one lone Sassenach for them all to advise.

The Scottish clubs were furious—just as twenty years later the Rugby clubs of Wales were to watch in angry frustration as the Rugby League scouts waved their chequebooks at the amateur talent of the valleys. The only way to stop a player going to England to play football for money was to pay him money to stay behind in Scotland, and the rules against that sort of thing were even stricter in Scotland than in England.

For the 1883 Cup Final Blackburn Olympic actually gave their players time off work to train at Blackpool; in the same year, for the final of the far less prestigious Lancashire Association Cup, Darwen and Blackburn Rovers each had a spell of training at the seaside. Lancashire Football Association, in a deeply embarrassing position as upholders of amateur integrity up to its neck in a seething tide of professionalism, placed a belated ban on the signing of Scottish footballers. The Football Association themselves expelled Accrington for offering an inducement to a player, and other suspensions followed; but they were no more than token gestures. To mete out the same treatment to every team suspected of irregularly inducing outsiders to play for them would create civil war within the Association and do irreparable damage to the 'one universal game' so close to Charles Alcock's heart.

The split could easily have come in 1884—the same split between dogmatic amateurism and *laissez-faire* professionalism that was to cripple the progress of Rugby football in the 1890s. William Sudell, a rich cotton manufacturer and the founder of Preston North End, not only claimed that professionalism was in no way harmful to football and that everybody knew it went on anyway; he also called a series of meetings of Lancashire clubs, culminating in a revolutionary gathering in Manchester at which he proposed to form a British Football Association to include 'clubs and players of every nationality'. Twenty-six Lancashire clubs, plus Aston Villa and Sunderland, supported him.

Within a month Alcock, acting for the F.A. with speed and point, had succeeded in pouring a little oil on the waters. At a meeting of an F.A. sub-committee, which took place diplomatically in Manchester, he proposed to legalise professionalism 'under stringent conditions', with the proviso that no professional team should be eligible for his beloved F.A.

Cup. The latter condition was a forlorn gesture from a man who knew that the era of the amateur was coming to a close; that season was to end with Queen's Park of Glasgow, perhaps the greatest of all British amateur sides of any era, losing the Cup Final for the second year running to a Blackburn Rovers side bristling with Scottish professionals. (Three years before, in 1882, Lord Kinnaird celebrated Old Etonian's Cup victory by standing on his head in front of the Oval pavilion: not for the remainder of the century did a team from the South carry the trophy off.)

But professionalism was still illegal, and Alcock's proposals for creating a relatively smooth passage towards its inevitable acceptance were years ahead of the current F.A. thinking. At two successive meetings in January and March 1885 they turned his plan down flat. In Scotland, too, the Scottish Football Association sat on its throne and bade the waves retreat —the only effect of its intransigence was to drive more and more talented Glaswegians to the factories and the football fields of Lancashire and the Midlands.

So Alcock, tireless as ever, went away and drew up yet another set of proposals for the adoption of professionalism; this time the F.A., with little alternative, accepted them. His regulations for the payment of foot-ballers were, as Percy Young notes in his *History of British Football*, very close to the provisions laid down at the time for the employment of professional cricketers. This was not surprising; besides having guided the fortunes of British Soccer for twenty years, Alcock had at the same time—since 1872—been secretary to Surrey County Cricket Club, where he remained for a total of thirty-five years through the period which saw Surrey rise to the very top rank of county cricket. He supervised, at Surrey's headquarters at Kennington Oval, the most important sports centre in the country at that time, where Cricket, Soccer and Rugby internationals were all held. He personally wrote and edited all twenty-nine annual issues of James Lillywhite's *Cricket Annual* between 1872 and 1900; he founded *Cricket* magazine in 1882, and edited that as well; he wrote prodigiously on both cricket and football for Fleet Street news-papers, and his writings on the winter game are quite as authoritative as those of any other contemporary commentator, and considerably better attuned to the attitudes of the day.

The regulations he drew up for the professional footballer could have been written by M.C.C. There was a clause requiring a player to live within six miles of the club for which he was to play, a clause forbidding transfer from one club to another during the course of the season without special permission, a clause requiring all pros to be registered by the F.A., even a clause forbidding professionals to serve in the committee of the

Association or any of its affiliated associations—a typical piece of contemporary class distinction, implying somehow that professionals would forget to take their caps off in the committee room or might spit on the floor.

There were, predictably, no such gestures from the Scottish Association. They had a rush of Puritanism to the head, banned England's sixty-eight registered professionals from playing in Scotland, and talked self-righteously about keeping 'the evil out of the Association'.

Considering the inevitable conservatism of an organisation such as the F.A., the new regulations amounted to a liberal and conciliatory gesture to change; for the professionals themselves the situation was less satisfactory. When propserous cotton kings take the trouble to confront a large and powerful organisation on behalf of the underprivileged part-time professional footballer, there will always be a lurking suspicion that the professional footballer is not going to come out of the deal quite so well as the cotton king. So it transpired: before 1885 the professional footballer had been something of a free agent, a seller of his own talents to the most attractive offer. Now he was the pawn of a dozen overbearing regulations which gave him no bargaining power whatsoever, not even the right to pack his bags and play elsewhere. He was at the mercy of a club committee, and of that committee's evaluation of his worth to them at any given date; and he was paid wages, again not subject to negotiation, that were laid down by a committee of men who had never worked for wage-packets in their life. The arrangements accepted by the clubs were very much to the advantage of the clubs. The players themselves were not consulted, and not until the 'maximum wage' was abolished in the early 1960s, and the High Court had established the rights of the professional, was this hold of club over player to be satisfactorily relaxed.

The instinct of the Scottish authorities was to remove themselves as far from the debased English habits as possible. They were given a good exuse by a notorious match in the early rounds of the 1886–7 F.A. Cup. Queen's Park had become famous for the relish with which they disposed of English clubs in the F.A. Cup's early rounds, and it was in this mood that they received Preston North End at Hampden.

In the years that have followed it has not been altogether a rarity for one team to kick the other all over the park at Hampden, but for an English professional team so to treat the pride of the Scottish amateur game was not well received. Preston's 3–0 victory concluded with the Queen's Park centre-forward helped off, dazed after a thundering tackle from behind; at the final whistle 15,000 spectators invaded the field in fury at the Preston team, surrounded the pavilion, and dispersed only after they learned that

Jimmy Ross, a Preston Scotsman and the villain of the piece, had left the ground disguised in a long ulster with a hat pulled down over his face.

Despite this early departure of Queen's Park, Scottish clubs enjoyed a good run in the F.A. Cup that season. Seven of them had entered a good run in the F.A. Cup that season. Seven of them had entered the competition; Partick Thistle reached the last 16 by virtue of an 11–1 victory over Cliftonville, and a new name to the competition, Glasgow Rangers, talented and (discreetly) professional pioneers of a highly distinguished tradition, got to the semi-final where they fell to the eventual winners and the first team from the Midlands to get their name on the Cup—Aston Villa.

But the Preston North End performance still rankled. At their annual meeting that summer, the Scottish Football Association decreed that no club belonging to S.F.A. could also belong to 'any other national association'—the Scots turned to isolationism to preserve their amateur purity. There had been talk that year of the possibility of forming a British League, with the best of the Scottish clubs competing against the more powerful English ones on a regular basis; Scotland's peremptory withdrawal from English competition made any further discussion futile.

It was a Scotsman, nevertheless, who was to introduce English football to its present-day pattern. In the 1880s the fixture lists of the major clubs were in complete disarray. London clubs played other London clubs by long-standing gentlemen's agreement. Clubs in the North and Midlands, who had been only too pleased in their formative years to play any sort of game under any sort of rules with local opposition of whatever standard, were now no longer content to give up their Saturday afternoons playing local church youth clubs when they needed a thousand-strong home crowd to pay the wages of their resident Scotsmen. A good run in the F.A. Cup, or a prestige friendly match, could prove a welcome money-spinner, but the clubs were becoming more aware that worthwhile competition, and regular gate receipts, would come only when the best teams played the other best teams regularly every season. The man who pressed these ideas with the most persistence, and formed a clear plan for their successful adoption, was William McGregor, a successful draper from Perthshire who had set up business in Birmingham and taken an active interest in both Aston Villa football club and the Birmingham Football Association.

In March 1888 he circulated a number of the country's major clubs with proposals for the foundation of the 'Association Football Union', to comprise ten or a dozen of the most prominent clubs in England, who would arrange 'home and home' matches each eason (the idea, curiously,

came from America, where such a system had been working effectively
for some years among baseball leagues). The clubs he listed, with a pointed
lack of tact, included most of the big names from Lancashire and the
Midlands, omitted all Scottish clubs, all clubs from the south of England
and all amateur clubs.

After various meetings, letter-writings, numerous applications, a name-
change in order to prevent confusion with the Rugby Football Union and
a number of mollifying proposals to include such clubs as Notts County,
Stoke, and the then most prominent amateur team Old Carthusians, the
Football League was formed in 1888—a somewhat anomalous body,
playing to F.A. laws, yet already in a position to wield far greater power
than the senior organisation. The twelve founder members began their
first season that autumn. Six clubs were clustered in South Lancashire,
three huddled in and around Birmingham, and the others in their lonely
outposts—Derby County, Notts County and Stoke. These were so over-
awed, apparently, by their physical isolation from the main bunch that
they ended that first season in tenth, eleventh and twelfth positions
respectively; Preston North End, on the other hand, enjoyed a quite
uniquely successful season, the most dominant ever recorded by a professional club in England, by winning the F.A. Cup without conceding
a single goal, and the first League championship by eleven clear points
without losing a single match.

Having arrived in such style, the professional clubs took the game over;
they packed the uncomplaining crowds into their inadequate grounds;
they were well reported in florid style by a fast-growing Press; they
inspired enough confidence among the banking profession to raise the
money for vast, ugly, monolithic stands and terraces, some of which are
still accommodating similarly uncomplaining crowds today. For possibly
the only time in football's established history the game was wrested from
the control of the South—London, as far as football was concerned, had
become a suburb of Lancashire. In 1893 and 1894 even that tradition of all
footballing traditions, the F.A. Cup Final, was reluctantly allowed out of
London by the F.A. For once in his dual career as secretary of both the
F.A. and Surrey County Cricket Club, Charles Alcock was confronted
with a conflict of loyalties: the Association were determined for the Cup
Final to be played in London, but Surrey were getting worried about the
effects on their pitch of the huge annual crowds. Quite rightly, Surrey
won the argument, and the F.A., without a Stamford Bridge, a White
Hart Lane or a Highbury to turn to, settled for Fallowfield, Manchester
Athletic Club's ground, for the twenty-first anniversary final of the F.A.
Cup in 1893, and for Goodison Park, Everton, the next year.

The two northern Cup Finals had each attracted far greater attendances than any at the Oval, but the F.A. were determined to bring
the season's greatest occasion back to the capital, and chose the huge,
natural bowl at the Crystal Palace at Sydenham in South London,
justifying their choice by attracting 48,000 to the 1895 final. Even so, the
Cup Final was still the South's solitary share of top-class football. In
Charles Dickens's *London Guide*, published in 1879, the author (the
novelist's son) claimed that five times as many people participated in
the Rugby code in London as played Association Football, and despite the
early domination of London amateur players in the Cup and in internationals, the real support for the game was in the North. While the
disputes over professionalism were raging in Lancashire in the 1880s,
the Southern clubs remained aloof from accusations and counter-accusa-
tions about inducements and training and sinecure factory jobs for
promising centre-forwards.

Had anyone noticed, however, it might have seemed significant, when
the works team of the arms factory at Woolwich formed themselves into the
Woolwich Arsenal Football Club in 1886, that the captain was a Scotsman
called David Danskin; that by 1890 other Scotsmen seemed to have been
able to find work at the Royal Arsenal (which the club now called itself)
and that a couple of other players had moved there from Wolverhampton.
Nottingham Forest generously sent the Arsenal players a set of red shirts,
and in 1891 the club agreed—the first club south of Birmingham to do so
—to adopt professionalism and leave the London F.A.

It was a brave step. The nearest professional opposition was at least
100 miles away, and travelling such distances would put a strain both on
Arsenal's finances and on the patience of any opponents who could be
persuaded to make the journey south. Luckily, within two years regular
fixtures were assured. In 1892 the successful Football League launched
its Second Division, and a year later Royal Arsenal were admitted. Their
example provided the spur that was needed in the South. At the suggestion of Millwall, where local dock workers had emulated Arsenal by
turning professional, the Southern League was formed, to include such
teams as the St. Mary's Church Football Club, which had recently
changed its name to Southampton, and North London's first professional
team, Tottenham Hotspur.

With the professionals so markedly in the ascendant, the amateurs were
doing well even to remain in contention. They were still running the game
with a regard for the traditional niceties, and they were still wary of a
system which paid men for taking part in what they had always con-

sidered as nothing more than manly relaxation. ('Are you all Englishmen?' asked Major Marindin in the West Bromwich Albion dressing room after he had refereed their victory over the Scots-heavy Preston in a Cup semi-final of 1887. 'Yes, sir', came the answer. 'Then I have very much pleasure in presenting you with the ball. You have played a very good game and I hope you will win the Cup.') But with the spotlight on the new League, an amateur side had to be exceptionally talented to make their presence felt. The Corinthians had this talent, and in the 1880s and 1890s were playing the best football ever played by amateurs, better even, for a year or so, than the great Queen's Park teams. The club had been formed in a flush of English patriotism in 1882 in an attempt to shore up English football against the all-conquering Scots. The Corinthians began as a scratch side comprised of players picked from leading amateur clubs who could thus play together and get used to each others' style of play—an intelligent attempt to combat the well-drilled cohesion of the Scottish teams of the day.

Had the rules of the club allowed them to enter for the F.A. Cup, professional domination might have been less emphatic. In 1884 the Corinthians took on the Cup-winners Blackburn Rovers and humiliated them 8–1; in 1886 the England team which drew 1–1 with Scotland (a year after the legalisation of professionalism) included two players from Blackburn Rovers and nine from Corinthians. Eight years later, the England team that beat Wales 5–1 was composed entirely of Corinthian players.

And the public, then as now, loved a talented amateur. The eye had been caught, of course, by Nick Ross, the great full-back who moved from Preston to Everton just before Preston's 'double' season, and Ernest Needham of Sheffield United and, at the end of the century, young Steve Bloomer of Derby County. But even when young prodigies were changing hands at fees as high as £250, the real heroes were the gentlemen: W. N. Cobbold, the great dribbler, who hated heading the ball and who was so reluctant to take a tackle that he swathed his legs in rubber bandages and ankle guards; the Walters brothers, two pioneers of constructive defence, who gave up football at the request of their father after their younger brother had been killed during a game; G. O. Smith and Charles Wreford-Brown, the former one of the great forwards of all time who won more caps for England in his day than any professional, the latter a versatile footballer who played goalkeeper, centre-half and forward in three consecutive seasons and who is credited with having coined the word 'Soccer'. All these were Old Carthusians, too, and as such enjoyed a fifteen-year period of superiority in amateur club football, beginning with their victory in the F.A. Cup in 1881 and culminating in 1894 with their win in the newly founded F.A. Amateur Cup. In the final flush of amateur pride it was these men, rather than the professionals of the North, who truly epitomised English football.

In Scotland, the amateur predominance was at last succumbing to the inevitable. In 1891 the clubs followed England's lead and formed a league. Early proposals had once again conjured such phrases as 'evil in our midst' from the Scottish Association, but, as J. H. McLaughlin of Celtic said when proposing the formation of the League: 'You might as well try to stop the flow of Niagara with a kitchen chair than endeavour to stem the tide of professionalism.'

For the first two seasons of the Scottish League the game was still, in theory at any rate, an amateur one; but payments were made quite openly to players, and by 1893 the S.F.A. had no alternative but to give in: the drain of their players, a sorry run of results by the Scottish team, and eventually the Association's utter impotence as the rules were flouted in their face, had made their position untenable. Only Queen's Park held out, refusing to join the League until 1900, but their run had been a glorious one. From their formation in 1867 until the coming of professionalism they had run Scottish football virtually alone; they had come closer than any other Scottish team to winning the English F.A. Cup; they had provided the core of international team to humble England; they had won the Scottish Cup nine times, and they had provided Scottish crowds with an attractive and fast-moving game which was supported with an unprecedented fervour. But in 1896, the first year that the Anglos (the Scottish professionals in the English League) were eligible for selection for Scotland, Queen's Park provided only one member of the national team. But the balance was restored, Scotland ended their losing run and there were 50,000 at Celtic Park to see them do it.

In 1895 Charles Alcock had retired as secretary of the F.A. to concentrate on his writing and his services to cricket (he was still Surrey's secretary when he died in 1907). In his years with the Association the game had progressed from an ill-considered ritual played by a closed society of leisured amateurs to an established fixture of the British social scene, a game played and, what is more, watched by the mass of the working people, and a sport on the threshold of acceptance by the rest of the world.

Tactically, it had changed beyond recognition. Mass dribbling had given way to constructive passing. The old skills of walking the ball to the opposing goal-line had given way to the dramatic skills of powerful shooting. Heading had been introduced and adopted as a vital secondary weapon of both attack and defence. Massed attack and defence had disappeared as tactical positioning made the fullest use of available space; specialist skills had been developed by the players, and it was no longer necessary for the defender to attack and the attacker to defend.

As in all football games, the players had learned to exploit the laws to the full, and there had been a consequent necessity to strengthen the power of the officials: offences for which free kicks could be awarded had been steadily increased; and in 1891 the Irish F.A. proposed the adoption of the penalty kick for foul play within twelve yards of the offender's goal line—still, at that time, the only free kick from which a goal could be scored direct. The sole arbiter of such offences was now the referee. The two umpires had been banished to the touchlines, retitled linesmen and had their powers reduced to advising the referee on offside and throw-in decisions. The cross-tapes of 1872 had been replaced by the crossbar and, in 1892, the goal was given that extra, dramatic ingredient by the addition of goal nets. Football had progressed, in fact, to something very like the game we can watch today, and had done so in England, even to the extent of changing from a hobby to a profession, without the distressing public rows or the alienation of whole sections of the country which once appeared inevitable.

It had been largely a domestic growth. Scottish enthusiasts had invaded the stronghold of Rugby in Belfast in the 1870s and laid the foundations of the Irish F.A. In Wales, particularly in the Welsh Marches near the Shropshire and Cheshire borders, a pocket of footballing talent had developed, as impressive for a few years as the pockets of Rugby genius being unearthed in South Wales. But the Football Association had never been seriously concerned with sending out missionary tours to promote the game abroad in the way that the Rugby fraternity had begun to. Apart from occasional clubs springing up among English and Scottish communities in the Empire or in Europe and South America, Soccer remained a game played by Britons for Britons to watch. The international championship which England, Scotland, Ireland and Wales had disputed since the early 1880s, was still effectively a World Championship; it would not remain so for long.

3

the missionary spirit

Rugby Football: 1863 to 1896

From the moment F. W. Campbell and his supporters walked out of the Football Association in 1863, the distinctions between Rugby football and the 'dribbling' game were clearly defined for the first time in twenty years. Ever since the early 1840s well-meaning men had been racking their brains, sitting on endless committees and writing and rewriting the laws of football in an attempt to satisfy the supporters of two incompatible games. What is more, right up to the time that the talks finally broke down, there is no doubt that both 'carrying' and 'dribbling' men were determined to find a common set of rules satisfactory to all sides. Campbell and his followers must have appeared stubborn, ungrateful, even a little foolish to pass up the chance of joining a 'universal game'. To those present-day supporters of either code who care to imagine what football might have become had either side agreed on a compromise over the 'carrying' law, Mr Campbell's stubbornness must rank as heroism. Without him and his colleagues neither Association Football nor Rugby Union would have evolved as we know them now.

How close the two factions come to this compromise can be gauged by looking again at the crux of the 1863 dispute; the law about carrying the ball was still a matter of contention, but the 'dribbling' men had already given in over players catching a kicked ball; over granting a free kick after a fair catch; over the 'Rugby' off-side law by which all players had to be behind the ball; over the touchdown and the subsequent conversion attempt at goal; over goals of infinite height—all of them part of the Rugby game, all conceded because the majority sincerely wanted to keep the Rugby men inside the Association. The real row came, not over carrying, in fact, but over hacking, which Campbell had defended with supercilious jibes about his opponents' lack of guts, but over which he proved quite intractable. Yet within two years of that final split between Rugby and Association delegates, Campbell's Blackheath Club had itself abolished hacking and was calling for its suppression elsewhere. A merger of the fortunes of Soccer and Rugby had been as close as that.

Blackheath had launched the English traditions of club Rugby in the 1863–4 season with a match against Richmond, but within a couple of seasons, they were cancelling club fixtures against sides who insisted on retaining the 'hacking' rule; Richmond, too, proposed to abolish hacking in 1866, and subsequently both clubs declined to play anyone who tolerated it. Even before the formation of the Rugby Union in 1871 hacking had largely died out of club football, though it was retained at Rugby School, where kicking an adversary on the shin was presumably still considered character-building.

Without the expertise of dribbling that the Rugby-playing clubs had abandoned to the Association, the game in the 1860s was in a particularly unlovely stage of development. 'Hard. blind shoving' was the only proven formula for success, and none of the clubs had yet devised a less strenuous way of scoring tries. The sides, in most cases, were composed of twenty men each, and fifteen of these were usually forwards; their job, far from heeling the ball back to their own backs in the modern manner, was to keep it at their feet or in their hands and force it through the other side's pack. Two backs would guard the goal, a threequarter would wander about waiting for anything to burst loose from the maul, and the halves, on the rare occasions when they gained possession in open play, would as likely charge back into the heat of the scrimmage as attempt to open up the game by breaking up-field.

The only scoring that counted was a goal, made either by a well-directed fly-kick during open play (known as a field goal) or by converting a touched down try—the ball was punted out, from the point at which the try was made, to a colleague who would then kick at goal in the face of the charging defenders (a practice long defunct, but one which has left left its traces in modern American Football where the extra point after a touchdown is kicked in open play with a clutch of hefty linemen pounding at the kicker's legs). The long traditions of football at Rugby School had not succeeded in establishing even the moderate ebb and flow of play that the Association game could boast, and invigorating though it may have been to play, as a spectacle it must have been deadly dull.

It was not, however, without its followers. Many public schools had adopted the Rugby game, and large numbers of their pupils became so attached to it that they were prepared to contemplate winter afternoons playing Rugby even after it had ceased to be part of their curriculum. In the eastern part of Scotland and in Ireland, particularly, football had been developing along Rugby lines for some years, quite untroubled by the tense negotiations conducted, ostensibly on their behalf, over the question of how the game should or should not be played. Dublin University

had a club by 1854, and Rugby had been introduced at Edinburgh
Academy as early as 1851; by the mid 1860s Fettes, Loretto, Merchiston
and others were already engaged in the annual round of school matches
which have provided bread and butter for the writers of school stories
for a century and more. In 1858 a club was formed by the old boys of
Edinburgh Academy, the Academicals, and their lead was followed by
West of Scotland, Edinburgh University, Glasgow Academicals, Royal
High School Former Pupils and Merchistonians, who were all well
enough established by 1871 to consider themselves representative of
Rugby football north of the Border and an adequate pool from which to
select a national side.

The desire for an over-all body to regulate the game came from the
English clubs, and it became a pressing need in the light of the game's
bad publicity after a Richmond player had been accidentally killed during
a club practice match. Prompted by Blackheath and Richmond, a meeting
was called at the Pall Mall Restaurant in Cockspur Street, near Trafalgar
Square, in January 1871; twenty-two clubs sent delegates, twenty-one
actually turned up (the Wasps representative missed the opportunity of
founder membership by going to the wrong hotel and drinking too much
before he realised his mistake), and within two hours they had formed
the Rugby Football Union and delegated E. C. Holmes, the Richmond
captain and a barrister, to draft the Laws of the Game.

No sooner had this news reached Edinburgh than the six established
clubs, already fired by reports of the early representative games of Soccer
between Englishmen and Scotsmen living in London, challenged the
Rugby Union to a match in Scotland. In complete contrast to the evasive-
ness of the Football Association when confronted with the identical
challenge from Queen's Park, the Rugby Union accepted, and the match
was arranged for 27 March—rather less than nine weeks from the day the
Union had been formed.

Four thousand people arrived at the long, narrow pitch at Raeburn
Place, Edinburgh, to see forty men dispute the first international football
match of all time. Each side scored a try, Scotland converted theirs into a
goal and won the match. The Scottish try, in fact, would not have been
allowed had the match been played in England: their forwards picked up
the ball at a five-yard scrum, drove the whole scrummage into the goal
and then fell on the ball. This was illegal in England, and the protests of
the visitors were loud and long. The issue was settled by H. H. Almond,
headmaster of Loretto School, originator of the early inter-school matches
and an umpire on this historic day, who awarded the disputed try to
Scotland on the arbitrary but psychologically sound grounds that 'when

an umpire is in doubt, I think he is justified in deciding against the side that makes the most noise. They are probably in the wrong.'

The international matches between the home countries were to punctuate the spread of the game in the following decade as they have punctuated the development of Rugby ever since; with competitive club Rugby largely unknown in Britain until well after the Second World War, the home internationals have provided the only regular opportunities for assessing the progress of the game's skills and tactics in a century of otherwise disjointed and diverse club fixtures. Commentators who found their Soccer excitement in the vicissitudes of the F.A. and the Scottish Cups, turned again and again to the internationals for their Rugby stories, looking for the drama—and often for a measure of violence—that went unremarked in the club games. The early Scotland–Ireland matches, for example, were remarkable for the feelings they kindled in players and spectators alike. The first match between the two countries, played in 1877, was staged in Belfast in the middle of one of those not infrequent ideological disputes between Ulster and Leinster, which resulted in only two Leinster men being played alongside the thirteen Ulstermen. Scotland overwhelmed the Irish by six goals and two tries to nil. Belfast saw another Scottish victory in 1879, and in 1883 four Irishmen were carried off in the heat of battle: Wallis with a broken ankle, Whitestone and MacDonald with wrenched knees, and Morrow with 'concussion of the brain.'

But in 1881 a tremendous game saw a glorious Irish victory, their first ever and their last against Scotland for more than a decade. After a dramatic start when Graham of Scotland and Spunner of Ireland both received black eyes and two other players got involved in a boxing match, the game developed into a fiercely fought stalemate. A nil–nil draw looked likely when a piece of mishandling by an Irish back put the whole Scottish pack onside, including Graham, now nursing a kicked shin as well as his black eye by the Irish posts, who strolled across to the loose ball and touched it down. The kick was missed, and with hysteria mounting among the spectators, the Irish flung themselves at the Scottish line, only to be bundled into touch. Then a quickly taken line-out and two snap passes found the ball with Bagot, who dropped the winning goal. 'Such frantic excitement as these lightningly executed, triumphant moves evoked was never seen,' wrote a not unbiased Irishman who was on the spot that day, 'and men, women and children embraced each other indiscriminately. The spell of sorrow was broken and we returned to Dublin by the five o'clock train, supremely happy.'

This was ten years after England's first international against Scotland and six years since Ireland had first faced England in London. In those

ten years the game had spread furiously through the English provinces—
Lancashire, London, the West Country and Yorkshire and the North-
East, into Scotland's Border counties, into the smart suburbs of Dublin
and Belfast, and inevitably into Wales.

The foundations of the game in Wales have never been satisfactorily
excavated, despite the efforts of the most fanatical Rugby followers in the
one region of the British Isles where the word 'football' automatically
means Rugby. The public school of Llandovery has claimed the honour
of introducing the game to the Principality in the 1860s, but in Wales the
game has never been, as it has elsewhere in Britain and Ireland, built up
on the shoulders of the public school Old Boy and university undergraduate clubs. Rugby took root, by heaven knows what quirk of the
Celtic character, as a game of the people. The early clubs were town clubs,
clubs for working men, and clubs founded independently many miles
from each other. Llanelli and Cardiff, Swansea and Newport, the 'Big
Four' of Wales, were typical—hard, industrial towns breeding tough men
with little enough leisure. In England or Scotland these men would have
played Soccer (in Cardiff, indeed, the local football club opened the Arms
Park in 1870 to play Soccer), but in Wales the booming game was Rugby,
which spread from the towns to the villages and the valleys just as surely
as the dribbling game did in England, giving the other three home
countries a decade's start, yet taking to the game with a dedication that
gave them parity by the late 1880s and the lion's share of superiority ever
since.

Rugby was not a game that came naturally. It was a game that had to be
taught by men who loved it, frequently by men who had grown up with
it at school, before it could be fully appreciated. It was a game to play
rather than a game to watch, an acquired taste without, from the outside,
any obvious attractions that the far less hazardous Association game did
not offer. But it was also a game which bred missionaries, and while the
Football Association sat at home embellishing the national game with
Cup competitions and league championships, leaving the Empire and the
foreigners to pick up the game from itinerant civil engineers or the Royal
Navy on shore leave, the Rugby Union and its supporters carried the
message through a receptive Empire. The result was that the game was
firmly entrenched in Australia, New Zealand, Canada and South Africa—
often having dispossessed other, less tenacious football codes in the process
—long before Soccer received enough advice or encouragement to establish a foothold.

In Australia, for example, enthusiasts had founded a Rugby Union even

before there was one in Wales, in 1875, and by the early part of the 1880s
New South Wales were well enough organised to be sending a touring
side to New Zealand where the game had not been received with quite the
same readiness as it had in Sydney and its environs.

Public school emigrés from Britain had brought the kicking game to
New Zealand in the 1860s, and by the time the Rugby Union was being
formed in the old country, Soccer was taking a firm hold in such clubs and
colleges as played anything at all. But in 1870 Charles John Munro, son
of the Speaker of New Zealand's House of Representatives, returned from
school in England to his home in Nelson, a small, isolated port on the
northern tip of the South Island. The townspeople of Nelson played
Soccer; they also played the then undeveloped form of Australian Football
which they called Victorian Rules; and they varied these with a now
defunct game of their own that seems to have been a combination of both
—quite enough, one would have thought, for the young men of one small
colonial town. But Munro had watched Rugby played in England, and
persisted in his conviction that his new 'foot-ball' was worth adopting.
On 14 May 1870, the Nelson Club played Nelson College in New Zealand's first match under Rugby rules. Later that winter the men of Nelson
braved the crossing of Cook Strait and took a team to Wellington, in the
North Island, where they founded a reputation for the consumption of
alcohol and a legend of having trudged about Wellington with goalposts
slung across their shoulders looking for a piece of meadow that was not
waterlogged.

The following year Wellington acknowledged the success of the Nelson
visit by founding a club of their own. In 1872 Nelson's captain moved to
Wanganui and founded a club there; and Auckland, who had also played
a hybrid version of Victorian Rules combined with Soccer, took up Rugby
in preference. In New Zealand the spread of the game was very much a
missionary effort; the communities of both Islands were isolated from
each other; railways were scarce, roads inadequate. The impact of a new
game could not be transferred 'up the road' to the next village as it could
in South Wales or even in New South Wales. It depended on men travelling from centre to centre, men keen enough to bully the local students or
schoolboys into changing their Saturday afternoon game for one that they
had never seen before. And it meant remarkable tours like the one undertaken by the combined Auckland clubs in 1875. They took a 1,500-mile
trip in horse-cabs and packet-boats to play five games, one of them as far
south as Dunedin (about as far from Auckland as Prague is from London).
'Our footballers started today for Kawakawa,' ran a typical newspaper
report, 'and if they get there, which is doubtful, they are going to play a

match.' The touring party can hardly be blamed, one feels, for losing all their five games.

Such were the difficulties of communication that Rugby was controlled by regional bodies (Wellington, Canterbury, Otago and Auckland all had governing Unions by 1883). The New Zealand Rugby Union was not formed until 1892, and then only to facilitate dealings between each of the smaller unions. But well before that, the New Zealanders had absorbed enough Rugby know-how to exchange tours with Great Britain.

In South Africa, as in New Zealand, other football codes had to be superseded before Rugby Union could establish itself as the country's one true religion. In Rugby scripture, Military v. Civilians played at Cape Town on 23 August 1862, is recorded as the first game of Rugby to be played in Southern Africa, a fact repeated with the same kind of Old Testament authority as the 1869 Princeton v. Rutgers game is quoted as the first American Football match. And just as Princeton–Rutgers was a Soccer match, it is equally likely that Military–Civilians was Winchester Football, and not Rugby at all. For one thing, contemporary drawings show the ball as being round (by no means conclusive, but significant); for another, Winchester Football, introduced by an Old Wykehamist, Canon G. Ogilvie, and known thereafter as Gog's Game, had become very popular as 'a healthy form of winter exercise' among the young men of the Cape. Military v. Civilians, whatever its rules, was a worthy herald for South African football. After an hour-and-three-quarter's goalless play a halt was called because 'the wind changed and this would have given the Military an unfair advantage which they were far too sporting to accept'. Ten days later the match was resumed for a further three-and-a-quarter hours, until darkness saw the Military victors by two goals to one.

The spread of the game in South Africa was not as dramatic as elsewhere in the Empire, but by the 1880s several clubs had been formed in the Cape, including the perennial rivals, Stellenbosch University and the University of Cape Town. With the Gold Rush in 1886, the game spread to the Transvaal, by which time the only province without a Rugby Union was Natal, the most 'English' area of South Africa and, at that time, the only major settlement in the Empire overseas to be clinging to a Soccer tradition in the face of Rugby expansion. It did not last; by the early 1890s Natal too had capitulated and a Rugby Union was formed. The game grew steadily more popular, and Soccer faded into insignificance.

Rugby's advance through the Empire was led, to a great degree, by men with a positive desire to convert the non-believer. In contrast, the game's strangest conquest was effected by example—by curious pupils watching uninvited, and being captivated by what they saw; stranger still, the pupil was temperamentally as far distant from the British Empire as it is possible to be, and spoke, for the most part, no English. The unwitting teachers were young executives of the London wine trade sent out to look after the important end of the business in the southern districts of France; their impromptu games of Rugby inspired Frenchmen to form their own clubs, and to this day the main support in France for the game has been in the South.

The Rugby that tempted Frenchmen to take off their berets and kick a ball about was in few respects the same 'hard-shoving' slog that had emerged from the hacking controversy of the 1860s. The early years of club Rugby had demonstrated that to make the game more acceptable for the players, let alone the spectators, it had to move faster and more freely. The stimulus for this came from the universities. Oxford and Cambridge played the first of their annual matches in the 1871–2 season, and within a year or two the fixture had achieved a status barely lower than that of the internationals. Its importance was reflected in 1875 when a decision by the two captains to play fifteen-a-side instead of twenty-a-side on the great day resulted in an exciting match and almost immediate and universal imitation, welcomed not only, one would imagine, by those seeking a more open game, but also by hard-pressed club secretaries and their many descendants, who had their weekly struggle of finding twenty men per team reduced by twenty-five per cent. The new formation used nine forwards, two halves, two threequarters and two full-backs, and the increased freedom in all departments of the game was further increased by the 'down' rule, now an integral part of the Rugby Union game but one which was never adopted by American Football and which Rugby League subsequently abandoned: it required a player to release the ball as soon as he was tackled, and not to play it again until he had left the ruck.

The reduction in the number of forwards brought an increase in open play, and with the loose ball more evident, footwork in the open by forwards became a tactical necessity with dribbling, hitherto the province of the despised Association Game, a new and effective art. Another practice, now forgotten, was 'foiking'—hooking the ball out of the side of the scrum with the foot, from between the legs of forwards still reluctant to heel the ball; foiking led to a counter-move, invented by the Bradford Club but perfected and exploited by Newport, of wheeling the scrum, a legitimate surprise tactic even today, but a formidable weapon when a charging pack of nine forwards with the ball at their feet could break away from a wheel with only half a dozen defenders between them and the line. Even in the early 1880s, when first Scotland and then the other countries converted their second full-back to a third threequarter, Rugby was still a pounding, kicking and carrying game; the significance of quick passing from hand to hand had not yet been realised.

The development of this potential, and with it a tremendous stride towards the sophistication of modern Rugby, was launched during half a dozen remarkable seasons at Oxford University, when the tactical ideas of two otherwise unconnected Rugby enthusiasts were fused into an invincible combination by the most powerful player of the age. In the early 1880s, Oxford was well provided with the former pupils of Loretto School. The headmaster, Dr H. H. Almond—the phlegmatic umpire of that first international in 1871—was a fanatical supporter of the game as played at his school, and something of a Rugby theoretician. There is evidence for supposing him to have been a supporter of the fast, open game, prompted by quick, disciplined passing and snap kicking (a clear parallel, incidentally, with the tactics being used so successfully against English teams at this time by Scotland's Soccer teams); certainly Almond was remembered by contemporaries 'in his quintuple capacity of Head-master, captain, forward, umpire and coach, rushing about the field crying out to his boys "Pass, pass, pass!" and "Kick, kick, kick!" ' And it was no coincidence that between 1880 and 1884 there were never fewer than four Loretto men in the Oxford XV against Cambridge.

At the same time, at the Blackheath Club, another accomplished theoretician, Arthur Budd, had seen that the reduction of the forwards from thirteen or fourteen to nine had left the game much freer for short inter-passing between them, and for short tap-kicking into open spaces. Budd had no influence at Oxford himself, but he did have a young protegé at Blackheath, Henry Vassall, who had just left Marlborough with the singular distinction of having been the last man to captain the school's Rugby Twenty and, the following year, the first to captain the Rugby Fifteen. Harry Vassall was a huge, fearsome giant of a forward with calf muscles thicker than most men's thighs and a fine football brain. He took Budd's theories to Oxford, where he won his Blue in 1879 and again in 1880, captained the University side in 1881 and virtually governed it in 1882. There he found the willing Lorettonians, some of his own schoolfellows and various other eager experimenters, and within a couple of years had perfected a devastating passing game which paid dividends beyond the dreams of any Rugby coach today.

Vassall looked on his half-backs not as suicidal runners, as they had

become in club Rugby, but as the vital links between the forwards and
the threequarters. He trained his pack to forget the old ideas of ramming
the ball forever forward at the opposition, and instead to get the ball *back*
to the halves, the halves to pass out to the threequarters and the three-
quarters to run fast and elusively. As a variation, he had introduced the
'kick and rush' attack by which his forwards, in line abreast, would charge
through the opposing backs with the ball at their feet, led by Vassal himself 'going like a traction engine'. It was a tactic he was thought to have
developed as captain at Marlborough when, after a boy had been badly
hurt in a maul, it had been expressly forbidden by the school authorities
for a forward to pick the ball up. So well was Vassal's side led, and such
talent did he develop, that during his career at Oxford, seventeen of his
players won international caps, and the University went three-and-a-half
years without defeat.

Vassall was further helped by the supreme skill of his two half-backs
(they played then not as scrum-half and outside-half, but together at the
base of the scrum; there were still nine forwards, and the ball left the
pack only when the scrum 'broke down' or the opposition charged or
kicked it through—too much for one half-back to cope with alone).
Grant Asher, a Scotsman from Loretto, was a powerful passer of the ball
and a hard, feared defender as well, a man with Rugby in his blood since his
early days at school, who took over Vassall's side as captain in 1884 and
produced, some people said, an even greater team. His partner, Alan
Rotherham, from Uppingham, had played Soccer at school, and only
started playing Rugby after some intense individual coaching by Vassall
and Asher. He became England's best half-back of the 19th century,
a clever runner, an accurate if deliberate passer, and a master of the newly
devised 'dummy'. (This was a somewhat heavy-handed ruse in retrospect:
Rotherham would raise the ball high above his head as he ran, in the
manner of an American quarterback, and shout out the name of one of
his threequarters; as the opposing forwards converged on the nominee,
Rotherham would drop his hands and run on with the ball. Astonishingly,
it seems to have been effective.)

These two half-backs, inheriting Vassall's tactics and supported at the
back by C. G. Wade, from Australia, and two more highly gifted Lorettonians, G. C. Lindsay at centre and the full-back Henry Tristram, made
even the most powerful opposition look so inferior that the spectators at
Oxford took to watching matches on the opponents' 25-yard line rather
than from half-way; they so captured the imagination of visiting Welsh
teams that their style and combination-work laid the foundations for the
improvements in Welsh football that began to bear fruit in the late 1880s

and has never wavered since. And that, for a team of young English and Scottish undergraduates, is a lot to answer for.

With the success of Oxford's passing tactics, it became increasingly important for the half-backs to get a fast service from their forwards, and the heel from the scrum became widespread, both feeding the backs fast and protecting the half-back as the ball went loose. The forwards, now that they were no longer concerned with kicking the ball forward through the opposing pack, were able to put their heads down and shove; the innovation was heartily scorned by older forwards of the iron-shinned brigade, but it gave the scrum a far more efficient, stream-lined look, and has changed little since.

Other patterns of the game were moving towards the shape we should recognise today. In the 1885–6 season Cardiff successfully experimented with four threequarters by dropping one of the forwards, and the national team followed suit. So, subsequently, did everyone else, not because they particularly wanted to (there were strong doubts expressed, and never entirely disproved, that the outside threequarters would be squeezed out towards the touchlines and so rendered ineffective) but because a team with only three threequarters could never defend itself for long against a team with four.

Towards the end of the century the half-backs, throughout Rugby's modern history the most influential players in a well-balanced team, assumed something like their present roles. The scrum was now well-knit and disciplined, and there was no longer any need for both half-backs to wait at the forwards' feet for a ball hustled out by the opposing pack. The forwards themselves by now usually packed with three men in the front row, two locks behind them, and three at the back. (Even so, 'first come first down' was still the order of the day; not until 1903 did the Welshman Travers begin to specialise as hooker in the centre of the front row, and even he, after Wales's triumph over the first All-Blacks in 1905, was still described in the press merely as 'a forward'.) In addition the channelled heel to the lone scrum-half was practised to perfection. This left the outside half—the stand-off or fly half, as he became known— enough room to launch the attack by running, kicking or passing to his threequarters: a simple enough theory but one which, even at the turn of the century, was not fully developed, and only reached full effectiveness in the Oxford University XVs with Adrian Stoop as the principal strategist.

Finally, almost ludicrously, the International Board in 1892 laid down what shape of ball Rugby was to be played with. Everyone knew, of course, that Soccer was played with a round ball and Rugby with an oval one, and had been since anyone had started to think about rules. However, it remained a fact that no Rugby law to that time had specified a size or a shape for its principal piece of equipment.

Why Rugby School played with an oval ball is just not known. The simplest answer is that an inflated pig's bladder is roughly oval in shape (doubters can verify this easily by removing the bladder from a dead pig, waiting until it is rotten enough to be pliable, and inflating it) and the first efficient footballs were the inflated bladders of pigs. However, if a pig's bladder is put into a leather case, the bladder will inflate to the shape of that case, so the outline of the Rugby ball was dictated by tradition rather than necessity.

We know, anyway, that by 1835 the ball was oval (*Tom Brown's Schooldays* speaks of the ball lying 'quite by itself, pointing towards the School goal'), and we know that certainly by the 1840s, and probably earlier, it was covered in leather to the shape of the bladder rather than the shape of a sphere. The balls were made for Rugby by the firm of William Gilbert, who were also bootmakers to the School; Gilbert used to hang the bladders until they were 'green' and stinking, then inflate them with his own lung power, gaining such a reputation in the process that one of his Rugby balls was on show at the Great Exhibition of 1851 as an 'Educational Appliance'. In the arguments over the rules of football which resulted in the Soccer–Rugby split, no draft proposals, not even, as far as can be established, any of the heated discussions, even mentioned the shape of the ball; it presumably did not seem worth worrying about at the time, though how Soccer would have developed with an elliptical ball, or Rugby with a spherical one, makes interesting speculation.

In any event, another man from Rugby, Mr Lindon, thought up a way in 1870 for making bladders out of rubber and inflating them with a pump, and there was never any serious proposal for adopting a different shape of ball. Its squat appearance in the early days, and even under the 1892 law, made it ideal for place-kicking and drop-kicking and only the later emphasis on running, passing and carrying persuaded the authorities to adopt a narrower, torpedo-like shape; accordingly, in 1931, its width was reduced by roughly 1½ inches.

In the first twenty-five years of the Rugby Union's influence the game, quite apart from developing in skill and popularity and being readily adopted by new converts throughout the pink areas of the world map, had become highly disciplined. It is, of course, a game which could be, and just occasionally is, destroyed if the inherent violence is not kept voluntarily in check. Luckily, from the start of the Rugby Union the

rules were strict and very detailed, and while giving the referee a certain
degree of latitude, they clearly set the limits beyond which players could
not transgress. The laws of American Football had got completely out of
hand in the 1870s and 1880s because coaches and college players alike were
given the opportunity to flout them: they ran in front of their ball-carrier
to protect him, barging defenders out of their way, despite the fact that it
was against the rules. The intercollegiate authorities, and the officials on
the field of play, were too weak to stand against it, so interference was at
first tolerated, then accepted in the rules, then regarded with horror
as students were maimed and concussed in the ensuing 'mass' plays.

Rugby kept this sort of 'revolution by default' firmly in check; the
referees who, as in Soccer, had relegated the two umpires to the boundaries
as 'touch judges' with even less power than the Soccer linesmen, were
usually experienced ex-players, and they were firm; the International
Board (a somwhat grandiose term, in those days, meaning England,
Scotland, Ireland and Wales) kept their hands firmly against the passionate competitiveness that, they must have felt, had contributed to the more
extravagant developments of the American game. They were fair, idealistic
men, deeply concerned about the quality of the game they had all played,
firmly in control of its development throughout the world, still untroubled
in their dreams by the devastating problems of professionalism which
were soon to be upon them.

Their concern was not, as with that of the Association Football authorities, to consolidate the game at home, but to stimulate it abroad. It was
already evident that Rugby had become a middle-class-oriented game in
Scotland, Ireland and the greater part of England, and was fast becoming
a religion in Wales. The International Board and their overseas equiva-
lents were now able to launch the one great attraction that Rugby held
long before any other of the world's football games—the overseas tour.
It needed money, of course, and it needed players who either could
afford the time off work or who came from an area where the boss might
be sufficiently interested to allow them the necessary freedom; but acting
on the precedent so successfully pioneered by England and Australian
cricket teams, the Rugby unions developed a system of reciprocal visits
that has done more than anything to keep alive world-wide interest in the
game.

The preliminaries to the great series of tours were acted out in Australia
and New Zealand. The Auckland coastal tour of 1875 had been a grotesque
prototype, in some ways a primitive foretaste of the time-honoured
British club tour (now, perhaps mercifully, on the wane) and its unreal
world of sing-songs, missed coaches, sub-standard rugger and being sick

in Somerset village streets at three o'clock on Easter Monday morning. But in 1882 a party of New South Wales Rugby men took the boat for a seven-match tour of the New Zealand clubs; two years later the New Zealanders replied with eight matches in New South Wales and Queensland, and the Australians were back in New Zealand in 1886. A pattern was set, only to be overturned in 1888 by the simultaneous launching of two gargantuan tours—one by New Zealanders to Britain, the other by Britain to the Antipodes.

The New Zealand and Native team, known generally but misleadingly as 'The Maoris', though the great majority of the twenty-seven-strong party were of British descent, undertook what is probably the most strenuous sporting tour in history. They were not officially sponsored by any New Zealand Rugby body, but were promoted by private sponsors in the hope of a profit from attendance receipts (one of the sponsors was the captain, Joe Warbrick). The party was away from New Zealand for more than a year—from June 1888 to August 1889—visiting the British Isles, France, Ceylon and Australia. In the British Isles alone they played seventy-four matches, winning forty-nine of them and beating Ireland in one of their three Internationals (they lost the other two to Wales and England). In all they struggled through a hundred and seventeen games, sometimes playing five in a week to keep the money coming in.

The other tour, the first British Isles team to be fielded and the forerunner of the celebrated British Lions tours, was not the idea of the Rugby fraternity at all. Three cricketers two of whom had been on the MCC's 1887–8 tour of Australia, were sure that a Rugby tour along the same lines as the successful cricket series would be popular and, with luck, profitable. They put their proposal forward to the Rugby Union, who were sympathetic but unconvinced. The lack of experience, and the lack of seasoned professionals, they felt, would make the venture too much of a risk. So the cricketers went away and organised a tour on their own. A. E. Stoddart, opening batsman for Middlesex and England and strong-running threequarter for Blackheath, went as joint captain with the Broughton Park forward R. L. Seddon; and two Nottinghamshire players of the highest class—Arthur Shrewsbury (whom W. G. Grace considered the best batsman of the age next to himself) and Alfred Shaw, the finest bowler of his day—went along as joint managers of a touring party with only twenty-two players. (The long-term results for Rugby were incalculable, but the short-term repercussions on the cricket front were less happy: a nine-month tour meant missing a whole English summer. Stoddart was an amateur and a law to himself, but Nottingham were furious about the defection of their two great professionals; Shaw was now in his mid-forties and nearing the end of a long career, but Shrewsbury, at thirty-two, was in the middle of a prodigious run of high-scoring seasons, and it took a long time for the ill-feeling to die down.)

Four months of the tour were spent on board various ships. In the intervening periods they played 41 matches in Australia (25 of them under the 18-a-side Victorian Football rules) and 19 in New Zealand. They won 27 of the 35 Rugby fixtures, losing only twice to provincial sides in New Zealand, and generally showed a quality of back play as yet undeveloped outside Britain. And the team's versatility can be judged by the fact that though none of them had ever played the game before, they won 14 of their 25 Australian Football matches.

The tourists played no test matches on this tour—the first overseas internationals by a British side being reserved for the visit to South Africa in 1891. This time the International Rugby Board gave its full blessing, though the South African Board baulked at the complexities of arranging their end of the tour, and it was left to the Western Province Union to conclude the arrangements, with a guarantee against loss by no less a Rugby enthusiast than Cecil Rhodes himself. 'Let them come', he said. 'I shall stand surety for any shortfall.'

They came all right, though the commemorative history of South African Rugby, brought out by their Board to mark its seventy-fifth anniversary, might leave one in some doubt; in a vain attempt to rewrite the past, the compilers omitted all details of the 1891 tour. One can understand their reticence, for W. E. Maclagan's party of only twenty-one players steamrollered everything that opposed them. Before the voyage out Sir Donald Currie, then head of the Castle Line, gave Maclagan a cup to present to the team that 'put up the best showing' against the British tourists. As side after side capitulated to the Britons' speed and expertise, and the virtually unstoppable running of Blackheath's R. L. Aston at threequarter, the cup became more and more of an embarrassment. In the end it had to go to Griqualand West because they had lost their match by only a goal (they subsequently presented it to their Rugby Board, and it now represents the major trophy for inter-provincial competition).

The British tourists played 19 matches and won them all, including three tests. Aston ran in for 33 tries, a total never approached since by a British player abroad, and the Lions scored in all 224 points against one solitary try in reply—a record equalled only by the unbeaten All-Black tour to Britain and France in 1924, and for defensive invincibility not matched even by them.

In 1896 the Rugby Board sent another tour to South Africa. In many ways it was as successful as the first—played 21, won 19, drawn 1, lost 1—

conceding only 45 points against the 310 they scored. But the one defeat that carried as much significance as any of the 19 victories, proving that the unselfish policies of expansion by the Rugby men had at last had its effect, and giving notice that the pupils from New Zealand and South Africa were now fully capable of holding their own with the masters (so much so that after the 1896 tour the British Isles tourists had to wait seventy-five years before beating either of those countries in an international series on their home territory).

For the first time the Irish had a contingent in the touring side—five of them forwards, with a well-developed scrum-wheeling technique that bewildered almost every team they encountered—led by Tommy Crean, whose one curb on his countrymen's high spirits appears to have been to restrict them to four glasses of champagne at lunch on match days. But even the champagne and the scrum-wheeling know-how deserted them on 5 September 1896, when South Africa scored the only try of the game, inflicted on Britain her first Test Match defeat, and presaged a tremendous upsurge in the South African game in particular and overseas Rugby in general.

As Rugby neared the end of the century, it could look back on some twenty-five years of development that contrast significantly with those of Soccer's own evolution. The games themselves had both taken tremendous strides, developing techniques of attack, defence, specialisation and sheer individual expertise that could hardly have been foreseen when Rugby men parted so decisively with the young Football Association. But the attitudes of the men who ran the game ensured that the the two British brands of football would tread quite separate paths to popularity. Both Association and Rugby administrators were from the same background— public school, usually university, usually one of the leading amateur clubs. The Association men, under Charles Alcock, recognised that the popular appeal of their game was spreading so fast that their major task was to improve the administration of the game at home—to sanction and administer crowd-pulling competitions, to build up domestic internationals, to control the early years of professionalism as best they could. With all this on their plates there was little time to concern themselves with the propagation of the game abroad, and the few goodwill tours that did take place were undertaken by individual clubs. As a result the administration of world Soccer developed slowly, haphazardly and out of the control of the countries who had invented the game and understood it best.

The Rugby men, on the other hand, were proud of the social cameraderie which their game had, almost by its very nature, developed. In New

Zealand, Australia, Canada, everywhere Rugby was played, the instinct was to take a train or a boat or a horse-bus or, if necessary, a camel caravan and find other people to play against—preferably men of similar background, preferably a long way off. And if there was no one there who knew the game, they would play amongst themselves in the hope of kindling interest among the spectators.

It was a laudable attitude, but a blinkered one. The Soccer men did not avert their eyes from the growing working-class attraction to their game; the Rugby men did. They failed to understand the fierce pride engendered in the Northern and Midland cities by the successes of their own football teams; that club Rugby in the South was not the same as Rugby between rival towns in Yorkshire; that warm-hearted exchanges on deserted fields were no substitute for hard competition between glory-seeking heroes egged on by partisan supporters in the stands. Soccer's appeal is so universal, so simple, that the inward-looking attitudes of its administrators in the 1870s and 1880s were no tragedy; the game spread in spite of them. But Rugby's attractions, if they were not absorbed at school with Latin and Greek and Algebra, needed intelligent and careful encouragement. With this understanding, Rugby might have become a national preoccupation on the scale of Soccer, as it succeeded in becoming in the more enclosed communities of Wales and New Zealand and South Africa. Without it, the game was to suffer a disastrous setback in the late 1890s which broke Rugby in two and from which neither half has yet fully recovered.

4

an american revolution

American Football: 1869 to 1900

Organised football came late to America. Even by the early 1860s, when the young gentlemen at Oxford and Cambridge were beginning to come to some sort of agreement about how to conduct this new pastime to everyone's satisfaction, the game in America had discovered no recognisable form for itself. There was no grass-roots tradition in the towns and villages of the Eastern seaboard, and few, if any, of the rollicking, disorganised, English and Scottish village games seem to have survived the passage across the Atlantic; perhaps the village footballer was not the type to seek a new world; certainly the formative years of the United States, when British agricultural traditions were carved into the American countryside, were grim, hard, and lonely. Farms were remote and isolated, villages were trading centres rather than cosy united communities and a New England farmer certainly did not see so much of his neighbours that he would consider spending every May Day screwing their faces into the New England mud in the name of friendly competition.

Such football as had arisen in American in the early years of the 19th century had come mainly from the exchange of academic tradition between the two powerful English-speaking nations. The schools for the sons of the American bourgeoisie were understandably similar to the schools for the sons of the British rich, and as British schoolboys retained their playing-field and cloister games for their leisured years at university, so American schoolboys enlivened the hours on campus with the team games encouraged (or, more likely, tolerated) at their English-oriented schools. We are told that in 1820 (when William Webb Ellis, at thirteen years of age, was still three seasons away from his triumphant piece of opportunism) a form of kicking football, called 'ballown', was played at Princeton. There are sporadic accounts, too, of other forms of football being played in various Eastern Colleges during the first half of the century—all differing in the details of their rules but all tending to the kicking tradition, with the handling used as a convenience for stopping the ball rather than as a means for carrying or propelling it. All the games were internal

affairs, too; intercollegiate sport, for so many decades to be the preoccupation of the American press and the American middle classes, was as yet
unknown.

There is some suggestion that the games were a good deal less gentlemanly than the variations being played in Britain at the time. The Harvard
authorities were forced to prohibit football from the campus altogether
(it seems, by all accounts, to have been more of an initiation test for freshmen than a game for general participation; perhaps Harvard was only
trying to restrict organised bullying), and at New Haven, Connecticut,
it was the town rather than the gown who took a repressive hand, for the
city fathers forbade Yale students to play football on the public green.
Both these bans were introduced around 1860, but football in a more
conventional form was making rapid progress, and it was from the third of
the Big Three universities that the constructive steps came.

The years of enlightenment, of good clean clashes between good clean
college boys, of glorious victory and honourable defeat in the crisp autumn
air for the sake of the old school, are measured by all true-blooded Americans from November 1869, when the first intercollegiate football game
was played between Princeton and Rutgers University at New Brunswick,
New Jersey. Two seasons earlier, in fact, in 1867, Princeton men had
drawn up a code of rules limiting the sides to twenty-five players each,
and Princeton University had played a game against the Princeton
Theological Seminary that very year. The conventions accepted at
Rutgers were slightly different, and, being the home side, their rules were
used in the Princeton match. And it is curious, particularly in the light
of the subsequent elevation of this game as the unassailable watershed of
America's football tradition, that in virtually every respect the two teams
were playing Soccer. They used a round ball, their aim was to put the ball
through the opposing goal (rather than touch it down, as a Rugby tradition
would demand), and no running with the ball was permitted. (The Princeton rules, under which a return match was played a week later, also
allowed a free kick after a fair catch as in the current English Soccer rules;
Rutgers rules, in the tradition of Gaelic Football, allowed players to bat the
ball with their hands as well as kick it.) There was no time limit on the
game—the two captains decided that the first to score six goals would be
the winner; Rutgers won 6–4.

The game began at 3 p.m., undeterred by an old Rutgers professor who
pedalled up to the scene on his bicycle, watched the proceedings for a
moment, then stalked away shouting, 'You men will come to no Christian
end.' One of the players, John W. Herbert, wrote of that first game some
sixty-five years later:

On the arrival of the players a few minutes before the game was called, they laid aside their hats, coats and vests. Neither team was in uniform, although some Rutgers players wore scarlet stocking caps.

The players lined up on each side, the organisation of the twenty-five being the same on both sides. Two men were selected by each team to play immediately in front of the opponents' goal and were known as the captains of the enemy's goal.

The remainder of each team was divided into two sections, the players in one section were assigned to certain tracts of the field which they were to cover and not to leave. They were known as 'fielders'. The other section was detailed to follow the ball up and down the field. These latter players were known as 'bulldogs'. They were easily recognisable in the evolution of the game as the forerunners of the modern rush line. I played in this division as I was a good wrestler and fleet of foot . . .

After the return game at Princeton (the rules had been amended so that eight goals were required for victory, and Princeton won 8–0), the authorities at both colleges got together to prohibit a decider. But the football tradition was well-founded, and no year has passed since that autumn of 1869 without American colleges playing football against each other. In 1870 Columbia University, New York, joined the intercollegiate group and two years later Yale played Columbia in a twenty-a-side game at New Haven. In October 1873 these four founding colleges met in the first Intercollegiate Rules Convention, a meeting that might, and—considering the enormous influence these four giants had over football in its infancy— probably should, have established the pattern of American college football for the rest of the century. The delegates agreed uniform rules along the lines of British Association Football, spoke warmly, no doubt, as youthful sportsmen will at social gatherings, of future games between their respective colleges, and possibly looked forward to converting the footballers of the other great north-eastern university, Harvard, away from the strange running-and-carrying 'Boston game' that they were reported to have been playing up in Cambridge, Massachusetts, since the lifting of that 1860 ban. The seal, so it seemed, was placed on the success of the kicking game when a team from England called the 'Eton Players'—playing, we can assume, something not far removed from the Eton Field Game—played a match against Yale. Yale beat the tourists 2–1, but were highly impressed by their opponents' enthusiasm for the freedom of movement given by the eleven-a-side game, as compared with the Intercollegiate Convention's twenty-a-side.

The various bargainings, persuadings and tantrums that ensued before the apparently entrenched Soccer rules gave way to the basic principles of America's present carry-and-rush game were many and heated; but, in the truest tradition of American innovation, they were done with energy and they were done fast. In the winter of 1873, in such American universities as cared, Soccer was the accepted game. By November 1876 the tables had been turned, Rugby was adopted, and American Football was on its rampaging way.

The initial credit must go to Harvard. Because of their infatuation with a carrying game they had been excluded from the deliberations—and the fixture lists—of the game's other four protagonists. They turned, for competition, to McGill University of Montreal, who played to conventional British Rugby rules with the refinement that tries—crossing the opponents' line with the ball to earn a free kick at goal—could be counted in the result if the goals were equal. Harvard and McGill played three games, the first to Harvard rules, the other two to Rugby rules; and Harvard (who won two and drew the other) were captivated by the Rugby conventions. They adopted Rugby rules with enthusiasm and, with a healthy desire to put one across the old enemy, challenged Yale to a game of Rugby. And Yale, in their turn, were won over to the running and spirited tackling of the Rugby code; they adopted the rules as their own, and at the same time persuaded the Harvard men to adapt the new game to their eleven-a-side formation.

This game was watched, in its turn, by two Princeton men who took the good news back home and gave such a glowing account of it that Princeton adopted Rugby rules on the spot; on 23 November 1867, at Massasoit House, Springfield, the delegates of Harvard, Yale, Columbia, and Princeton (Rutgers had now been left behind in the hectic manoeuvrings of more powerful opponents) formed the Intercollegiate Football Association. The Rugby Union code was adopted, though with rule 7 reading: 'A match shall be decided by a majority of touchdowns. A goal shall be equal to four touchdowns, but in case of a tie, a goal kicked from a touchdown shall take precedence over four touchdowns.' The round rubber ball was replaced by the oval, leather-cased one. And, much to the disgust of the Yale representatives, the sides remained at fifteen men apiece.

A week before this meeting was held, a seventeen-year-old freshman played his first game at half-back for Yale, in their now annual and ferociously contested match against Harvard. Walter C. Camp was this teenager: the first great name to be thrown up by the new game, the Father of American Football, and one of the very few men in history who can really be said to have changed, single-handed, by his own imagination and energy, some part of his country's way of life.

Camp was barely out of high school when Rugby was officially adopted at Yale; at the next convention of the Intercollegiate Football Association he was Yale's representative. By the time Camp attended his last Rules Committee, in the spring of 1925, college football was America's winter obsession, college football players were heroes, college football coaches as powerful as five-star generals, and American Football a game unique in the world in a way which would have been quite inconceivable to the carefree runners and kickers of 1876. And without Walter Camp it is possible—even likely—that American Football would never have happened.

Walter Camp's life story, even from the land of idealised success stories, is almost too perfect to be true. That he was half-back on the Yale football team for six years (there was no limitation in those days) seems consistent with his later pre-eminence in the control of that growing sport; and given his prowess at football, it is only with mild surprise that we learn that he was the fastest schoolboy runner in all New Haven.

But he was also a baseball player of class, numbered among the very first to master the art of pitching a curve; as a hurdler he is given credit at Yale for having invented the present hurdle stride; he swam competitively, with success, at distances ranging from short sprints to five miles; he was something of a tennis player in the years before the game really caught the public imagination; he rowed in the Yale eight. He captained the University at baseball and football; he was a member of the team at every sport at which Yale competed.

After two years as a post-graduate at Yale Medical School, during which his sporting career continued at its customary pace, he turned to business, joined the sales force of the New Haven Clock Company as a salesman and—almost inevitably, one feels—rose effortlessly to become chairman of the board. And when not selling clocks to the people of Connecticut, he found the time to become one of the great football coaches, creating victorious Yale elevens season after season. He rounded off this picture of unsullied, respectable New England success by marrying well and fathering a son who played football for Yale and a daughter who, almost surprisingly, did not. 'And,' says an obituary tribute published in the *Football Guide* of 1925, a publication which Camp founded in 1883 and edited until his death, 'he gave generously of his time to the civic and charitable movements of the city of New Haven.' It is not recorded whether he ever relaxed.

A comparison which Englishmen can draw, and which even Americans can appreciate, is between the respective careers of Camp in America and C. B. Fry in England. As sporting phenomena both are unique. Fry's achievements included setting the world's long-jump record, playing

Soccer for England, playing Rugby at the highest level, and making some 30,000 runs in first-class cricket. Charles Fry also ran a boy's training ship, edited his own magazine, represented India at the League of Nations in Geneva, and turned down an offer of the Crown of Albania. He was an intellectual, too, which makes him, in a curiously satisfying way, very much an English phenomenon. Camp, quite apart from the achievements listed so far, succeeded by his own imagination, his own gifts of persuasion and his own conviction that he was *right*, in transforming an enjoyable game played and watched by East Coast college boys into an entirely different, man-made, utterly riveting game played and followed through the length and breadth of his country. And that seems to make him, in the same curiously satisfying way, very much an American phenomenon.

The first major attack on the Rugby rules was made in 1878 when Camp, still only nineteen years old but showing all the assurance of a hard-bitten union negotiator, attended the second rules convention as a member of Yale's delegation. From the start of the meeting he behaved much as if he had invented the game and considered himself at liberty to change the rules as he wished; he demanded that the convention reduce the size of the teams to eleven-a-side. The convention, not to be dictated to by an aggressive young upstart however good a half-back he might be, voted the motion out. And the following year they repeated their rejection of the eleven-a-side rule proposed by Camp, as well as another unconventional idea he had put forward—that of counting 'safeties' (the 'touching down' of the ball behind one's own line in order to get a free kick out) as points against the defending side.

Camp had also begun to work out in his own mind, though without discussing it in open committee, one of the fundamental changes in the shape of the game, a change that was specifically alien to the spirit of Rugby. The Rugby scrum, as a method of putting the ball into play after a stoppage, was a necessary convention if 'open play' was to be maintained. The scrum gave, and still gives, a moderate advantage to the side putting the ball in, but at the same time left the outcome (as to which side would in fact gain possession) so much in doubt that both teams had to be prepared for attack or defence until the last moment. It was not orderly, but it was exciting, and it added an extra dimension to the game.

Camp was in this, as in almost every stand that he was to take on the rules of the game, in favour of orderliness. Once a team had possession, he argued, they should be given a full opportunity of planning a manoeuvre with the ball; and to do this, they should be allowed to put the ball into play unhampered. It meant, a British chorus would now argue, the death of open, see-sawing play, of defence turned by brilliant inspiration into attack, of sudden, thrilling turns of fortune. On the contrary, a million Americans would retort, it meant the development of brilliantly conceived, dazzlingly executed attacks countered by finely deployed, perfectly drilled defence. The arguments are futile, Camp had his way.

His big day was 12 October 1880, at Springfield, at the annual inter-collegiate convention. It began with the now customary proposal by Camp and his Yale supporters to reduce the teams to eleven, and, surprisingly enough, the motion was accepted. He then delivered carefully worded proposals for further changes in the rules. A scrimmage, he ordained, would take place when the man in possession put the ball into play by kicking the ball or 'snapping' it back with his foot. The man who received it, the 'quarterback', would not be allowed to run forward with the ball. The meeting accepted the motion unanimously, and also confirmed that the game would—as it had ever since—be played in a much more re-stricted area than any of the other major football games. The size of the field was set at 110 yards by a mere $53\frac{1}{3}$ yards, a long, narrow arena which would rarely countenance the long, lateral passing that has given Rugby so many of its thrills and so many of its heroes.

It wasn't long before Camp and his (by now thoroughly converted) convention colleagues found themselves profoundly embarrassed by their new rules. Camp had expected that the opportunities presented by un-hampered possession would result in field-long moves prompted by long runs and high, ground-gaining punts. It can have been less than encouraging for him to play in the Princeton games of 1880 and 1881 under his proud new rules; Princeton's strategists were not prepared to kick the ball into the air for Yale to gain possession. They employed, instead, their 'block' game, which meant nothing more sophisticated than getting hold of the ball at the earliest opportunity and hanging on to it indefinitely. Their strategy had not got as far as devising ways to attack while in possession, so the 1880 game petered out into a scoreless draw. The following year the farce was varied slightly in that while Princeton retained the ball without scoring in the first half it was Yale who retained the ball without scoring in the second half. It is open to argument, of course, as are all such sporting assertions, but there must be a good case for assuming the Princeton–Yale game of 1881 to have been the dullest football match of any kind played anywhere ever.

Walter Camp saw that it was not good, and out of chaos he brought forth a system of 'downs'—if, in three attempts, the team in possession had not advanced five yards, possession would be surrendered. This proposal, accepted by a relieved convention in 1882, formed another fundamental of the American game that has never altered (in 1906 the distance to be gained in the three 'downs' was doubled to 10 yards, and in 1912 the attacking side was given an extra play in which to make the yardage—10 yards in 4 downs. So it has remained). With this principle— the necessity of earning your right to retain the ball once you had gained possession—came another of those characteristics that appear ludicrous to the uninitiated and wholly indispensable to the *aficionado*. This is the gridiron, the officials' ruler marked out in parallel lines the full length of the pitch at five-yard intervals to help them in the mathematical tasks that Camp's new rule had imposed upon them. They certainly needed a bit of help; their job was becoming an extremely difficult one. Theoretic- ally the captains were the only players allowed to dispute a referee's decision, but with the increasing complexity of the rules, many of which were as difficult to interpret for the players as they were for the spectators, the spectacle of a referee surrounded by furious, gesticulating players after every decision became more and more common. It took some time, too, for the five-yard markings to become generally accepted: the referee kept note of the forward progress of the team in possession by dropping a handkerchief at the point where the ball was last put into play, and by measuring with the eye from there to the next down; it is not surprising that in the heat of the battle the referee's attention could be diverted in one direction while the handkerchief was kicked advantageously in another.

In the early 1880s the ever-watchful Camp was becoming impatient with the scoring system. It had up to now closely followed the Rugby system of quantitative scoring—one type of score being balanced against another, with a field goal being worth more than a touchdown, and a goal —a 'converted' touchdown—worth more than any number of touch- downs, which were only taken into consideration in the case of a tie. (In Rugby, at this time, the rule was even more severe: a 'try' was worth nothing unless converted, and had no value even as the decider in a stale- mate). It is no wonder that this led to anomalies from time to time, and the last straw seems to have been provided by the 1882 Harvard–Princeton game, in which Harvard scored a touchdown but failed to make a goal on the try, and then scored a field goal; Princeton's only reply was a touch- down which was converted to a goal; each team claimed their goal as the superior one (the rules were not clear on the matter); the referee awarded the game to Harvard, and Princeton went off in a temper, refused to accept the decision and for years afterwards insisted on claiming the match as a Princeton victory.

Camp's answer was a system of points about which there could be no such arguments: at the rules convention of 1883 the following were accepted: two points for a touchdown, four points for a goal from a try, five points for a field goal, one point (to the other side) for a safety. It is perhaps worth noting that this innovation marked the first instance of American Football leading where Rugby was to follow. In all his other legislation so far, Camp had been moving away from the slow but determined evolution of Rugby Union. In this case he had put his finger on what was clearly, whatever the code followed, a weakness in the system. Three years later, in 1886, after a breakaway dropped goal in a Middlesex–Yorkshire match defeated a whole cricket-score of unconverted tries for Yorkshire, the Rugby Union brought in their own system of numerical scoring.

Apart from some minor adjustments to the rules, American Football remained uncharacteristically static over the next five years. The game as it stood then must have been an extremely attractive one, played as it was by strong, young students with a keen sense of intercollegiate rivalry. To the spectator of 1885, American Football must have looked very like the game played before Rugby League crowds in the North of England in the 1970s—not so well-disciplined or so skilled, to be sure, but as fast and as open as the best high-scoring League games are now, quite as physically uncompromising in attack and defence, probably just as untidy in some of the set pieces. Tackles were still made, Rugby-fashion, round the waist; passes from hand to hand were still given laterally; punting to gain ground had returned after Camp's three-downs rule had made it futile to hang on to the ball after an attack had been halted. The quarter-back's job in the 1880s was not unlike the dummy-half's in today's Rugby League, and the use of backs to work the ball across the field and through the opposition's lines was still a practical proposition. The formations at the start of each play differed somewhat, and the American refinement of measuring ground gained (rather than the Rugby League's set scrummage after every sixth consecutive tackle) give the games a different emphasis, but in most essentials American Football had by then been steamrollered by Walter Camp as far from its parent Rugby Football as the Rugby League game had reached in the late 1960s. The main difference being that Camp had taken three years since the first breakaway and Rugby League took about seventy.

The game of the 1880s may have been a splendid spectacle, but it was also a game that was losing its innocence. The evidence we have seen so far shows a new sport ruled by the iron hand of a benevolent and imaginative dictator; but Walter Camp and his rules conventions, young and energetic though they were, remained no more than legislators. We have already noted the heavy burdens placed on the single official; it was now becoming clear that the referee was buckling under the weight and in danger of losing control of the game. Walter Camp and his fellow delegates had undoubtedly seen this weakness—after all, they were all still engaged in playing, coaching or supporting college teams—and there is little doubt that many of them positively exploited it. Certainly they did not take the obvious step—to double or treble the numerical strength of the officials, or at least give them umpires or line-judges to help. (Rugby, even in the early 1870s, had controlled a game with a referee *and* two touch judges, all of whom were empowered to call the two opposing captains into their deliberations if any real dispute arose.)

The off-side rule was the point at which the game eroded. The rule was quite explicit, as it still was and still is in Rugby: players were prohibited from taking any part in the game if they were in front of the ball. In America it became a common trick for backs to run alongside the ball-carrier to fend off tacklers (whose job was not particularly easy anyway, since they were not allowed to tackle below waist height). The rules of the game at this date may well have been less than clear about deliberate obstruction, and referees certainly made no positive step towards controlling the practice. It did not take a lot of imagination for the already ingenious college coaches to push the rule just a bit further, to encourage the interfering backs to run slightly *ahead* of the ball-carrier and thus, in effect, clear a path for him. The referees did nothing to prohibit this blatant piece of off-side play; within a couple of seasons it was accepted as common practice, as was the counter-measure, worked out by defenders in some desperation against this powerful new attack, of tackling the ball-carrier low, well below the waist. By 1888, both were legalised, as was blocking an intending tackler out of the way, with the one strict proviso that linemen should hold their arms at their sides while protecting the ball-carrier, rather than spread them wide.

What the legislators expected from this change in the laws is something of a mystery. There does not appear to have been any school of opinion at that time which was actively dissatisfied with the attractive, open-running game; and anyone of foresight must have realised the probable consequences of accepting the blocking tactics as a *fait accompli* and thereby legalising them (Camp, indeed, was very much opposed to the new rule, and both spoke and voted against it; he had little support). The inevitable happened. Within the space of a few games, the pattern of football had been turned back to front. The emphasis passed immediately from the man with the ball to the men round it; instead of ball and carrier swooping and jinking down the field to gain yardage, tightly-knit groups

of blockers, arms held grotesquely at the sides, piled in to similarly compact groups of would-be tacklers. Power had taken over from finesse, and
such was the reluctance of backs to risk any movement without their
echelon of outriders that the game became ludicrously contracted. There
had been critics who felt that the narrow, 55-yard-wide pitch was too
tight for the running, passing game of the early 'eighties; there were few
now who would not admit that the game could be played down the length
of a school cloister, just as it had been fifty years before at the old Charterhouse in London—and even then the players would barely have touched
the sides.

The advent of 'interference' as the most powerful weapon of attack
heralded, for the time being, a decline in the influence of Camp and the
rules committee. It was several years before the game was to be changed
by regulation again; instead, the new rules had ushered in the era of the
tactician. For virtually the first time in the game's short history, Camp was
not the only man in the vanguard of development. Other names began to
make themselves heard: Deland of Harvard, Woodruff of Pennsylvania,
Stagg of Chicago—the strategists of a game in which players had, for the
time being, taken on the role of cannon fodder in a battle fought by generals
on the sidelines. For the coaches the task at the start of every new season
was to drill their players in a series of new tactics designed to surprise
and smash their way through the opposing defence. By the end of the
season they had found ways of chopping down their opponents' attacks,
and in turn their own subtle manoeuvrings had been countered by the
opposing coaches. So they had to spend the next summer thinking up
something else.

The search for openings in the opposing defence was futile without
power to force gaps in it. And power interference was at its most effective
when the maximum number of men were travelling at maximum speed.
Even before the legalisation of interference, the team at Lehigh (and also,
so they claimed, the team at Princeton) devised a gambit at kick-offs
whereby, instead of booting the ball into the arms of the waiting opposition, all standing at least ten yards away, the kicker tapped the ball into
his own hands and, surrounded by his team-mates, bullocked his way into
the opponents' territory. Princeton used it against Pennsylvania in 1884,
when it was still technically illegal, but after the 1888 rulings it became
standard practice for putting the ball into play.

In 1892 Lorin F. Deland, a chess expert but never a football player,
devised for Harvard's annual blood match against Yale a tactic that put
real power into the so-called Lehigh V. At the start of the second half,
without either side having scored, the Yale defence was deployed on their

55-yard line expecting the now conventional charge from the Harvard
45-yard line. But they were puzzled to see only Trafford, Harvard's
quarterback-captain, stay on the 45; the rest of his team fell right back to
the 25, five of them on the left touchline, five on the right. Trafford
signalled the game to start, and, arms interlocked and accelerating at every
stride, the two groups charged diagonally across the field towards their
captain. As they converged on him, now moving at high speed, Trafford
tapped the ball into his own hands, joined in the now unified mass, and
ploughed into the Yale line.

The first Flying Wedge, as this highly organised slice of violence came
to be called, did not in the event result in a touchdown for Harvard.
The Yale defenders regathered their wits with commendable speed, and
dragged down the charging mass ten yards short of their line. Indeed,
Yale scored the only goal of the game and won 6–0. But Deland's flying
interference was a sensation; every coach in the business had a go at it
with one variation or another. At Pennsylvania George Woodruff, himself
one of the earliest proponents of interference as a player at Yale, devised
a slightly more sophisticated flying wedge, by which some of the players
joined the juggernaut *behind* the ball-carrier. Now he was not only protected on all sides, but he could be treated, for convenience, rather like a
sack of potatoes: once battle was joined he was pulled from the front and
pushed from behind to gain that few extra yards advantage. Amos Alonzo
Stagg, perhaps the most inventive of all the 19th-century coaches, devised
a series of devastating formations by which mass momentum play could be
launched not only from the free-running but infrequent kick-offs, but from
the very scrimmage itself. His 'ends back' and 'tackles back' formations
involved linemen retreating from the scrimmage line at the snap, envelop-
ing the carrier and ramming him, as before, through the opposing defence.

Momentum plays could not, by their very nature, last long. Within the
very few years in which they were permitted, they became as ludicrous
as they were dangerous. There were stories of flying wedges hurtling in
perfect formation across the field with each man gripping a suitcase
handle sewn into the trousers of the man in front; certainly the same
suitcase handles were sewn onto the shoulders and back of ball-carriers'
canvas jackets, the more effectively to drag them through the grasp of
tacklers. There was no finesse, either, about stopping a flying wedge;
you prayed, shut your eyes, and dived in amongst the feet, groping for the
man with the ball (unless you were 'Pudge' Heffelfinger, Yale's legendary
6 ft. 4 in. guard, in which case you would dive over the top of the wedge,
presumably with your eyes open, to grasp the ball-carrier by the neck).

Deland's Flying Wedge was first used in the autumn of 1892. By the end of the 1893 season, the whole game was in uproar. The injuries had been frequent and appalling; both West Point (Army) and Annapolis (Navy) had banned football altogether; Yale and Princeton, the very aristocrats of football in America, were urgently advocating the abolition of mass momentum; Harvard and Pennsylvania (with large and still eligible graduate departments to call on) were still in favour of retaining it; there were threats of diplomatic relations being broken off among the very colleges that had created the game. In the spring of 1894 representatives of the four met at the University Athletic Club of New York, and buried the Flying Wedge and all its most blatantly violent offshoots without regret. Now, at the kick-off, the ball had to travel at least ten yards towards the opponents' line unless a member of the receiving team touched it first. No more tapping the ball into your own hands while waiting for the Marines to appear at full gallop on either side. The end of a painful couple of seasons.

But not a decisive end. Flying interference had gone, but momentum play from the scrimmage still lived on, though with the compromise proviso that no more than three men might group behind the line of scrimmage, and they no more than five yards back. The compromise was a failure, the rough play continued. Cornell University restricted its team to home games; Yale and Harvard's clash that year was uncompromisingly vicious on both sides; the press and the public became as angry as the competing colleges; and in 1895 the rule of the Big Four—Princeton and Harvard, Pennsylvania and Yale—who had between them held a dictatorial sway over the giant advances of American Football since 1876, was at an end. As they split up, fuming at each other over their own inability to control the violence they had allowed into the game, the 'Commons' took over from the 'Lords'.

Almost immediately a 'Big Ten' conference was called, represented by colleges from such unfashionable backwoods as Illinois and Michigan and Wisconsin and Minnesota. They had, at their first attempt, no more success than their elders and betters at finding a solution to the mass play problem, but a year later they met again, and the rules of 1896, accepted with reluctance by the humbled aristocrats who would have found no one to play against if they refused, finally drew the teeth from mass momentum. The new rules, couched in pedantically precise language, meant in effect that the lines of scrimmage, which were now to comprise at least five players per side, would be stationary at the moment the ball was snapped. Another bludgeon had been plucked from the hands of the college coaches, another problem posted to test their ingenuity.

. . .

At the end of the 19th century American Football had been a game in its own right for a mere twenty years; in 1900 Walter Camp was still only forty-one, still the energetic and inventive football theoretician, still looking ahead with proposals for further modification in the laws; and still, despite the inevitable shifts of power in the administration of the game, the figurehead of American Football, inseparable from any move, good or bad, that had effected the game's breakaway from the tradition of Rugby.

These twenty years, despite Camp's unifying presence, were times of extraordinary activity—quite literally years of revolution. It had been, in this period, rare for the game to go three clear years without a major change in the rules, and for the players the era can only have been desperately unsettling, a series of seasons when all they can have wanted to do was to play football in the way in which they had learned to enjoy it, and when all they were allowed to do was follow the uncertain experiments laid down by a committee of well-meaning alumni of Harvard, Yale and the like. Great names, of course, did emerge on the field: the great, all-powerful Heffelfinger; Yale's Frank Hinkey, the 'disembodied spirit' with an uncanny ability to slide through any interference and collar his man; Amos Alonzo Stagg and George Woodruff, both members, with Heffelfinger, of Camp's awe-inspiring Yale eleven of 1888; Pennsylvania's guard, Thruxton Hare.

But these men, for all their power and speed, and for all their individual charisma for the supporters of the 1880s and 1890s, could never be much more than cogs in a machine. No football game at any time has had less room for flair and imagination among players; teams were drilled round an idea formulated in the imagination of their coach. It is no coincidence that most of the greatest names in 19th-century football were those of the destroyers—the fearless tacklers, the uncompromising blockers. The elusive runner, whose speed and fast thinking and deceptive passing were ensuring the lasting popularity of every other football code from Melbourne to Manchester, had become a pawn. Indeed, to launch many of the plays called in the 1890s there was no need for a ball at all: it had become little more than a symbol by which to identify the ball-carrier after a snap; after that it was the man, not the ball, that had to be thrust forward towards the opposing line.

Not that football before the turn of the century was boring. No game keenly contested in front of passionate crowds can be dull, and the ingenuity of the coaches and the finely-honed reactions of their teams kept the crowds very much on the edge of their seats. Once the restrictions had been placed on the most blatant of the mass momentum tactics, the so-called 'deception plays' took on rather more importance. In a tightly knit battle, fought nose to nose with very little variation in the efforts used to break the opposing line, sleight of hand was needed when thrust of shoulder had lost its effect. The results were a delight to watch.

Perhaps the classic joke of American Football is the mythical scene of twenty-one players lying in a tangled heap on top of each other while the twenty-second lopes down the far touchline with the ball stuffed under his shirt—the ultimate triumph of a deception play. In 1890, we are asked to believe, this was actually accomplished against the great men of Harvard by Y.M.C.A. Springfield, a college with the one true distinction of being the first to give a coaching job to the greatest of all trick-pulling coaches, Amos Alonzo Stagg. By 1890 Stagg's highly effective 'turtle-back' routine was attracting, as all scrimmage-line attacks eventually did, equally effective defences. The turtle-back involved the whole team crouching over in a tight ring, much as they do in the huddle between plays today, as the ball was snapped into it; the mass would then move right or left, with the ball-carrier hunched in the middle, and crash through the opposing lines when it found a gap. The only defence to this was concentrated blocking, forcing man after man out of the 'turtle' until the ball-carrier could be exposed to the tackle. In the Springfield–Harvard game the 'turtle' thundered as usual towards the wing, one man hunched in the centre protected by his team-mates, with the whole Harvard line in pursuit, each blocking for all he was worth, no one noticing the one Springfield man who had been shed by the 'turtle' only moments after the snap and who was now lying as if injured on the ground. Once the tumult had moved far enough away for comfort he stood up, to reveal that he had been lying on the ball all the time, and ran down the opposite wing for a touch down.

It was this sort of variation to the high-speed intricacies of mass attack and mass defence that kept the crowds coming to what was still, despite its rapid advances, very much a junior member of the American sporting scene. The game, even by the time that control passed out of the hands of the East Coast colleges, was still played only in a limited number of schools and universities; the administration was still a strictly amateur body and, indeed, the public demand for sporting success that had resulted in professional Soccer in England and, somewhat later, in Scotland, and had in 1896 split the Rugby establishment in two, barely had expectations beyond the college game in the States. The fans looked for no more lasting tradition than could be provided by the *alma mater* herself and by the man who coached the *alma mater*'s football team. The heroes were transient memories—even more transient after the qualification rule that restricted a student's playing career to his undergraduate years. He was an

All-American choice one year, a retired footballer the next. In England
we can talk of the great Scottish Soccer team of the 1880s, or the great
Arsenal side of the 1930s, knowing that the nucleus of each of those sides
was a permanent, integrated knot of players who could build up a tradition
of perennial excellence. In America they talk of the Yale team of 1888, or
the Pennsylvania of 1897. The greatest heroes of college football stood
against all-comers for only three years at the most; the greatest heroes of
Soccer or Rugby frequently lasted fifteen years. And this is something the
Americans accepted well into the professional era—it was the mid
1920s before they started looking for long-service heroes.

The fact that their career was a comparatively short and a comparatively
glorious one did not, however, mean that life was particularly easy for
the 19th-century footballer. He would certainly, for example, envy his
counterpart of today, with his mere dozen games a season, with half of
every game—or more—resting on the sidelines, with whole squads of
coaches and trainers and masseurs to tell him what to do and to patch him
up after he has done it. John W. Heisman, the distinguished coach of the
early 20th century, once wrote of his playing days at Brown University
and at Penn. It was a time when teams on tour would play three games on
successive days to defray expenses; when there would be no more than
four substitutes for the entire tour; when the game was a full ninety
minutes long, without breaks at quarter- and three-quarter time; when
anyone who wore home-made padding was regarded as a sissy, and when
the only head protection was long, uncut hair.

We didn't have many sweaters in those days, but we all wore snug
fitting canvas jackets over our jerseys. You see, tackling in that day wasn't
clean-cut and around the legs as it is today. All too often it was wild,
haphazard clutching with the hands, and when runners wore loose gar-
ments they were often stopped by a defensive player grabbing a handful
of loose clothing. Some players wore pants, or jackets, of horse-hair.
When you made a fumbling grab, you lost your fingernails . . .

Line charging. Very little scientific thought had been put on that
department before the dawn of the present century. Nearly all linemen,
as a rule, lined up squarely against those who played in the same position
on the opposing team. They didn't crouch or squat or play low. They
mostly stood bolt upright and fought it out with each other hammer and
tongs, tooth and nail, fist and feet. Fact is, you didn't stand much chance
of making the line . . . unless you were a good wrestler and fair boxer . . .

The substitution rule was strict, too, though not so strict as in Soccer
or Rugby which then—and for more than half a century later—forbade
substitution altogether. In America at the turn of the century, substitution

was allowed on much the same basis a it is in international Rugby matches today: when the referee was satisfied that a player was genuinely injured. Abuses of the rule were common, and substitutes became an important part of any team; but it was to be many years before substitution became accepted as part of the tactics of the game, and it took a tough player to remain on his feet after playing a full ninety minutes of 19th-century gridiron.

It is not surprising that a grotesquely idealised picture of an early football squad began to emerge: an all-powerful coach in godlike command of the life of a university, served with selfless devotion by a dedicated band of loyal American youth. It was a picture that the image-makers loved to paint, and success on the football field had already become far more prestigious than success at examinations. The less idealistic truth is exemplified by the early years of Alonzo Stagg's coaching career, a story that must have been typical of dozens of campuses away from the money and the limelight enjoyed by the privileged few. When he arrived at Chicago from Springfield in 1890 to take the high-sounding title of 'Director of Physical Culture and Athletics', Stagg found himself in the unenviable position of being a football coach at a college without anywhere to play football. The problem was not solved, as he might have justifiably expected, by the university granting him some money to have a site cleared. He had to pass the hat round himself: a collection among faculty members raised 490 dollars, the student body contributed 281 dollars, and an athletics meeting that Stagg organised raised another 95 dollars. They begged a square block of vacant land, and were granted its use at a peppercorn rent; Stagg and his volunteer students levelled the ground themselves, nailed up the boards, erected the goal posts (these had been donated by a local timber firm), laid the turf, and, after a couple of months, inagurated the field with a baseball game. The changing rooms (a contractors' old hut) Stagg bought out of his own pocket, and they managed to get out of debt by accepting advertising on the boards round the inner side of the fence. Then he had to set about training a football team.

By 1900 American Football was unrecognisable as the Rugby Game which had spawned it twenty-five years before. There were still one or two vestiges of the parent game that survived: the line-out was still employed when the ball went out of bounds, though it usually degenerated into an untidy maul; the punt over the heads of the defending line, followed by a rush in pursuit, was still the staple means of gaining ground if the conventional snap and charge failed (it was, as it was in Rugby Union for so long, much more common on days when the ground was wet and slippery); and the game still lacked the one magic ingredient without which, arguably, it would never have gained the following it enjoys today —the forward pass. But Rugby had been left far behind in almost every other department, with the one significant exception that Rugby was a game enjoyed by boys and men from the ages of twelve to thirty-five or forty; American Football was not, and by its new nature could really never be, a game played for sheer enjoyment. An American Football player who was not fully fit was asking for hospital; it was a game for the specialists, for the young and strong and fearless. If a sane man stopped to think about American Football, he would never set foot on the field.

The game also called for special qualities of a less conventional nature. Stagg's Chicago team arrived at the penultimate game of the 1897 season at the head of the championship, needing two final victories to clinch it. On the night before the Wisconsin match, Chicago's outstanding back and specialist punter, Clarence Herschberger, challenged his captain Walter Kennedy to an eating contest—the result to be determined by weighing each player before and after the food and the winner to be the man who had put on most weight. After an evening of mind-boggling endeavour, Kennedy had put on $7\frac{1}{2}$ lb., Herschberger a mere 7 lb. And instead of retiring with a glass of bicarbonate of soda to contemplate the next day's vital game, Herschberger, somewhat disgruntled by the decision against him, ordered and consumed a further thirteen eggs. Stagg was convinced ever afterwards that the match would have been won, rather than lost 23–8, had not Herschberger been seized with gastritis an hour before the kick-off and carried away to bed.

It was a game for survivors, too.

5

splendid isolation

Gaelic Football and Australian Football: 1858 to 1970

The football games that swept across the world in the last third of the 19th century were all, more or less, Made in England. Rugby, Association Football, American Football, were all the direct or indirect descendants of the old, primitive village game that had then been polished, reorganised and codified in the Junior Common Rooms of Oxford and Cambridge or the privileged atmospheres of old boys' clubs in London and Sheffield and Edinburgh. But two other major games of football, both of them quite divorced from the 'English' games and, though related, quite distinct from one another, were becoming increasingly popular. In Ireland, the recent resurgence of Nationalism had led to the sectarian encouragement of Gaelic Football, and in the State of Victoria two enterprising young athletes had devised an entirely new form of the game which has come to be called Australian Football by the purists and Australian Rules by everyone else.

Gaelic Football
Ireland's traditions of rural football are quite as long and no more respectable than those of England and Wales; some form of inter-village skirmishing had become a regular sight in medieval times in all the Celtic strongholds of North-Western Europe: *La Soule* was played in Normandy, hurling in Cornwall, *knappan* in Wales, football in England and the Border regions of Scotland. Ireland was no exception; the traditions of the old team games were so strong (or, alternatively, they were considered so valuable) that alone in the British Isles the Irish were not plagued with the tiresome football prohibitions that dogged England and Scotland for centuries. In Galway, moreover, a statute of 1527 specifically laid down that while quoits and handball and hurling were prohibited on pain of a fine of 8*d*., only the 'great foot ball' was permitted. Despite this ban, in fact, it was hurling (with a small hard ball and sticks, on the principles of hockey, rather than the pure hands-and-feet game of Cornish hurling) that remained the more popular game in Ireland.

In 1720, however, the Irish poet Mathew Concanen wrote an account, in mock heroic verse, of a great football match between the rival towns of Swords and Lusk, and in that century, too, football was played at Trinity College, Dublin, every evening in the college park. It is significant, though, that it was the 'commoners', the less wealthy students, who played, and not the more aristocratic 'fellow-commoners'. As for long periods on the British mainland, the game had become rather too rough for the fashionable young gentlemen to play; it was a hard, rural game to be played on lush rural farmland. 'Caid', the game was called in the early 19th century, and it was played in Antrim and Donegal and Kerry and many regions in between. It was parish-to-parish football with teams of un-limited size, play of unlimited duration (or until the sun went down), and apparently of unlimited violence—a game, in fact, very close to the rural English pattern without the mid-19th-century search for a common set of written rules.

By the 1880s, however, the traditional Irish football was in danger of foundering beneath the rival attractions of the imported English games of Soccer and Rugby, which were both played at the schools, universities and clubs in Ireland's major towns and cities. The Irish Football Associa-tion, and with it the attractions of the Irish Cup, had been founded in 1880, and the following year the Combined Irish Rugby Union was formed from the already well-established Irish Football Union (for clubs from the Southern provinces) and the North of Ireland Rugby Union. Com-pared with these comfortable, English-inspired organisations, the country-side parish-to-parish games appeared ever more primitive and ever less attractive.

Their salvation came from two men, tackling the problem on two fronts. After a particularly bloody encounter between thirty-four men of Tip-perary and thirty-four men of Waterford, Maurice Davin of Carrick-on-Suir, Tipperary, and Michael Cusack, of County Clare, then living in Dublin, got together with Davin's brother Daniel and some of the leading players to draw up a code of rules in an attempt to restrict the wholesale violence. So far, so good: sensible, level-headed ideas to convert disorgan-ised mayhem into semi-disciplined rough-and-tumble with many similari-ties to the very early rules of Soccer. But the method of broadcasting their new rules to their Irish fellow countrymen was of immensely greater significance to the future of that sport and to the sport of Ireland in general. For perhaps the first time since football had been banned in England because it interfered with archery practice, politics was brought firmly and unashamedly into sport.

Davin and Cusack called a meeting in the billiard room of the Hayes Commercial Hotel at Thurles, in Tipperary, 'to encourage and promote every form of athletics that is peculiarly Irish; to draft laws for promotion and conservation of every Irish native sport; and to revise, encourage and draft rules for the native pastimes of the Gael'. The response was hardly overwhelming: five men turned up at the meeting: two journalists, two local athletes and a Templemore building contractor, John K. Bracken, whose other chief distinction is that he was father of Churchill's wartime Minister of Information, Brendan Bracken.

If the five supernumeraries were less than distinguished, the two principals were men of some considerable standing. Maurice Davin's fame as an athlete had spread far beyond Ireland. He had held a world record for throwing the hammer, he was a long-jumper of note, and he was equally renowned as an amateur boxer, an oarsman and a cricketer. Michael Cusack, on the other hand, was a political firebrand. 'Citizen' Cusack, as he liked to call himself, and as James Joyce immortalised him in *Ulysses* in his later years, when he was a fixture on the Dublin scene, was at the same time an athlete and a Rugby player, an intense advocate and defender of all things native to Ireland, and an implicit believer in the ultimate victory of Irish Nationalism. It was his idea, almost certainly, not merely to define rules for Gaelic football (and at the same time the even more Irish and lethal game of hurling), but to form a Gaelic Athletic Association to promote Nationalist ideals through the preservation of traditional Irish games.

The meeting made up for what it lacked in numbers with a truly Irish flamboyance. Without a blush it approached three of the foremost Irishmen of the day requesting their patronage: Charles Stewart Parnell, the most charismatic of all Irish politicians; Michael Davitt, a Nationalist hero whom the Irish called a patriot and the British a fanatic, and who had just served seven years in an English prison for gun-running; and Dr Croke, Archbishop of Cashel.

All three men agreed to be patrons of the new Gaelic Athletic Association, and it was a letter from Archbishop Croke to Cusack that set out the passionate, insular and, in many ways, reactionary foundations upon which Gaelic football was to evolve:

One of the most painful, and at the same time one of the most frequently recurring reflections that, as an Irishman, I am compelled to make in connection with the present aspect of things in this country, is derived from the ugly and irritating fact that we are daily importing from England not only her manufactured goods but, together with her fashions, her accents, her vicious literature, her music, her dances, her manifold mannerisms, her games also and pastimes, to the utter discredit of our own grand national sports and to the sore humiliation of every genuine son and daughter of the old land.

Ball-playing, hurling, football-kicking according to Irish rules, 'cast-ing', leaping, wrestling in various ways and all such favourite amusements may now be said to be not only dead and buried, but, in several localities to be entirely forgotten and unknown. And what have we got in their stead? We have got such foreign and fantastic field sports as lawn tennis, polo, croquet, cricket and the like, very excellent, I believe, and health-giving exercises in their way, still, not racy of the soil but rather alien on the contrary to it as are indeed, for the most part, the men and women who first imported and still continue to patronise them.

These sentiments were couched in just the terms that the G.A.A. wanted to hear, and were certainly a forthright expression of encouragement for their aims. Yet, as far as football was concerned, they had little relevance to what Cusack and Davin had been attempting to do with the rules. The Archbishop had spoken with disdain of English games, and while he had not specifically mentioned them, he must have included Rugby and Soccer in his thoughts. They, after all, were the one real threat to the already declining sports of Irish football and hurling. Yet the rules that Davin and Cusack had drawn up for Gaelic Football and which one of the G.A.A.'s earliest acts was to ratify, had converted a long established game of the people to just the sort of game that the Bishop was complaining about. Gaelic Football à la Davin and Cusack was no more the true game of the Irish countryside than Association Football was the true game of the Northern English village—it had become an artificial, though prob-ably far more enjoyable, version of the old traditional game, and the new rules owed everything to laws tried and found effective by the players of 'foreign and fantastic field sports'.

The pitch was specified at 120 yards by 80 yards; the goal was, in those early days, a Soccer goal, 15 ft wide and 8 ft high, with no posts above the height of the crossbar; the only method of scoring was by kicking the ball through the goal. The rules make no mention of offside, so there probably was none; nor do they mention how long a player may handle the ball, though presumably, as goals and not tries were the aim, there was no such thing as Rugby's 'running in'. (The rules for hurling which were published at the same time, and which ever since have closely paralleled the rules for football, say that the ball may not be lifted off the ground with the hand; possibly that rule applied to football as well and, as today, players had to flick the ball to their hands with their toe.) One rather charming image is conjured up by Rule 5 (now long forgotten) by which the game starts with the players standing 'in two ranks opposite each other until the ball is thrown up, each man holding the hand of one of the other side'.

Some of the rougher edges were shaved off these rules by a revised list published in 1886: the sides were set at 'not less than 14 and not more than 21', 'point posts' stood at either side of the goal, so that high shots and near-misses, counting a point each, could be considered if the score in goals was equal; the goal was enlarged to 21 ft wide with a crossbar 10½ ft from the ground; the playing time was fixed at one hour per match; and wrestling and handgrips, which had hitherto provided a bit of extra entertainment for the spectators, were prohibited.

The game was taking shape fast, and the rush of village hurling and football clubs from all over Ireland to join the Association had been quite overwhelming. It is somehow characteristic of the Irish temperament that in the midst of this enthusiasm, and the successful start of the foot-balling championships that still endure today, the G.A.A. nearly argued itself out of existence. The row, as so many Irish rows, was between militants and moderates. The militants were determined to keep a strong, political hand on the Association, and though an early G.A.A. rule to ban from their competitions all athletes competing at meetings organised by other organisations was shelved for the time being, a series of internal squabbles over relations with the Irish Amateur Athletic Association, and a public exchange of intemperate letters between Michael Cusack chief militant) and Archbishop Croke (surprisingly, perhaps, chief moderate) resulted in the fiery Cusack being voted out of the secretaryship and into open conflict with the Association.

That was in July 1886. The following year, in a somewhat small-minded reprisal after the discovery that certain prominent Nationalists had been shadowed by the police, the G.A.A. prohibited any member of the Royal Irish Constabulary from membership; other dictatorial actions by the Association's Central Executive, including the suspension of the Dublin County Committee, led to the temporary resignation of Davin himself from the presidency; the clubs' loyalties were divided—some siding with the conservative Nationalists and the clergy, others with the 'physical force' elements of the rampant Nationalists.

After a series of convoluted exchanges, of another spate of letters by the Archbishop Croke, and after Davin had been elected as chairman of one split limb of the Association and a militant as chairman of another limb, there was an uncharacteristic calm. Another convention was called, Maurice Davin was re-elected to the official Presidency (he finally walked out two years later after vigorous cross-examination over the state of the G.A.A.'s rocky finances), and the members got on with the interrupted job of building up the Association and its games.

As so often happens, the administrative quarrels had taken their main toll in the one area where both sides were in perfect agreement—the promotion of the Irish games; in 1889, the year when Davin resigned as President, the entries for the All-Ireland championships were painfully small (only three counties contested the hurling, and the football fared little better); the county and provincial competitions were getting hopelessly behind schedule, so much so that some fixtures were being held as much as two years after the arranged date. The Central Council was still at odds with the clubs; there were now some 1,700 of these, from 26 counties, yet an appeal for £1 per club to help pay off the G.A.A.'s £850 debt met with no response at all. On top of this came another political storm—the Parnell crisis, on which the G.A.A. for the first time, and quite contrary to the principles of its foundation, began to pass political resolutions: 'That this Convention is resolved to support the policy of independant opposition and freedom of opinion under the leadership of Mr Parnell.' Again the G.A.A. split into factions; again football and hurling were virtually forgotten in the political turmoil that followed Parnell's death and the subsequent general election. The crowds grew smaller, competitions dwindled, the roll of affiliated clubs had dropped within two years to a meagre two hundred and twenty. Once again people began to write obituaries for the G.A.A.

But the Association has been nothing if not resilient. In 1893 it determined to reorganise its countrywide structure, and slowly the tide began to turn. It was a slow business; money was still very short, though the Association now had enough funds to pay its secretary, and internal differences of opinion were still liable to end in resignation and recrimination. But slowly the number of affiliated clubs moved back towards the high points of the 1880s. In 1896 the Central Council organised a series of exhibition matches of hurling and Gaelic Football at Stamford Bridge, in London, and at the turn of the century the Irishmen of London had made enough progress in the games of their homeland to be able to field teams as a province of the G.A.A.

It was 1903, however, before the Association could look over a year's events with satisfaction rather than with reserved optimism. Money problems had at least been eased, the formation of a Provincial Council in Ulster meant that the whole country was administering Gaelic Games, and the authorities felt confident enough to establish a Junior All-Ireland Championship—open to all players who had not appeared for their counties in the senior grade. And it was the 1903 Gaelic Football Final, 'the game that made the G.A.A.', that at last kindled genuine public excitement.

Gaelic Football had advanced considerably since the early efforts by the G.A.A. to establish order and discipline. In 1892 the teams were reduced in size from twenty-one to seventeen, which made for a much more open game, and the value of a point was at last established, now being equal to one-fifth of a goal whether or not the score in goals was equal. Four years later a goal was made equal to three points, and has remained so ever since. The nature of the game was very much as it is now—a free, open game played in fast-fluctuating bursts punctuated by long kicking and spectacular leaping catches. The establishment of the 'point' for the near-miss between the point-posts or over the bar had placed even greater emphasis on long kicking, and on the tactical skills needed to place the talented kickers in a clear shooting position.

The pace of the game came with the development of dribbling—a curious, bobbing progress dictated by the need to flick the ball with the toe every few paces, but refined by the best players so that it hardly affected their speed; and with the multitude of ways of passing the ball that had been perfected by a long kick, a short toe jab, or a slapping or punching of the ball with the hand to a waiting colleague.

Play changed ends fast, and shots at goal were frequent; tackling was fierce and the rules to curb it erred, if anything, on the side of *laissez-faire*. On top of which there were virtually no stoppages. The referee blew his whistle only for fouls, which were listed as something of an afterthought in the rules (catching a player, tripping him, or pushing him from behind), or for balls going out of play. Even injuries suffered in the course of duty were not considered worth stopping play for (they are still ignored: there is no society for the protection of Gaelic footballers, and a characteristic sight is that of a player laid cold in the middle of the pitch, his manager and trainer working away at his side, and the game proceeding all round them at its customary pace). It was fast, furious, non-stop action for a whole breathless hour, and the celebrated 1903 'home final' was more breathless than most.

Its qualities were somehow enhanced by the fact that it was not played, because of exceptional fixture pile-ups, until well into 1905, and as it then needed three full matches to decide the winners, it was another five months before those winners could take their place in the All-Ireland final and beat a patiently waiting London Irish with ease. The great rivals of 1903 were Kerry, the Munster champions and over the years the undisputed masters of Gaelic football, and Kildare, the Leinster winners. They first met at Tipperary in July, and with a few minutes to go in the tightest of matches with the scores level, the game had to be abandoned after frantic spectators in the huge crowd had invaded the pitch in fury at a refereeing decision. In August, after the G.A.A. had ordered a replay, a record crowd of 12,000 watched another nerve-wracking display of top-class football—and another draw: Kerry 7 points—Kildare 1 goal and 4 points.

Before the second replay, the teams, fiercely amateur as were all sportsmen under the aegis of the G.A.A., took time off for special intensive training, causing the same sort of shocked sensation as when, back in 1883, it had been discovered that Blackburn Olympic had gone to Blackpool for special training before an English F.A. Cup Final. Crowded trainloads of supporters followed the Kerrymen from their kingdom to Cork for the decider in mid October. This time, in mud and rain, their champions proved the masters. Neither side scored a goal, but with the legendary Dick Fitzgerald, then only a lad of seventeen, but still able to bend free kicks like the latter-day Brazilians, Kerry won by 8 points to 2 and clinched a classic final. The gate had taken £270 that day, a far cry from the years when the G.A.A. were begging reluctant clubs to help them with their mounting debts.

From 1905 Gaelic Football's future was assured. The rules were further improved in 1910: the points-posts were abolished and substituted for them a Rugby-style goal (it had a goal net beneath the crossbar, and a point was scored for a ball kicked over the bar and between the uprights); and the 'parallelogram' was introduced—the equivalent of Soccer's penalty area marked in front of the goal, in which the goalkeeper alone received special protection. Soon, too, the sides were reduced to their current size—fifteen men—making once more for a faster and more dramatic contest. The results were immediate. The first All-Ireland Final after the reduction to fifteen-a-side attracted an all-time record crowd for a Gaelic Football match, and put £750 into the G.A.A. pockets.

Both records stood for about two months when the match, in which Kerry and Louth had played a draw, was replayed. The replay specialists from Kerry once more ran out winners—a magnificent team in the early years of the century, now captained by Dick Fitzgerald and fielding one of the great jumping-catchers of the game's history, Pat 'Aeroplane' O'Shea. This time they not only achieved the Association's first £1,000 gate, they also enabled the Association to buy, for the first time, its own permanent headquarters.

The major competition matches had been held at the City and Suburban Athletic Ground at Jones's Road, Dublin, since 1895, and with reasonable prospects of the spectator enthusiasm continuing, the Association had been trying for some time to raise the money for a permanent home. The majority wish was to buy Jones's Road for the G.A.A., though no such major decision would have been allowed through without an equally major dispute, and a not entirely disinterested lobby from Tipperary agreed that the cradle of the Association, the town of Thurles, should house its stadium and stage its championships. Their protests were, fortunately, overruled (it would have been about as convenient as rebuilding Cardiff Arms Park on the Pembrokeshire coast) and the unexpected riches provided by the Kerry–Louth finals of 1913 finally enabled the G.A.A. to buy Jones's Road, rechristen it after their letter-writing mentor, the late Archbishop Croke, and set up Croke Park as the undisputed world centre for Gaelic Games, as predominant in its particular sphere as Twickenham, Odsal and Hampden Park are in theirs.

As it had established itself in the sporting sense, so the Gaelic hurlers and footballers were establishing themselves at the forefront of the nationalist movement. Already, in 1904, the G.A.A. had permanently rejected all moves to interfere with 'the Ban', the controversial measure that had been voted in and out of favour ever since the earliest meetings in Thurles, and which would have a profoundly retrograde effect on Irish sport for the next seventy years. The Ban was simple enough: no player of G.A.A. games—in effect football and hurling—was allowed to play, or watch, or support 'foreign' games—in effect Rugby, Soccer, cricket or hockey. In addition, the G.A.A. had banned from their games all soldiers, sailors, policemen and members of the militia—that is, anyone working directly or indirectly for the occupying British and who might be suspected of spying on them.

The Ban, in theory, kept the G.A.A. as arguably the purest, and certainly the best supported, stronghold of nationalistic, anti-British influence in the whole of Ireland; in the ensuing years the games were to assume an almost mystic significance in the struggle for independence. Some manifestation of this was not unexpected: the enlistment of many hundreds of G.A.A. men in the Irish Volunteers in 1913; the rejection of the British call in 1915 to 'the hurlers and footballers of Munster' for recruitment into the ranks fighting the Kaiser; the Dublin footballers who fought with Patrick Pearse in the G.P.O. at Easter 1916. But on 21 November 1920, another of those shameful days that the Irish have been moved to label 'Bloody', football so stirred the sensitive Gaelic emotions as to assure a place in the country's heart.

It was not a championship, but an exhibition game at Croke Park between Dublin and Tipperary. It was played to raise funds to buy arms for the volunteers, and it was played on the very Sunday on which fourteen British Secret Service officers had been shot in their Dublin lodgings. Fifteen minutes after the start a contingent of Black and Tans carried machine-guns in at the canal end of the ground and, it seems, began to blaze away indiscriminately at the field of play and the 10,000 crowd round it. Some say twelve died in the shooting, some say fourteen; what is certain is that among the dead was Mick Hogan, a Tipperary back and, though the machine-gunners could not possibly have known it, a Company Commander in the Grangemockler Volunteers, active in the fight for Independence. There is now a Hogan Stand at Croke Park in his memory, but the place of Bloody Sunday in the lore of Ireland's favourite spectator sport is an even more telling memorial.

Australian Football

While the Irish were first developing, then deriving inspiration from, their national football game, a close cousin to Gaelic Football was growing in the State of Victoria. The rules of Australian Football, in fact, were first drawn up eighteen years before the formation of the G.A.A., and its adherents had few of the teething troubles that beset the Irish authorities.

Football had been recorded twice in Sydney in the early 19th century. The *Sydney Monitor* told in 1829 of 'the privates in the barracks . . . in the habit of amusing themselves with the game of foot-ball', and some years later the Queen's Birthday was celebrated with an attempt at 'a game of foot-ball which gave rise to sundry scuffles and broken shins to boot'. What these games were is impossible to say, but they were no doubt undisciplined and most probably imported relics of the old village games of the British Isles, and they were played in New South Wales, where in the later part of the century, the Rugby code was to have a long period of prosperity.

The foundations of the game in Victoria, however, were Gaelic. The Irish had come in their thousands to the goldfields of Ballarat and Bendigo, and by the 1850s were reported by a local paper to be playing a game that seemed to be 'a combination of many games, including football, wrestling and general rough house'. Gaelic Football was not yet centrally controlled, but it had a freedom of space and a freedom from petty restriction that appealed both to the miners themselves and the Irish soldiers at the local garrisons, and the matches that did take place were evidently rugged, wide-ranging and relatively unsubtle.

New games, however, are not established by a mass of people enjoying themselves but by men committed to the task of teaching them to others. The rules of Soccer were agreed so that all clubs could play the same game; the rules of Rugby so that more players in more countries could enjoy what the schoolboys of Rugby had sworn by for years; the rules of Gaelic Football were to be codified so that the affiliated clubs in the Gaelic Athletic Association could all share a common nationalistic bond. The rules for Australian Football were written because a young man called Tom Wills returned home to Geelong, Victoria, in 1856 after being sent to school at Rugby, and advised his friend Henry Harrison not to take up the game that had been the pride of his school, as it was 'unsuitable for grown men engaged in making a living'. The inference, presumably, was that Rugby was too dangerous a sport for anyone with responsibilities; it is ironic, in that case, that the two men sat down to invent a code of football of their own, and came up with one which, apart from American Football, is the hardest and most bruising of all football codes, with fewer rules than most, and one which strikes an outsider as the last conceivable game to recommend to a grown man engaged in making a living.

Both Harrison and Wills were prominent sportsmen in and around Melbourne. Harrison was an athlete, excelling in long-distance and middle-distance running and hurdling, and he also played a lot of primitive football in Melbourne and Geelong. Wills, his cousin, was principally a cricketer, and on his return from England he was a member of the first Victoria team to play an intercolonial match against New South Wales. (He was also the coach of the first cricket team to tour England from Australia, the remarkable Aborigine party of 1867, the more surprising for the fact that his father had been a victim of an Aborigine massacre in Queensland only a few years before.)

As well as considering the current forms of football as too dangerous for men with responsibilities, he also saw it as too risky a way for cricketers to keep fit during the winter months; they needed some sort of vigorous exercise, though, and he, Harrison and two local newspapermen (mainly Wills, apparently—he was not a good committee man and was inclined to become short tempered with anyone disagreeing with him) were looking for a code of football rules that would suit their purpose. Their first effort in this direction does not survive, and nor does the game that resulted from them. There was no defined area for the playing field, the laws about conduct were very hazy, and the scope of the game so enormous— goals were placed about a mile apart, and there were forty people on each side—that it was virtually unmanageable. Nevertheless, these rules sufficed to launch the history of Australian Football with what is always regarded as its first match: Scotch College Melbourne, v. Melbourne Grammar School on 7 August 1858. By all accounts it was not a great success. It had been arranged that the first side to kick two goals would be the winners, and on that afternoon, before the break for lunch, Scotch College went one goal ahead. But when darkness ended play it was still the only score, and a fortnight later they resumed. Still Scotch College could not clinch their victory, and still Melbourne could not reply. They finally decided on a draw a week later after another stalemate afternoon, much to the relief of everyone concerned.

The definitive rules, on which the modern game is based, did not come until 1866, by which time a number of clubs had been formed in Melbourne and Geelong for which the vast areas demanded by the earlier rules—not to mention the vast teams needed before a game could be played—were becoming a hindrance. The 1866 rules borrowed chiefly from Rugby Football and Gaelic Football, as well as from some of the Football Association rules in force at the time: the size of the pitch was reduced to a mere 200 yards long and 150 yards wide (there was as yet no specification as to its *shape*); throwing the ball was not allowed, and running with it was virtually abolished by reducing the runner to only seven yards between each bounce of the ball; tripping was not permitted, though players could be held if they were in possession of the ball and pushed with the hand or body 'if they were in motion'. The conduct of the game was left to the captains of either side, who could award penalties for breaches of the rules.

The rules worked well, and more clubs in the Melbourne area began to play the game competitively. Australian Football holds one aspect of its history in common with the American Game (in other respects they are about as disparate as any team games can be): the early years of its existence were littered with law revisions that gradually, but extensively altered its entire nature. In 1867 the round ball that had previously been used was replaced with the oval Rugby ball; in 1869 victory for the first team to score two goals was replaced by the more familiar system of victory for the one scoring most goals in an allotted time; in 1872, in another full-scale revision of the rules, umpires were introduced, ends were changed at half-time, and it was no longer possible to score by charging the ball *en masse* across the goal-line—it had to be kicked.

Uniquely, too, the game had done away with penalising teams for kicking the ball out of play. In all other forms of football the team putting the ball out over the touchline forfeits some sort of an advantage to their opponents—by giving them the put-in at a scrum (Rugby League), the throw at a line-out (Rugby Union), a free kick (Gaelic Football), a free throw in any direction (Soccer), and so on; in Australian Rules the umpire (later the job was taken over by the boundary umpires) would stand on the boundary line where the ball had left play, turn his back on the players and hurl the ball in over his shoulder.

By now, almost without exception, the playing field was oval. Cricket grounds in Australia in the major urban centres had now become enclosed, and to make full use of the space available, while still leaving enough room for the paying customers, the footballers used the whole area of the ground. It meant, however, that there was no goal-line as such, only the goal itself; that, in turn meant that a shot just missing the goal (two single posts seven yards apart) would gain a tremendous advantage from the umpire's throw-in, which would inevitably lob the ball back into play within easy striking distance of the goal. So Wills and Harrison (still, in the 1870s, very much in the driving seat) positioned posts on either side of the goals. 'Near misses' which went between the goal and these posts would allow the defending side to kick the ball out into the centre of the field—not yet, not until the late 1890s, would a 'near miss' earn a point.

In Victoria, Australian Football flourished virtually unopposed. The attraction was its speed—virtually non-stop, regular end-to-end switching; large open spaces for big kicking; and the spectacular high-catching 'mark', the leap to catch a soaring ball which, if the ball had travelled ten yards without being touched on the way, entitled the catcher to a free kick. The regular revision of the laws had made the game far less ponder-ous, certainly more open and less stylised than either the Soccer or the Rugby being played at the time.

In 1877 the clubs around Melbourne formed themselves into the Vic-torian Football Association, and the first serious attempts were made to expand the game beyond the narrow locality in which it had grown so popular. From the earliest days the Australian footballers have always been anxious to export their giant of a game at every opportunity; it is surprising that so far it has only twice been adopted for any length of time outside Australia (up to the First World War in part of New Zealand, and in the late 1960s in the Australian-governed islands of Papua/New Guinea), and even in Australia itself it has had to struggle for ninety or more years to gain a firm foothold in either New South Wales or Queensland. But they did try. At one time, before the Rugby missionaries took hold, there was a chance that the game might take hold in New Zealand; on the formation of the Victorian Association teams were sent to play matches in Sydney and in Adelaide; soldiers transferred across Australia from the gold-mine garrisons in Victoria to other duties in Western Australia took the game to Perth. The next year South Australia formed an Association, and in 1879 the first inter-state ('inter-colonial' in those days) match was played at Melbourne between Victoria and South Australia.

Other ventures were less successful. On the death of Tom Wills in 1880 (he committed suicide after years of heavy drinking and, finally, alcohol-ism) Harrison had determined to realise the greatest ambition of his cousin: to make Australian Football a worldwide sport or, failing that, an All-Australian one. Harrison's reputation as 'Father of Australian Football' is based on the work he accomplished between 1880 and the turn of the century, as he travelled to Britain, to Europe and to New Zealand in vain efforts to get the game on some sort of footing abroad. In Australia he met with less frustration. He had been a founder-member of the Victorian Football Association, and in 1896 he was a leading official with the breakaway Victorian Football League, an organisation with a vastly improved administration that was eventually to dominate all major competitions and produce almost all the greatest 20th-century players. He became the first chairman of the Australian Football Council, and he did much to assure the prosperous future of the game by agitating over the years for the establishment of a Schools' Football Association to follow cricket's example by introducing the Australian game to every school and organising interstate school games.

Perhaps his greatest triumph, though it may have become apparent only eighty years later, was to organise a series of matches between a non-Australian touring party and the club sides of Victoria, South Australia and New South Wales—an achievement that was not paralleled until the Gaelic footballers of Kerry made their Australian tour in 1970 and played a game combining both Australian and Gaelic rules as part of their programme. The foundations had been laid during Harrison's abortive European visit, and when, with the Rugby Union's blessing but without its financial support, A. E. Stoddart's Rugby tourists made the first major Antipodean tour by a British party, Harrison was able to persuade them to play some of their matches under Australian rather than Rugby Union rules.

In the event, the tourists played twenty-five Australian Rules games quite apart from the more serious business of sixteen Rugby matches in Australia and another nineteen in New Zealand. They did not come entirely unprepared; touring Australian cricketers had given some advice, and the Australian authorities had sent over some rule-books to help in the initial training sessions. In addition, when the party arrived in Victoria they were allotted some of the foremost Australian footballers, as well as the experience of Harrison, to brush up their techniques. But the tour was a remarkable success; the crowds were good, the games were by no means one-sided, and the takings were respectable.

In the opening match at Melbourne Cricket Ground—already the premier venue for major football matches—the Carlton Club and the tourists attracted almost 30,000 spectators; by the end of the tour, an exhausting one involving thousands of miles in travel and a game once every two days, they had won fourteen games and lost only eleven, and had already caused talk of a regular tour by British teams to play the Australian Game, and even of a combined Australia and New Zealand football tour of Britain. It was not Henry Harrison's fault that all these high hopes of expansion came to nothing; it was something of an achievement to have raised them in the first place.

At the time of the British tour, the Australian Football goals were still no different from those Tom Brown and his schoolfellows had kicked towards at Rugby in the 1830s—two tall posts without a crossbar, the simplest of all football targets. In 1897, in yet another major revision of the rules, points scoring was introduced; they clearly derived their new system from the Gaelic Game, though without restricting the height of the goal with a crossbar. They converted their 'behind' posts, originally given a role equivalent to Rugby's corner flags, to that of secondary goalposts, equivalent to the now extinct 'points-posts' of Gaelic Football. And as in Gaelic Football, a near miss was now to count as a point at some fraction of the value of a goal struck through the two centre posts.

So the Australian football field, as well as being uniquely shaped and uniquely large for a playing area, is unique in having four goalposts at either end at 7-yard intervals—six points scored for a shot at any height through the centre posts, one point—a 'behind'—for a shot at any height between the goal and the outer posts (or for a shot that goes in the *goal* after touching another player or a goal post). Immediately the scores rocketed to cricket proportions (even today it is quite normal for between 150 and 200 points to be scored in an afternoon) and the attraction of the game rose with it.

Another lure for the spectator—and an early, effective method of playing on the personality of a sports star—was provided by an annual award for the 'fairest and best' player in any year. The idea was first introduced by South Australia with the Magarey Medal, but the other State bodies all followed suit, providing a welcome focus on individual skill in a sport where to an uninitiated spectator the field might look, with its thirty-six players anything up to 200 yards away, no more than attractive ballet by nondescript, identically-costumed dancers.

The emergence of stars into the game, together with the intense rivalry generated among the top teams in the Victoria Football League and the inter-state rivalry in the South and West, was bound to lead to all the disruptive practices of player movement which had already been dogging professional Soccer in Britain and was soon, on an even greater scale, to deprive Australia of many of her finest Rugby players as they were lured to the newly independent Northern Rugby Union in Great Britain. The rancour that these transfers caused was the primary reason for forming the Australian National Football Council, the first over-all body the game had had, in 1906, and the Council's immediate action was to tighten up the inter-state clearance and permit rules. They also organised the Australian Championship, a series of inter-state matches played at regular intervals in the state capital cities, and usually won by the all-powerful Victorian Football League.

The Championship has remained ever since a curiously uncertain competition; in theory it is the supreme test to determine the best state in Australia, but in practice it causes excitement only in the marginally less fanatical states of Western Australia, South Australia and, more recently, Tasmania. For the football fans of Victoria the Championship has had much the same appeal as the International Championship has to English Soccer fans. In Britain, an England *v.* Northern Ireland international is an occasion of only marginal significance, certainly bearing no comparison with, say, an F.A. Cup semi-final. The same is true in Victoria; the real crowd-pullers have been the V.F.L. premierships—the semi-finals and finals of the Melbourne clubs—rather than the worthy but somewhat irrelevant round of inter-state matches which, so often, merely serves the purpose of finding out who is second best to the Victorians.

By the time its development was interrupted by the First World War, the game which had been invented from scratch by a cricketer and an athlete had established itself firmly on the imagination of the Southern states of Australia. Australians, like Texans, like to dwell on the gigantic proportions of their country, and the citizens of Melbourne, whose rivalry with Sydney for the distinction of being Australia's Number One city seem always to have been conducted from a position of weakness, are possibly more Australian in attitude than anyone. In Australian Football they had found the biggest of all football games with enough excitement to satisfy even the chronically sport-hungry Australian, and with larger-than-life heroes to match.

As the Australian and New Zealand troops left to fight for their Empire in 1914, the current hero was a tall Tasmanian ruckman called Roy Cazaly, playing in the Victorian Football League for South Melbourne. His great skill was the powerful, springing leap to a high ball, which he then palmed down in true ruckman style to his waiting colleagues. His name and his leaping caught the imagination of all Victoria, and as the War began 'Up there, Cazaly' was the catch-phrase of the moment—so potent, indeed, that 'Up there, Cazaly' endured as the battle-cry of the Anzac troops in the appalling Gallipoli Campaign of 1915. It would have surprised even Tom Wills that Australia's household name at that time was neither cricketer nor swimmer, athlete nor jockey, but the player of a game that fifty years ago had not even existed.

Gaelic Football

With the formation of the Irish Free State and the eventual emergence from the Civil Wars that followed, the immediate political purpose of the G.A.A. was over. Nationalism had triumphed, and the players of Irish Games could claim with some justification that they had done their bit to achieve the victory. But the G.A.A.'s task was now a far less tangible one— to fight for all things Irish is considerably less easy when Government, Parliament and Civil Service are already Irish than when these institutions are run by an oppressor from outside.

As late as 1946 the Gaelic Athletic Association were being begged, in print, to forget the championships and the American tours and the 70,000 strong crowds at Croke Park, and to concentrate once again on the grass-roots of the Gaelic Games. True, all proposals to do away with the Ban on foreign games after independence had been decisively squashed, but purists were afraid, with reason, that the fast-growing popularity of hurling and Gaelic Football right across Ireland, North and South, was leading to a series of 'high-class annual gladiatorial shows' and bringing all the temptations of big business into what should be, essentially, a part-time rural pursuit. In every county, the complaint continued, two or three quality teams were gaining all the publicity and luring the best players away from the minor clubs—thus making the strong team stronger and the weak even weaker. As the gates at the big Sunday afternoon games swelled, so fewer players were seen hurling and kicking footballs on the village greens. 'Only by cultivating the mediocre, by having more people playing the games instead of watching others play will a general and even standard of excellence ever be attained.'

One can feel sympathy with the writer, the anonymous compiler of *Sixty Glorious Years of the G.A.A.* The drift from the land, and the slackening of the old rule requiring players to turn out for their own parish teams, had certainly been a factor in the centralisation of hurling and football talent. But idealism and sporting success rarely go together, and the runaway popularity of Gaelic Football as a game inevitably meant an emphasis on success, on winning, on 'gladiatorial shows' rather than on quiet inter-parish encounters in the white-walled villages after Mass on Sundays. A purist might have argued the same case in Wales, where the humble Rhondda Rugby villages have suffered for decades from the depredations on their best talent by the glamorous clubs of urban Wales; Gaelic Football's popularity, like Rugby's, feeds on the success of the best players and the best teams, and without the great county teams of Kerry and Dublin, Wexford and Galway, and without the senior clubs that built up the talent for these teams, it could never have gained its present status as a genuine national sport.

The expansion after independence followed closely the patterns evolved by the other successful football codes. With the annual knock-out Cup as the principal crowd-puller, a National League was formed for 1925, and an inter-provincial championship, the Railway Cup, competed for by Ulster, Munster, Leinster and Connacht, was inaugurated in 1927, the year Maurice Davin died.

In 1931 a new tradition was started when Kerry, the All-Ireland champions, were rewarded with a tour of the Irish communities of the United States (they went again in 1933, and in 1932 an American team, as well as South African and British representatives, took part in the short-lived revival of the Tailteann Games, the old Gaelic equivalent of the Greek Olympics). The Depression Years were not, perhaps, the most auspicious times to start a regular traffic in footballing spectacle, but the visiting teams were as popular in New York and Boston as they were in Dublin, and the visit of the footballers and hurlers to the Gaelic Athletic Associations across the Atlantic has become almost an annual affair.

At home, too, the crowds who had once been so reluctant to support their country's traditional games were now proving a problem for the organisers. At the Association's Golden Jubilee Finals in 1934 there were 50,000 people at Croke Park to see Cavan beat Kildare in the All-Ireland Final. In 1938 the figure had swelled to 70,000, and filled the new double-tiered stand erected to the memory of Michael Cusack; by the end of the War Croke Park was again too small. Appeals for the cultivation of the mediocre, for bringing back the game to the parishes, had taken little account of passionate interest that Gaelic Football had captured among committed and noncommitted Gaels alike. In 1944, sixty years after Cusack and Davin had called their meeting at Thurles, an unprecedented 79,247 paid to see the Connacht champions, little Roscommon, beat the mighty Kerry. War, even in neutral Ireland, had left the train service in a shambles; so men thumbed lifts in lorries carrying peat to Dublin, others walked to the capital, setting out days before to cover the ninety miles in time. And when the underdogs had taken the trophy with a point in the last few minutes, there were bonfires blazing along their route home to the reception in Roscommon Town.

The nature of the game itself had undergone only one significant change since the early years of the century. There had always been a certain amount of controversy over the rule about passing the ball. In the early days of the game passing was largely ignored, progress was made by individual rushing with slick, hand-to-toe control of the ball, or by the age-old monster-kicking to high-catching target-men in forward positions. The rules did not allow the ball to be thrown, except by the goalkeeper, but they did allow it to be hit with the hand to a colleague. Punching the ball clearly put more power and distance into the pass, but in the early 1940s, among the Ulster counties, there developed a highly skilled system of weaving, close formation attack based on quick, accurate short passes—and the accuracy of these passes depended on tapping the ball with the flat of the hand rather than the closed fist. The method reached perfection in 1942 when Ulster won the Railway Cup for the first time with a display of graceful, flowing teamwork that had never been seen in a major competition before. (The G.A.A., of course, had never recognised the Border between Northern Ireland and the Republic. The six counties together with Cavan, Monaghan and Donegal—the old province of Ulster—competed on an equal basis with the rest). In 1943 Ulster won the Railway Cup again, and again their delicate hand-passing gave them the advantage over the more forthright methods of their Leinster opponents.

In 1945 Kerry proposed to the Association's Annual Congress that the hand-pass be abolished, a majority voted for the motion, but not the necessary two-thirds; later, however, the Central Council conferred with referees and gave its interpretation—that the ball must be struck with the fist. Next year, after a long debate and some intense lobbying from Ulstermen, the Congress overruled the Central Council and reinstated the hand-pass. Finally, in 1950, a half-hearted motion repeating the proposal to ban hand-passing reached the Congress almost unnoticed. The men of Ulster hardly bothered to lobby support, and to everyone's surprise the motion was carried. Henceforth, the ball could only be punched or kicked, and a particularly subtle feature of a game not overburdened with subtleties was lost.

Gaelic Football, nevertheless, was continuing to spread its horizons. In 1947 it had made the dramatic gesture to Irishmen overseas of playing the All-Ireland Final in New York—with a crowd of 35,000 at the old Polo Grounds standing bareheaded for 'Faith of our Fathers' and every household in Ireland tuned in to Michael O'Hehir's commentary over the Transatlantic cable.

It was not altogether a satisfactory match; the baseball area was a little too small for a football pitch and the raised pitcher's mound tended to get in the way. The Kerry players, who eventually went down to Cavan by 2 goals and 7 points to 2 goals and 11, were also somewhat disconcerted by the booing which greeted a heavy tackle on one of the Cavan forwards—in Croke Park such strong-arm stuff would have passed unnoticed. Nevertheless, the game was an inspired piece of public relations by the G.A.A., and strengthened links with America, as it would in the 1960s with Australia, at a time when it was important for such a well-supported game not to sink into closed-door insularity.

Australian Football

The dangers of insularity had always worried the Australian Football authorities too. While the game had continued on its triumphant way in Melbourne, Victoria State, Western Australia and South Australia, and while crowds there had risen to astonishing numbers, the difficulties of selling the game outside these particular breeding grounds had beaten even the most determined missionaries. They had no doubt about the qualities of their property—had not C. B. Fry, a man who had played both Soccer and Rugby at the highest levels, said that 'the Australian Game is easily the finest form of football ever invented—the most athletic to play and the most exciting to watch'? But its size, as always, was against it; existing sports grounds with any sort of permanent spectator accommodation were all far too small even to simulate the tremendous scope of the game. Only cricket grounds provided the necessary space, and cricket clubs were understandably reluctant to have 36 men in studded boots leaping and tumbling all over their carefully groomed wickets.

After the First World War the game had improved in technique and in organisation as well as in popularity; it had produced such unforgettable stars as Haydn Bunton, who was signed by the V.F.L. club Fitzroy in 1929 at the age of 18, and was immediately banned for a year because Fitzroy were found to have offered him a pair of football boots as an inducement to play for them. Quite unaffected by this setback, Bunton won the Brownlow Medal—V.F.L.'s award for fairest-and-best player—in three of his first five seasons in senior football, and, transferring to Western Australia in 1939, won that State's fairest-and-best award three times in the next four years.

While Bunton was an elegant and subtle player, Jack Dyer, his contemporary, was a tank, credited with having broken the collar-bones of more than a dozen opponents in his 310 first-class games with the Richmond club, merely because they had got in the way of his shoulder charge; he was known as 'Captain Blood', but the shrewd football brain behind his bruising image brought him the successful player-managership of Richmond. And South Australia produced its own special hero, the master goal-kicker Ken Farmer, the Don Bradman of football, who kicked an amazing 1,419 goals in his 224 league games, more than six a match; by 1970 the 100 goals per season mark had been passed fourteen times in South Australia—and eleven of those were achieved by Farmer,

17 The high mark: Australian Football's most dramatic ingredient is demonstrated by one of its first masters, Dick Lee of the Collingwood club, in 1914.   *Herald-Sun, Melbourne*

18 Leaping in unison: Bill Mohr of St Kilda comes off best during a
match in the 1920s. Note the guernsey, the sleeveless shirt now inseparable from Australian Football.   *Herald-Sun, Melbourne*

19 Stepping high: the legendary Haydn Bunton in full flight. Fast, strong, agile, safe-handed, Bunton won an unsurpassed tally of Australian Football honours in the 1930s. *Photographic Library of Australia*

20 Transatlantic Rugby: the United States XV of 1924, one of only three entrants for the Paris Olympic Games and thus, by beating Romania and France, the last and reigning Olympic Rugby gold-medallists. In this warm-up match in England they beat a Devonport Services side 25–3.

Radio Times Hulton Picture Library

21 Antipodean Rugby: the all-conquering New Zealand tourists of 1924–5 in a rare defensive formation during their 19–0 defeat of Wales. Pouncing on the ball is the impregnable George Nepia, greatest of all full-backs.

Central Press

23 Welsh defiance: for Rugby tourists to Britain, the ultimate testing ground is South Wales, and a win against a Welsh club XV is harder earned than many an international victory. In 1951 the South Africans survived this crashing try by Bleddyn Williams to scrape home 11–9 against Cardiff. *Popperfoto*

22 Welsh genius: Lewis Jones, prodigy of post-war Rugby, incomparable runner and kicker for Llanelli and Wales. At twenty-one he plunged his country into gloom by signing professional forms for Leeds, in the Rugby League, for whom he kicked a remarkable 1245 goals in only 384 matches. *Western Mail*

24 Welsh inspiration: feet are as important as hands on a Rugby
field—a demonstration of tactical kicking by Cliff Morgan, mercurial
fly-half for Wales and the British Isles throughout the 1950s, in a
match for Cardiff against Swansea towards the end of his career.
Western Mail

25 Welsh capitulation: the magnificent French pack forms round
their captain, Lucien Mias, at Cardiff Arms Park in 1958. France won
the match 16–6, their first victory in Wales since the two countries
first met in 1908. *Associated Press*

26 Irish luck: an instinctive one-handed save by the Kerry goalkeeper Dan O'Keefe from a close-range Laois shot in the All-Ireland Gaelic Football semi-finals, 1937.

27 Irish fire; a determined attack meets rock-hard defence—
Meath forwards in the Armagh goalmouth at Croke Park,
Dublin in 1953. *Bord Failte Photo*

28 Going for the man I: in Rugby League football, the man
with the ball must be stopped, no matter how it's done or how
many men it takes to do it. One man against the odds during the
Salford v. Barrow Challenge Cup Final at Wembley, 1938.
Central Press

29 Going for the man II: by contrast, the man with the ball must under no circumstances lose possession, no matter what persuasion is offered. A Kiwi forward hangs on tight in enemy territory, Great Britain v. New Zealand at Swinton, 1955.
Radio Times Hulton Picture Library

30 Racing for the line: a rare sight in Rugby League—a wing threequarter in the wide open spaces; Warrington's Australian-born hero Brian Bevan gallops for a try in the Cup Final victory over Widnes, 1950. *Popperfoto*

31 Looking for the ball: a perfect scissors movement by Great Britain sets their winger Billy Boston (left) on his way, with three New Zealanders outmanoeuvred, bewildered and running in the wrong direction, Swinton, 1955.

Radio Times Hulton Picture Library

32 How to tackle a Kangaroo: pick him up, turn
him over, and drive him headfirst into the pitch. An
unsubtle moment from Great Britain's victory over
Australia at Wigan, 1959. *Associated Press*

a small man in a game for giants who kicked so weakly with his left foot that he developed a 'boomerang' shot with the outside of his right to make up for it. In the South Australian league, whole sections of the crowd would change ends at half-time just to stand behind 'Farmer's goal'.

With men of this calibre on show, it was not surprising that by 1928 66,000 people were prepared to queue for an ordinary Saturday afternoon league match in Melbourne, or that, ten years later, a record 96,834 were at the V.F.L. Grand Final at the Melbourne Cricket Ground. In the 1950s and the 1960s attendance records were broken again and again; before the V.F.L. introduced a system of seat reservation for the Grand Finals in 1957, fans were willing to camp outside the ground for a week to ensure a good view of the match. And in 1970, when Carlton came from behind to beat Collingwood in the last quarter of the Grand Final, there were 121,696 roaring fans there to watch them do it.

Successful experiments with floodlit games were begun in 1950 for inter-state matches—something of a technical triumph, it takes a lot of artificial lighting to cover an oval 200 yards long and 150 yards wide—and in 1962 the V.F.L., rightly guessing that even the vast terraces of Melbourne Cricket Ground were soon going to be too small for the winter demand, paid half a million dollars for a 212-acre plot of land at Waverley, fifteen miles out of Melbourne, where they modestly proposed to build 'the best football ground in the world'. The first major football final was played there in 1972, and the game's previous dependence on the hospitality of the State cricket authorities can be gauged by the fact that this was the first such final ever to be played on a ground owned by a football club. Eventually, when the stands are complete the new Victoria Football League Park will hold up to 160,000 spectators, and the League has no doubts at all that it will frequently be full.

The rewards of the game have been well regulated, too. It is virtually impossible for any but the most accomplished player to make enough money to live from football. The game has been semi-professional from an early stage, but the ordinary team man is paid on an unusual sliding scale depending not on how good he is but on how many senior league games he has played. Thus, in the Victoria League in the early 1970s, players were paid 35 dollars a game for their first 50 matches, 45 dollars a game up to 100 matches, and 55 dollars a game up to 150 matches. The maximum, for any match after the 150th, was 65 dollars a game, but in fact not many players reach far past this total—the physical pressures are enormous, and players giving such long service to their clubs have generally, by that time, reached the position of player-coach, captain or vice-capatain, at which elevated status players are allowed to negotiate their own salaries with their clubs. In addition to match payments, the clubs also put money into a provident fund for the individual players, and despite the fact that almost all players have jobs outside the game, they are all guaranteed something on their retirement from football.

As in professional Soccer, American Football and Rugby League, big money has changed hands in the transfer of players, but the players have not in theory been allowed to share any of it; and recently a rule has been introduced granting free transfers to players after ten years' service with any single club. For the players, the one chance of riches is the winning of the 'fairest-and-best' medal. It is a curious habit, singling one player out of many hundreds for adulation—not unlike the long-established American habit of selecting All-American teams every year; but even the Americans pick a full team, the best man for every position—the Australians heap the whole publicity machine on to one player alone, and his business manager gets to work at once. The rewards for Victoria's Brownlow Medal winner can amount to between 10,000 and 20,000 dollars in advertising and endorsements, and also assures the player of enough lasting hero-worship to guarantee a generous round of testimonial dinners on his retirement.

In the 1950s and 1960s Australian Football at last began to advance outside its traditional backyard. In 1954 teams from New South Wales, Canberra, and Queensland joined the Australian Amateurs in a sort of second division of the Australian Championship, and in 1957 the North Queensland side played the first 'inter-country' game of Australian Football since 1888 when they travelled to Port Moresby to meet Papua. Already the major league clubs had been persuaded to play various important fixtures in the country areas of their states to bring the game to a wider audience, and their efforts were gradually being answered by even greater response from the backwoods, with fans travelling hundreds of miles from the bush to see the premiership finals.

It was an important time for a publicity drive. The game itself was probably at the most spectacular stage of its history: the high marking, the enormous kicking and the fast, physical challenge had already been there; in the 1950s it gained another dimension through the genius of the game's most celebrated post-war star, Graeme 'Polly' Farmer. During his 370 major league games in Western Australia and Victoria, this giant, part-Aborigine ruckman had discovered—just as the Ulsterman had discovered in the Gaelic game in the 1940s—the potential of the handpass· Australian Football rules had always allowed players to punch the ball with a closed fist, but until Farmer's day it had remained a defensive measure, generally used in desperation when a clean catch was impossible.

Farmer turned the handpass—punching the ball from his hand to a team-mate—into a devastating tactical weapon. He had improved the punching technique from a clumsy lunge to a skill with either hand from a distance of ten yards, and, more relevant, could capture a high ball, lure a posse of defenders towards an anticipated kick, and punch the ball thirty yards to a fast moving colleague to change the direction of attack in an instant and add considerably to the attraction of the game.

This made the increased promotional effect opportune; what made it necessary was the fast-changing nature of Australia's population. Immigration after the war was almost entirely from Europe, and though a great proportion of these came from Britain, where at least the sporting traditions might command an interest in the alien game, almost every other male immigrant would have been reared at home on a diet of Soccer relieved, in a few instances, by the two Rugby codes. It is yet another measure of the confidence with which Australian football was advancing that there has been no significant dip in the spectator figures for the Australian game.

Television has redoubled the interest. In Melbourne on a Saturday, the five or six Victorian league games will pull in the average total gate of 180,000, and then, replayed on TV, command early evening prime time in front of enormous home audiences. Television records gigantic viewing figures even for such run-of-the-mill duties as the voting by the League's umpires for Victoria's 'fairest-and-best' of the year, and in recent years has managed to find viewers in the traditional Rugby states of New South Wales and Queensland who are eager to transfer their allegiance to Victorian League games on a Saturday.

The 1960s saw even more ambitious efforts to spread the word. Under Australian direction the game took a firm hold in Papua/New Guinea, where an official competition was inaugurated; both Melbourne and Geelong clubs went on private club tours to the United States, and games were played in Tokyo, Honolulu and San Francisco. In Europe an exhibition match was staged in that most unlikely hotbed of Rugby Union, Bucharest. And in 1967 came the series of exchange visits with Gaelic Footballers. The Australians began it with two matches in the autumn of 1967 when they played Meath, the All-Ireland champions, and Mayo at Gaelic Football, and beat them both. The Australians were a combined side, picked from half a dozen of the V.F.L. clubs, and the one concession they were allowed was that they (and, for the occasion, their opponents) could pick the ball from the ground rather than flick it up with their toe.

Extraordinarily, when Meath celebrated their All-Ireland victory by touring Australia the following spring, the Australians' powerful, flowing, disciplined football that had so impressed the Irish at Croke Park, was completely overshadowed by the Irish non-stop running. The Australians were, to be sure, playing on a smaller pitch with an unfamiliar ball, and aiming at a far smaller goal than they were accustomed to; but for the semi-professionals of Victoria to lose by 7 points to 3 goals and 9 points to the Gaelic team in front of 30,000 of their countrymen was something of a setback, emphasised a week or two later by a repeat of the defeat in a 90-degree heatwave.

In 1970 the Kingdom of Kerry followed in Meath's footsteps. Kerry were without the now-ageing Mick O'Connell, one of the great Gaelic footballers of all time and a vital cog in the Kerry machine for many years; but the Irish champions once again showed that even a mighty Victoria team, under Australia's latest super-star Ron Barassi, could not raise themselves sufficiently to beat well-drilled, sweetly moving tactics in an alien game. In Adelaide, perhaps even more significantly for the future, Kerry agreed to play half their game—still to mainly Gaelic rules—with the oval Australian ball (it's a slimmer, slightly longer ball than the one used for Rugby, with rounder ends and weighing slightly more).

The Australians, it was said, would be so far ahead at half-time that it would be pointless playing the second half. In fact the teams were level at half-time, 2 goals and 2 points to Kerry, 1 goal and 5 points to South Australia; and with the round ball in use in the second half, Kerry walked away with the match with ease. There were certainly prophets in Adelaide that day who were predicting, for the not too distant future, Australia would be playing Gaelic internationals in Ireland and the Gaels playing Australian Football internationals in Australia.

Another possibility, that the Irish and the Australians might agree on a compromise game which both can play on equal terms, is very remote. Both the Australian Football Council and the Gaelic Athletic Association are heirs to long and important traditions. For common ground to be reached, one or other nation would have to agree to alter the shape of their ball, which is too fundamental a change to be made lightly, and many other, less vital conventions would have to be abandoned on both sides. What is more likely is that Irishmen will learn to play to Australian rules with sufficient expertise for the best Gaelic footballers to hold their own in Australia, and the Australians, likewise, will take time to train at the Gaelic skills in order to be able to play in Dublin without demanding concessions in the rules.

Certainly the Irish have opened the way to such contact—and, even more important, to contact with Rugby and Soccer players in Ireland—by at last dropping the Ban. The exclusivity of the G.A.A., their insistence on the use of the Gaelic forms of proper names, on the use of Irish materials for all contract work, on the use of the Irish language on all official documents, had all been maintained with a certain fierce pride. But the Ban on all contact with foreign sports, had become something of an embarrassment. Jack Lynch, All-Ireland winner at hurling and Gaelic Football and a future Prime Minister, had once been suspended from the Association for watching a Rugby match; so had the Republic's first President, Douglas Hyde; Eamon de Valera himself had been vehemently attacked by the G.A.A. for a similar lapse. And the spirit of the Ban had become quite untenable; it was no longer any use protecting their fellow countrymen from the insidious sight of corrupt English-inspired unfortunates playing Soccer or Rugby when every other household in the land could—and did—watch them by turning on their television sets. The World Cups of 1966 and 1970 were watched and marvelled at by Irish men and women who ten years before had never seen a Soccer match in their lives. And the G.A.A. had come mighty close to a breach of the laws themselves by their welcome of the Australian tourists in 1967 and their bending of the Gaelic rules to suit the visitors.

In 1971 thirty of the thirty-two counties voted at grass-roots level to recommend the Ban's abolition. On Easter Sunday at the annual Congress of the G.A.A., the President Pat Fanning, himself still a supporter of the Ban, announced its demise: 'Let there be no sounding of trumpets as the rule disappears. Nor should there be talk of defeat. If victory there be, let it be victory for the Association.'

Sounding of trumpets, in fact, would have been very much in order. Ireland's football, Gaelic, Rugby and Soccer, could only benefit from the removal of these barriers; there is now no conceivable danger to the following that Gaelic Football has built up from Derry to Cork, or from Dublin to Galway; and the skills of a different code played in the city schools and colleges can only enhance those learned under the tuition of the Gaelic Athletic Association in the farms and on the hillsides.

6

wonder of the world

Association Football: 1900 to 1953

While the Irish, the Australians and the Americans remained reasonably content for their games to progress in isolation, Association Football was allowed no such exclusiveness. In the first fifty years of the twentieth century Soccer developed from a popular British pastime with a growing crowd appeal to a world obsession of unprecedented dimensions—a game providing a common language to link Upper Volta and South Korea, Australia and Paraguay, Iceland and Sri Lanka, a game with 16 million registered players and many times that number playing five-minute or five-hour kick-abouts on every other spare piece of flat ground in the world, a game that has found so many players that it has had to register 300,000 referees to look after them, and a game that attracts up to 140 countries to enter the one great Open Soccer Championship—the World Cup.

The explosion of world Soccer was no more than a magnified repeat of what had happened in Britain since the early 1870s. Between the launching of the first F.A. Cup competition and the early rounds of the thirtieth, in the autumn of 1900, membership of the Football Association (and it must from now on be remembered that both the F.A. and the Rugby Union had never, and would never, see the need to add the word 'English' to their supremely arrogant titles) had grown from 50 clubs to some 10,000. Two hundred and seventy of them were entering each year for the Cup; every village and every factory worth its salt supported a team, a field and a couple of sets of goalposts; and almost all of them were organised— quite unlike their counterparts in the Rugby Union—into some sort of league competition.

The middle-class origins of the Association, though still nominally in command at the top, had all but faded from major competition. Though such scholarly and patrician figures as C. B. Fry would still find the class to play for a professional team in an F.A. Cup Final, the new clubs were the product of working class enterprise, of youth clubs and church organisations, sometimes even from other clubs formed to play other games:

Burnley grew out of a Rugby club, Tottenham Hospur, Crewe Alexandra, Sheffield Wednesday all from cricket clubs.

· In the South, too, the amateur tradition had succumbed—in the more competitive reaches of the game, at any rate—to the attractions of professional football. The clubs that followed Royal Arsenal into the field made an uncertain start, but the ultimate justification for the founders of the Southern League came when Tottenham reached the final of the F.A. Cup in 1901 to attract a hitherto unheard of crowd of 110,820 to Crystal Palace (and another 30,000 to see the replay at Bolton, when they beat Sheffield United 3–1 to become the first and only non-league club to carry off the Cup). The money had become something of an attraction, too. Many of the leading clubs were doing so well from their gate-receipts that even those formed with no intention of seeking a profit were sitting back and watching their bank balance grow. At one match in 1904 Aston Villa took over £14,000 at the gate; several such clubs became incorporated under the Joint Stock Companies Act (the F.A. itself did so in 1903, with a capital of £100) and some even paid a dividend.

Despite their evident success as entertainers, however, the professional footballers were denied any but the most meagre share in this prosperity; they were hard-worked and very poorly paid. They had little security, and at a few days' notice could be bought and sold at the whim of their club committee—to be transplanted, quite possibly, hundreds of miles from any home they had begun to build up. Their skills and their hard apprenticeship never gave them the respect due to other accomplished tradesmen—in 1899 the entire England team, including one of the most polished and gentlemanly individuals ever to wear the white shirt, G. O. Smith, were barred from a Birmingham hotel before their international with Scotland until the hotel's manager was given assurances by the F.A. that the footballers would not outrage the comfort of the other guests.

No. 163. Right or left full back [ran an advertisement in *Athletics News* in the 1890s]. This is one of the most likely youngsters I have ever booked. He gives reference to a well-known pressman, who has recently seen him play and knows what he can do, and has a high opinion of his abilities and future prospects. Just note—height 5 ft 11 inches; weight 12 stone; age 20. There's a giant for you—this is a colt worth training.

One hopes that No. 163 went to a good home, though however well his 'future prospects' turned out, he cannot have had an easy life. The great Welsh forward Billy Meredith, one of the two or three finest professionals to emerge in British football between the formation of the League and the

First World War, used to recall the rigours of the week, not untypical for a talented footballer, in which he won his first cap for Wales in 1895.

On the Saturday, after a nightmare sea-crossing, he played for Wales against Ireland in Belfast; then another night of sea-sickness on the way back; on the Monday, the Wales–England match at Queen's Club, in London; on Tuesday, home to Chirk, in North Wales, for a day's work down the local coal mine (Manchester City did not pay him enough to feed him *and* provide the allowance he had to give his ageing parents); on Wednesday, up to Manchester for a home game with City; on Thursday and Friday, shifts down the pit; on Saturday, up the road to Wrexham to play for Wales against Scotland. For those three internationals (each one, incidentally, was drawn) he was paid £1 per game. Throughout his thirty-year career Meredith averaged £4 15s. a week from football.

Yet the Press and its correspondence columns raged at the very idea of footballers being idolised by their public. Letters expressed fury at collections being taken for footballers at the end of a successful career, or at their being followed by adoring small boys along the streets, or at their being received at town hall banquets.

Spectators, too, though they presumably saw what they came to see, were treated in the same cavalier manner. Huge terraced cattle-pens were built in Glasgow and the northern towns and cities of England where the maximum number of football supporters could be accommodated at the lowest possible cost for the shortest possible time with the fewest possible facilities. Sometimes the stands or the terraces gave way, as at the Scotland–England international at Ibrox Park in 1902, when 25 people were crushed to death; more often they were merely uncomfortable, over-crowded corrals where ever-increasing 'record crowds' were a feather in the cap of the management, and where, for want of an alternative, you urinated down the raincoat of the man in front of you.

Improvements, when they came, were as breathtaking as they were isolated. At Stamford Bridge, headquarters of the old London Athletic Club, H. A. Mears built a stadium that seated 5,000 spectators (and, he boasted, accommodated another 95,000 standing; luckily the boast was never put to the test), and founded Chelsea Football Club with a reputation for exciting play and intriguing inconsistency. And at Old Trafford, where Manchester United had moved in 1910, the players had billiard rooms, massage rooms, a plunge bath and a gymnasium, while a sixth of the 80,000 spectators were under cover and there were attendants to usher the more affluent to their new tip-up seats and the new tea-room.

The players, too, looked for improvements (those many hundreds of professionals, that is, who were not idling in the billiard rooms at Old

Trafford). In 1898 the predecessors of that pampered Manchester United staff had been influential in forming a Union of Professional Footballers, which then proceeded to do nothing for ten years. But in 1908 Manchester United played Newcastle United in a match to raise money for a provident fund for the Union, and incurred the disapproval of both the League and the F.A. In the coming year, they further upset the authorities by seeking affiliation to the Federation of Trade Unions; in a thoroughly unimaginative and high-handed way, the F.A. and the League thereupon suspended the Chairman and Secretary of the Players' Union and called on all footballers to resign from it.

This determination to isolate footballers from the general work force was primarily to guard against a football strike, which would bankrupt the clubs in no time; but a strike-call is precisely what the F.A.'s action precipitated, particularly after they had refused to allow the matter to be taken to arbitration. The players announced they would not play in the opening matches of the 1909 season, a threat that sent the clubs scurrying to sign up every promising amateur they could lay their hands on, and the expected compromise was not reached until two days before the season's first Saturday.

It was ostensibly a victory for the players, who got recognition for their Union, back pay refunded and the suspension of its officers rescinded. But within a couple of years the players had been forced to accept the 'maximum wage' agreement from the League as well as from the F.A., and even on the resumption of regular football after the First World War players could receive no more than £8 a week, dropping to a mere £6 during the summer. It was improved to some extent by talent and place-money by the League, and the F.A. also guaranteed a modicum of security by stipulating a minimum wage as well, but this maximum permitted wage, which the League clung to for fifty years, was rightly seen as discrimination against top-class players. The F.A.'s and the League's argument was that inflated wages for players in the leading teams would drive the lower-division clubs into bankruptcy; it was probably true, but it was poor consolation to the crowd-pulling professionals who left the game pensionless after fifteen years with no more savings than might buy a share in a tobacconist's shop.

While the British footballers and their employers were arguing over the fruits of Soccer's expanding popularity, other nations were beginning to notice the same desire to play and watch the game that the English and the Scots had experienced thirty or forty years before. The game was simple enough and agreeable enough to have found a small place in the hearts of any group of young Britons in exile during the 1880s and 1890s; it was no surprise that they should play Soccer together in the winter just as they would almost inevitably play cricket together when the sun came out.

Throughout the nations of Europe, from Denmark to Hungary, from Imperial Russia to Portugal, virtually every pioneering football club was founded by the British. Despite the various mediaeval traditions of football—particularly the elaborate, courtly rituals of the Italian *Calcio*—there was no surviving tradition of the game on the continent by the mid 19th century. A party of Oxford undergraduates made a visit to Germany in 1875, but no club appears to have been founded outside British jurisdiction until 1876 when a group of British businessmen in Copenhagen formed the English Football Club.

By 1879 the Danes had taken to the game with such enthusiasm that the Kopenhegen Boldklub was formed, first playing a version combining the rules of both Rugby and Soccer, but later settling with Soccer. Within five years there were fifteen clubs competing in a knock-out competition, and in 1889 the Danish F.A. was formed. Denmark remained a major force in continental football right up to the First World War, after which their size and their reluctance to adopt the strong, physical European methods told against them. Denmark took the silver medal at the first two Olympic Soccer tournaments—losing to the United Kingdom in 1908, after beating France by 17–1 in a semi-final, and to England in 1912; and in 1910 they were the first international side ever to defeat an England team, when they beat an F.A. Amateur XI 2–1 in Copenhagen.

In Germany, the pattern was much the same. The Bremer F.C. in Hamburg was founded by expatriate Britons in the 1880s, and there was an Anglo-American Club in Berlin at about the same time. The first club there to play specifically to Association rules was the English F.C. at Dresden, formed in 1890. Ten years later, when the German Football Association was founded, there were four hundred clubs playing the game.

British mining engineers—and there were few developing countries where they could not be found distributing the fruits of Victorian technology—took the game to Romania and to Spain; in Russia, at a mill in Orekhovo-Zuyevo owned by two brothers from Lancashire called Charnock, a football team was developed in the 1880s good enough to attract crowds of 15,000 and to play matches against visiting foreign clubs. In Austria, it was the gardeners imported from England to tend the estates of the Baron de Rothschild who founded the Vienna Club and played in their noble employer's racing colours of yellow and blue; in 1894 they played the first football match in Austria against yet another team of expatriate Englishmen, the Vienna Cricket and Football Club (now FK Austria Vienna); the 'Cricketers' won 4–0.

And in Italy, too, that most un-British of footballing nations, it was the British who played the first matches and joined together in exile to form the first clubs; the British Genoa Cricket and Football Club is still known by its anglicised name of Genoa rather than the Italian 'Genova', just as A.C. Milan, another of the pioneer clubs, still resists any temptation to call itself A.C. Milano.

The pattern was almost universal. By the turn of the century there were few cities in Europe without a football club, and half the countries had already established national associations. British influence had seen the game off the ground, and then organisation, fixtures, development and discipline had been left to the foreigners to work out for themselves. At no stage in the early development of European Soccer did the Football Association attempt to set itself up as the central government of the fast-growing game; there were critics, not unnaturally, who felt it should behave in the paternal manner of the Rugby Union and the International Rugby Board, to keep a hand on the Soccer tiller to guarantee British standards in the world game. It would have created quite incalculable animosity had the F.A. heeded this sort of advice; on balance, they did well to leave things alone.

In fact, once football had gained a foothold in Europe, the Europeans were eager for all the contact they could get with British clubs. The tours which had characterised Rugby for so long now began to sprout on the Soccer calendar—a decade or so of friendly international club-to-club contact which faded with the decline of the powerful amateur teams and has been revived in the professional game in the last few years chiefly to keep professionals employed during the summer months. For this short period, though, British expertise flourished across the young football fields of Europe. Richmond Football Club toured Hungary in 1901 and beat a representative side 4–0; Oxford University scored 15 goals against Vienna on Easter Sunday in 1899, and won another match 13–0 the next day. In 1904 the Corinthians made a particularly significant tour in Hungary and Bohemia, where the improving techniques of the European clubs were reflected in the fact that the tourists were held to 7–4 and 4–1 victories in two games against Slavia Prague. They returned through France, where they were actually 4–2 in arrears with 23 minutes to go in the second half when their captain, G. O. Smith, led an inspired, pro-longed attack to win the game 11–4.

At the Second Olympic Games in Paris in 1900, a Soccer tournament was organised outside the official Olympic competition; there were only two entries, and Britain, represented by the amateurs of Upton Park, beat France. A few years later a Parisian team came to London to play the great Arsenal, and were overwhelmed 26–1, their single goal scored by a local Woolwich boy who came on as a substitute. But in 1905 a combined Copenhagen team beat Ilford twice, 8–1 and 6–1; and while continental sides were still no match for British national teams—the F.A. somewhat stand-offishly refused to play a full international against a continental side until 1908, when England beat Austria twice in Vienna 6–1 and 11–1— strong rivalries were developing between the European countries them- selves as the standard of their game improved. The first international out- side Britain took place in 1902, when Austria beat Hungary 5–0; in 1904 France and Belgium began a long series of keenly contested internationals with a 3–3 draw. Clearly, the British could not remain aloof for long.

Or could they? In that same year of 1904 Robert Guèrin, a Frenchman, came to England in an attempt to get the help of the Football Association, which they understandably considered of paramount importance, in forming an International Football Federation. Guèrin had long meetings with Lord Kinnaird and with the Secretary of the F.A., Frederick Wall, but to no avail. The F.A.'s current notion of football's international federation stretched no further than England, Scotland, Ireland and Wales, and no argument could persuade them to look wider; after their earlier diplomatic subtlety in not presuming to dictate terms to the new Soccer nations, this attitude might have appeared logical. But to the Europeans it seemed churlish, and the relationship of the British associa- tions with .'IFA vacillated between uneasy alliance and downright mis- trust from its formation that year—with Denmark, France, Belgium, the Netherlands, Spain, Sweden and Switzerland—until well after the Second World War.

Europe, however, were managing remarkably well without British guidance. In the first decade of the 20th century the new footballing nations began to produce their own coaches, managers and players to lay the foundations for the great national teams of the 1920s and 1930s. Two names stand out in this new theatre of the world game—one a Vien- nese Jew with a passion for everything British, the other an Italian student who acquired a love for football by watching Manchester United.

The Italian was Vittorio Pozzo, a Piedmontese who had been an athlete of some note before taking up football. He was studying in England, teaching languages part-time to pay for food, when he became captivated by the football he saw at Old Trafford and, in particular, the attacking centre-half play of Charlie Roberts. He had long conversations with Roberts, and later with Steve Bloomer, the Derby County and England forward, and from these few meetings he developed theories that were going to make Italy the most potent European force in pre-war world football. On his return home he was appointed Secretary of the Italian Football Federation, already with a first division swollen to an unmanageable sixty-four clubs. Pozzo's attempt to reduce the league to twenty-four teams was met with resentment and resignations, but he was entrusted with the Italian team entered for the 1912 Stockholm Olympic Games.

After a surprisingly successful run in the competition, the Italians went out to Austria—the team run by the Jew from Vienna, Hugo Meisl. Meisl had been a member of the original Vienna Cricketers, and in the early years of the century organised his football team from the bank where he was supposedly employed and which bored him to distraction. In 1911 he acquired, by an inspired choice, a British coach for his team, Jimmy Hogan, a moderate professional player with an imaginative football brain and an inborn love for the Scottish method of play—short, precise passing, running into space, five forwards up and an attacking centre-half feeding them.

Encouraged by Meisl, Hogan built a team good enough to beat Tottenham Hotspur in 1912, and experienced enough to beat Pozzo's Italians in that Olympic confrontation in Stockholm. (There Pozzo and Meisl met, organised an international club match between Juventus and the 'Cricketers' in Turin, which surprised everyone by being both exciting and good-tempered, and the following year staged a full Italy–Austria international in Genoa.)

Hogan and Austria advanced under Meisl's command. When the German F.A. tried to poach Hogan to coach their national side, Meisl baulked them by retaining him on a two-year contract. At the outbreak of war Hogan was first interned in Vienna, then bailed out and allowed to carry on coaching in what was then enemy territory, and afterwards permitted to move to Budapest to coach their leading club team M.T.K. English clubs had little time for theoretical coaching—the game, it was assumed, came naturally to Englishmen—and Hogan's coaching experiences in the 1920s at Fulham and Aston Villa were disastrous. But his continuing influence on the continent was enormous; by 1930 he was claiming that England's training methods were long out of date; in the same year his Austrian team was drawing 3–3 with Germany, and in 1932 were unlucky to lose 4–3 to England in London. Not until the late 1930s did the Football Association change its policy and appoint a full-time Chief Coach; their first choice was Jimmy Hogan. His methods received little attention till after the Second World War and achieved no real results until the 1960s, after English football had gone through a period of depressing mediocrity; had the F.A. heeded Hogan's advice a little earlier, those lean years might have been avoided.

While Soccer was capturing Europe's attention in those free moments the nations could spare from fighting each other, it was spreading like wildfire in the world's other major footballing continent, South America. The game had been introduced in Argentina, Uruguay and Brazil in much the same way as it had been launched in Denmark and Germany. As early as 1867, the year that Queen's Park of Glasgow came into being, a group of Englishmen founded the Buenos Aires Football Club in Argentina. In the 1880s the game was played at an English school run by one Alexander Watson Hutton, and the old boys, in the time-honoured British tradition, formed a football club (Hutton's interest in the game was rewarded when he became the first President of the Argentina F.A. in 1893). The Italians, too, had some influence in Argentina; the country had a large community of Italian immigrants at the turn of the century, and a tour by Pozzo's Torino Club in 1914 did much to spread the game's popularity and eventually to knit the Italian and Spanish attitudes into a powerful footballing force.

Uruguay began its life as a football nation with a club formed by an English professor, and others were founded by Britons building the country's railways. In Brazil there is a tradition of the earliest games having been played by British sailors, but the first real impetus seems to have come from a Brazil-born Englishman, Charles Miller, who returned to São Paolo in 1894 after a ten-year spell in Britain, taking two footballs with him. Soccer was virtually unknown there, even among expatriate Britons—the weather and the social climate were such that cricket was the gentlemanly game. But Miller started clubs at São Paolo Railways, the English Gas Company and the London Bank, and even persuaded the São Paolo Cricket Club to try the game. By 1902 there was a São Paolo League, and in Rio de Janeiro more English enthusiasts had founded the Fluminense Club.

Expansion in South America proceeded very much on European lines. In 1904 Southampton, who had already been the first professional team to visit Europe, made a short tour to Argentina. In the early years of the century Uruguay and Argentina started a long series of internationals; in 1910 the Corinthians—at a time when the F.A. were still highly reluctant to commit any sort of national side outside Britain—were invited by Fluminense to tour Brazil, and made such a favourable impression that a club in São Paolo was named after them (they returned in 1913, and conjured up all sorts of portents for the future of Brazilian football by being beaten 2–1 by a local Rio representative team); and in 1916 the three nations inaugurated the first South American Championships, and ushered in Uruguay's long domination of football in that hemisphere.

In one respect the South American game differed from the European. Until 1888 slavery had been legal in Brazil, and it would have been unthinkable in the early days of Brazilian football for the Negroes to have played in what were after all, exclusive middle-class clubs run by the British and the Portuguese. Uruguay had no colour bar—an important factor in the early dominance of their national teams—and only when the America Football Club of Rio deliberately flouted convention by employing a Negro player (thus driving some of their outraged players and supporters to transfer their allegiances elsewhere) did the barriers begin to crumble. Not until the 1930s, when the game was fully open to players of all races, did Brazilian football begin to hint at its true potential.

The football that was being adopted by club after club throughout half the world was by now very much a stable product. The rule-changes of the Football Association's formative years were extensive and, to an outsider, confusing. But by the time foreign clubs were learning the rudiments of the game, the formula for a fair, skilful, robust and exciting game had been achieved, and very little in the actual conduct of Soccer has altered since the 1890s. Such laws that have been modified, with one important exception, have been minor ones. Goalkeepers have been put through a number of nit-picking law-changes which have, in total, made very little difference to their jobs: their handling has been reduced to within the penalty area only; their position at penalty kicks altered from the edge of the 6-yard box to the goal line; their carrying the ball penalised after two steps (1919), generously increased to four steps (1931); their wardrobe (in Britain) required to include a yellow jersey for international matches; their unenviable role as Aunt Sallies reduced, also generously, by protecting them from most physical contact. Other minor alterations, like the compulsory numbering of players in League matches, have considerably improved the spectators' enjoyment of the game.

In the face of such changes Charles Alcock's concept of the 'universal game' still held good: football was played world-wide, but good sense in Europe, in South America and at home in Britain ensured that the laws were uniform in Huddersfield, Vienna, Montevideo and Oslo—no unilateral rule-revolution was going to split Soccer into factions as it had already split Rugby into American Football, Canadian Football, Union and League. The edicts of the International Board were generally followed to the letter by the associations abroad. This remained true even after the formation of FIFA; and it still held good in 1925 when unquestionably the most far-reaching piece of football legislation this century was passed —the alteration of the off-side rule.

Minor modifications apart, the rule had remained constant since 1866, nearly sixty years. It said that any player who, at the moment the ball was played to him or when he was otherwise interfering with play, had fewer than three opponents between him and the opposing goal-line, was off-side if he was at the same time in his opponents' half of the field. This rule had, on the whole, worked very well, particularly while defences consisted of two full-backs lying in a rearguard position protecting the goalkeeper, which gave every opportunity for spectacular five-man attacks to develop in midfield, supported by the long-lamented attacking centre-half of football's golden days.

The trouble with the rule, as it stood, was that it required a sort of live-and-let-live attitude from the players; once winning matches and points and championships increased in importance, someone was going to spot the flaw in the system. And it was this flaw that produced the off-side trap. The two backs would lie further and further upfield, one slightly ahead of the other. When an attack began, the forward of the two backs would sneak further upfield behind the line of the two forwards; from that moment, only the forward who held the ball was onside. The rest— anyone free to receive a pass—had been 'played off-side'.

The ruse was first exploited in the years just before the First World War, the years when Newcastle United were fielding the greatest side in their history, reaching five Cup finals and three first division champion-ships within eight years with unforgettable artistic football. In that Newcastle team was one of the game's great defenders, an Ulsterman called Bill McCracken, who in the last years before the First World War became notorious as Mr Off-side. He and Frank Hudspeth, his fellow back and an England international, infuriated opposing forwards, angered opposing crowds and, in the name of tactical football, produced some extraordinarily boring games. It was a standing joke for visiting teams at Newcastle Central Station to reply to the guard's whistle 'Blimey, off-side already', and the turf of St James's Park was said to have more grass in the goalmouths than it did in the centre circle, so efficient were the New-castle full-backs and their fast-learning imitators in their destructive skills.

It didn't help Newcastle back to their days of domination—they would have had to score goals, not just prevent them, to do that—but it did dreadful harm to the game. The seasons following the war were drab enough without unimaginative, defensive football, in which forty off-side decisions in a game was nothing out of the ordinary. The International

Board had to do something. They organised a special match in June 1925, under the auspices of the F.A. at Highbury between a team of Amateurs and a team of Professionals, and after an hour or so of desultory experiments with a couple of different off-side regulations they called it a day and held a meeting. The old off-side law was scrapped; the new one, reducing the necessary number of defenders between attacker and goal line to two, was adopted and put into effect for the 1925-6 season.

The change had not, principally, been made to increase the number of goals scored but to reduce the infuriating number of stoppages. But the immediate effect on goal-scoring was sensational. The clubs had been given very little time to adjust their defensive tactics to the new law, and for a month or two of the 1925-6 season the strong attacking sides ran riot. On the first match day of the season Aston Villa put ten goals past Burnley. Soon afterwards, Newcastle, just to prove that they could do it if they tried, beat Arsenal 7-0; Arsenal in turn beat Cardiff 5-0; Tottenham Hotspur and Huddersfield shared ten goals in a match. That first season, as managers and players struggled to adjust to the sight of front-running forwards lurking between their widely spaced fullbacks, 6,373 goals were scored in the Football League's four divisions, nearly 1,700 more than in the previous year.

The problems for defences, however, were by no means insuperable. The wily Bill McCracken, traditionally remembered as the start of all the fuss, had just been taken on as coach to Hull City; it can hardly be insignificant that Hull did not concede a single goal in their first five matches and, while finishing in the bottom half of the second division, had one of its best defensive records. The solution to the new off-side rule, however, is credited not to McCracken, whose role is traditionally that of the arch-villain of the whole episode, but by a gritty, dumpy Yorkshireman who was at this time approaching the heights of the most successful and influential career in British football since the retirement of Charles Alcock.

Herbert Chapman had played for Tottenham Hotspur before the Great War, as an undistinguished inside-forward; and had gone on to manage the then Southern League Northampton Town, and subsequently Leeds City, where he remained until the end of the war. After just eight games of the 1919 season—quite successfully, winning four and drawing two—Leeds were wound up by the League for making illegal payments to players. Their fixtures were transferred to Port Vale, their club records were never found, and their manager (who announced that he had burned them) was suspended for life, by all accounts a scapegoat for the Leeds directors. After a reasonably quick pardon he joined Huddersfield Town as manager early in 1920.

The West Riding of Yorkshire had felt the full force of the Rugby revolution, and managing a soccer team in what was now a hotbed of professional Rugby League was a difficult task. Leeds had been in considerable financial trouble themselves, and Huddersfield's gates were almost as disappointing. It was entirely through the efforts of Chapman that Huddersfield Town became *the* team of the 1920s. After only a few months under Chapman they had gained promotion to Division One and had reached the Cup Final, only to lose in extra time to Aston Villa; two years later they won the Cup. In 1923 they were League champions; they repeated the process the following two seasons, and in 1926 and 1927 they were runners-up.

At the peak of this tremendous run of success, in the summer of 1925 following Huddersfield's second championship and, incidentally, as the International Board were making up their minds to change the off-side law, Chapman moved south to Arsenal. Highbury in the mid 1920s housed a competent but as yet unremarkable First Division side. They had in their days at Woolwich been the pioneers of professional football in the South of England, but they had little real achievement behind them since they had joined the League as Royal Arsenal in 1893. They had won promotion from Division Two in 1904, had been relegated again in 1913, and had been somewhat fortunate that the extension of the First Division to 22 clubs at the end of the War allowed them back into the First Division without their being required to win promotion on merit. At the time Chapman was called in they had never attained higher than sixth place in the League, and they had never got to a Cup Final; just before the First World War, indeed, there had been plans to merge them with Fuiham, and they had been uprooted from their Woolwich home to join Tottenham Hotspur and Clapton Orient in North London. In both 1924 and 1925 they had narrowly escaped relegation.

Chapman began in the cavalier manner that in the 1970s would seem commonplace but that in 1925 must have appeared either foolhardy or supremely confident. He bought three of the most talented players in Britain: Scotland's goalkeeper Bill Harper, the Blackburn Rovers right winger Joe Hulme and the incomparable Charles Buchan, who had captained England, and since 1910 had scored 200 goals for Sunderland. (He cost Chapman £2,000 plus £100 for each of the nineteen goals he scored in his first season at Highbury, and probably a lot more under the counter.) In two years Chapman spent £25,000 on transfer fees. And in those same two years he had Arsenal in second place in the League championship (to have created both the champions—Huddersfield—and the runners-up was a unique achievement), in a Cup Final for the first time, and in the vanguard of a revolution in football strategy that has survived till today.

The revolution was forced on the game by the new off-side rule, but in Chapman it found an organiser to exploit it to the full. His first priority was defence—the two full-backs were now hopelessly vulnerable to fast-breaking forwards and had to have some assistance from the front. Inevitably an attacker had to be withdrawn, and the attacking centre-half of the 'good old days' became the 'stopper' centre back of the new era. He was there to blot out the centre forward; the full-backs could then stay wide to deal with the wing forwards; and any threatening forward movement by the inside right or inside left could be smothered by retreating half-backs.

And to counter this sort of defence in other teams—Chapman's imitators were not slow to recognise the efficiency of his plan—he advocated a far more direct approach from the forwards, particularly with the long cross-field pass that could unsettle the three-man defence pivoting on the centre-half.

Within ten years Arsenal had become a legend. Chapman continued to spend prodigiously. To find a replacement for Charles Buchan, who retired in 1928, Chapman cast eyes on Bolton's accomplished David Jack. Bolton demanded £13,000—tantamount in those days, when the record transfer fee stood at half that amount, to a curt refusal. Chapman haggled a bit, and, to the usual accompaniment of letters and headlines asking where it was all going to stop, Jack became the first five-figure footballer. Within a year Alex James, one of Scotland's 'Wembley Wizards' who had so tormented England's defences in 1928, arrived, for another £9,000.

Beside the ready money, which was already paying dividends at the turnstiles, there was the method. Chapman had appointed Tom Whittaker as trainer, who in turn brought in such revolutionary methods as sun-ray lamps and training régimes geared to the particular skills and requirements of each player. After five years of rebuilding and buttressing of confidence, Arsenal proved themselves capable of winning in the highest company. The vital test came at Wembley, by that time the unchallenged home of the F.A. Cup Final, the finest football ground in the world, and already endowed with a big match atmosphere quite unmatched anywhere in England. Here Arsenal's Eddie Hapgood stood on the bootlaces of Huddersfield's Alex Johnson for the whole match, and Arsenal's peerless forward line of Hulme, Jack, Lambert, James and Bastin brought the Cup to Highbury for the first time.

That was in 1930. The next year Arsenal won their first League Championship; the next they were runners-up in the League and losing finalists in the Cup; in 1933, 1934 and 1935 they were League champions again; in 1936 they won the Cup; in 1937 they were third only in the League; in 1938 they won the Championship again. It was a run of superiority unprecedented and so far unrepeated in English football, though the man who laid its foundation did not live to see the full flowering. Chapman died in 1934, his value and his significance in the English game unquestioned. He had, by his example, ushered in the era of the manager, the man who, in modern football, particularly successful modern football, personifies the club to a greater extent even than the players themselves.

Before Chapman's emergence in the 1920s managers were, as often as not, shadowy figures who ran the difficult end of the club's business, did what he was told by the directors, and made sure the pay-packets were correct at the end of the week. The football tactics, as a rule, were worked out by the players themselves, sometimes with the help of a player-manager or a tactically-minded captain. Games were played along traditional patterns, goals scored by skill, by inspiration or by teamwork born of long association between the players. From Chapman's arrival, the manager became all-important. He, not the players, decided how the game was to be played, how late the players could stay out at night, how much they should be paid, how the club's money should be spent. And it was he, not the players, who carried the can if the results did not please the club's directors.

Chapman had not only showed a genius for producing successful football teams. He also showed, long before his time, that a flair for showmanship could do much to bridge the wide gap between the football club and the spectators who kept it in funds. Chapman persuaded London Transport to rename the local tube station 'Arsenal'; he had a new stand and floodlighting installed; he had a 45-minute clock built (the idea was frowned upon by the F.A., and British clubs still maintain an incomprehensible aversion to such admirable gadgets); he experimented with numbers on players' shirts as early as 1928 (the F.A. didn't catch on till the Cup Final of 1933 and the League didn't require them until 1939); he made Highbury available to the F.A. for their coaching scheme for boys. But above all it was his football brain, adapting the capabilities of his players, their flair, their skills and their weaknesses, to the framework of the game and the known character of the opposition, that made him the first of the super-managers, men who, granted boardroom support, could guarantee a percentage of success for their club. The breed died, for the time being, with Chapman; similar mantles were assumed by some of the great continental managers and coaches in the 1930s and 1940s, and by those of Central Europe and South America in the 1950s. But they only reappeared in Britain in the larger-than-life Chapman mould in the late 1950s and the 1960s, with the Tottenham team of Bill Nicholson, the Manchester United side of Matt Busby and the Liverpool of Bill Shankly.

Chapman has his detractors. It took his genius to make an attractive and unforgettable team while at the same time putting the damper on the attacking football of the century's first 25 years by his ruthless use of the third back; his 'stopper', the first of a long and much maligned breed, was himself an attractive footballer, Herbie Roberts, one of the game's great headers of the ball and a rock in defence. But other managers had neither his flair nor his chequebook, and the third back game too often became a negative struggle, bearable for spectators if the forwards had the skill and the confidence to stage a sudden breakaway, quite deadly if they didn't. Commentators of the mid 1960s, deploring the negative tactics employed with such science and dedication to stifle the bewildering Brazilian-style attacks, were only seeing the logical development of the methods used forty years earlier by the imitators of Herbert Chapman.

Little though the British press or the British public cared, the development of organised football in Europe was proceeding quite as spectacularly as it was at home. After the successes of Jimmy Hogan in Austria and Hungary, British—particularly Scottish—coaches were constantly in demand to bring professional good sense to bear on the unlimited enthusiasm of the continental clubs. Arsenal's John Dick trained Sparta Prague of Czechoslovakia in the 1920s; and the rival Slavia Prague were managed for 33 years by the Celtic and Scotland goalkeeper John Madden. The Rangers wing-half J. T. Robertson had coached both Rapid Vienna and M.T.K. Budapest, though the latter had even more service from the ubiquitous Hogan, who coaxed them to a large proportion of their twelve consecutive championships in the Hungarian League between 1914 and 1925.

With the greater expertise came the demands for greater reward. All the continental teams were officially amateur until some time after the First World War, but it was well known that M.T.K. Budapest, for example, paid large sums both to obtain and to keep their players; even after such abuses had become widespread most European associations were able to agree to a system of regulated professionalism without the heart-searching that had characterised the English and Scottish transition forty years before. Nevertheless, it was not until 1925 that Czechoslovakia officially paid her players, 1926 for Austria and Hungary, 1929 for Italy and Spain, and 1932 when the French admitted professionalism to her league.

Even with paid footballers and a fast-growing football public, few European nations could match Britain's depth of top-class club football; it was from this lack that the first proposals were made that would result, eventually, in the European Champion's Cup. If the top clubs were so dominant in their own countries, it was argued, why not play in competition across national boundaries. In 1924 Hugo Meisl proposed a knockout competition for the best clubs in Europe. Interest was cooler than he had expected, but he persisted in his confident predictions of success, lowered his sights to the countries within reasonable reach of Austria, and in 1927 saw the launching of the Mitropa (Middle-European) Cup—a competition for the winners and runners-up of the leagues in Austria, Hungary, Czechoslovakia and Yugoslavia. It was won in two legs on aggregate by Sparta Prague 7-4 over Rapid Vienna.

Yugoslavia did not last long in the competition—their best teams had lost a lot of players to the more wealthy clubs of Western Europe—and Italy, whose national league had blossomed under the Fascist policy of promoting sport to the full, took Yugoslavia's place. The competition survived, with declining influence, throughout the 1930s (with the four competing countries being joined by Romania and Switzerland), generally dominated by the Austrian and Hungarian clubs; the Second World War, and subsequently the disruptions of the Iron Curtain, considerably reduced its status.

The 1930s also saw positive efforts to institute a European League. The idea came first from a long-retired French footballer, Gabriel Hanot, who had played in successful French and German club teams in the early years of the century, and who had been capped twelve times for France between 1913 and 1919. His first proposal was that two clubs from each European country should be entered in the league of a different foreign country each year—so that, for example, Tottenham Hotspur and Aston Villa would play in the French League while Stade de Reims and Olympique Lille would play in the English League.

The proposals were considered seriously, but they were wildly optimistic at that time, and, as the President of Racing Club de Paris, said that while Olympique Lille would be delighted to share the gate money at Tottenham, the converse would certainly not be true. He did, however, see a future for a European League, and proposed a cup competition with one club from each of 16 nations taking part. 'The biggest difficulty, obviously,' he said, 'would be to get the British teams in, but it's not an insurmountable one. The competition would be a sporting success, and bring in considerable revenue. The Final could take place at Paris.' It was a brave and, in some ways, prophetic idea. The European knock-out cup—

as opposed to a league—for the top club in each country would not be seen for another twenty years, but it did become a sporting success, it did bring in considerable revenue and, sure enough, the biggest difficulty was to get the English teams in.

For the time being, though, it was international rather than inter-club competition that was stirring the European Soccer nations on the Continent in a way barely comprehensible to the insular football administrators of the International Board. To England and Scotland, international games were of three sorts. Important matches which meant those against Ireland or Wales, who throughout the century have remained consistently inferior at Soccer to their bigger neighbours without ever allowing complacency. Vital matches, which meant England against Scotland, and as such a true test of world superiority. And other matches, which meant the occasional boat-and-train journey to a European capital to play a lot of foreigners in front of suitably impressed crowds, or occasional—very occasional—visits by awe-struck foreign teams to play against ill-prepared but generally superior British ones.

There were, it is true, occasional defeats away from home. In 1929 Spain became the first non-British side to beat a full England representative team—four goals to three in Madrid on a blazing hot day and a cast-iron pitch at the end of a long and exhausting tour. Was this the sign that foreign opposition might be challenging the inborn superiority of the English? Two years later Spain came to London—only the second foreign side ever to play a full international in England. They brought their prize goalkeeper, the india-rubber Zamora who was a national hero in Spain and reputed to earn £30 a week (the maximum wage for such as Alex James and Dixie Dean was then £8); the crowds surged to Highbury (20,000 of them to be shut out) and watched as Zamora stumbled through a 90-minute nightmare and retired in tears to the dressing room after letting seven goals past him. The English went back to their domestic competition, assured that the sun was not yet prepared to set on British football.

Earlier that year France had beaten England in Paris, but the French were trounced in their turn when they came to White Hart Lane in 1933. In 1932 the Austrian *Wunderteam* of Meisl and Hogan, who had held England to a 0–0 draw in Vienna in 1930, played a magnificent game at Stamford Bridge, and yet lost by four goals to three. And in 1934 a triumphant Italy, carrying their newly-won World Cup into the sacred halls of football, succumbed 3–2 to England at the so-called Battle of Highbury, a foul-tempered, ill-controlled match which did nothing to enhance the game.

Mussolini had expressed his dictatorial opinion that victory in London would be a 'triumph for Fascism'; and if that was not enough, the Italian players were said to be on a £50-a-man incentive bonus. Their centre-half Monti broke a bone in his toe in the opening minutes, and claimed he had been deliberately kicked; the rest of the game was lost in punching, kicking, butting, elbowing exchanges that left both teams bruised and exhausted, both blaming the other side for their dirty play, and England, 3–0 ahead at half-time, narrow victors at the end. Scotland, too, kept themselves very much to themselves in the 1920s and 1930s, and despite being well beaten in Rome by Italy and in Vienna by the Austrians, they, like England, maintained their unbeaten home record at the outbreak of the Second World War.

This invincibility had been maintained, however, by ignoring the two most prestigious areas of international football that the game had then to offer—the Olympic Games and the World Cup. FIFA had been formed in 1904 specifically to organise a world football competition, but for more than 20 years they were grateful to let the International Olympic Committee do the job for them; until 1930 the Olympic Games doubled as the World Championship of football, which worked well so long as the world game was predominantly amateur, but laid itself open to all sorts of abuses once the footballing nations were divided between those who paid their best players and those who pretended that they didn't.

The United Kingdom—once as Britain, once as England—maintained high enough standards in the amateur reaches of the game to take the gold medals with some ease at London and Stockholm, but it was clear by the end of the War that the depredations of the fighting and the absorption of all available talent by the professional clubs had left Britain's amateurs very weak; their 1920 Olympic team had little pre-tournament training, and lost to an undistinguished Norwegian team who then lost to the Czechs. The Czechs in their turn caused a major sensation by walking off the field *en bloc* during the final against Belgium after one of their players had been hurt in a foul tackle.

By 1924 the Uruguayans had arrived and the British had left. The former—a brilliantly coached combination of ball control and positional play—captivated the crowds in Paris to beat Switzerland in the 1924 final, and repeated their performance, after a replayed final against their old rivals from Argentina, in 1928. The British, grumbling about the widespread practice abroad of paying 'broken-time' payments to so-called amateurs, withdrew from the tournament in 1924 and from FIFA, with much the same objections, in 1928. As the British associations had withdrawn from FIFA at the end of the First World War in protest against her former enemies, and had returned to the fold only in 1923, their contribution to the central government of world football had been far from wholehearted. They did not, in fact, return again until after the Second World War, and their only appearance in any world competition after 1920 was a moderate display by Great Britain's amateurs at the Berlin Olympics in 1936 where the lost to Poland in the second round.

It had not taken Britain's withdrawal to alert FIFA to the increasing anomalies of the professional sides in the Olympic's so-called amateur competition; when the proposal came for an 'open' world nations' cup— from Henri Delaunay, another Frenchman with a persuasive manner—the only members of the Association to vote against it were those from that corner of Europe where amateurism was, and in most cases still is, the very root of the game's organisation—Norway, Denmark, Sweden, Finland and Estonia. FIFA awarded the staging of the first World Cup (named after their long-serving President, Jules Rimet) to the reigning Olympic champions, Uruguay, who proved that they could hold their own against professionals as well as amateurs by winning it.

The opening tournament was not a distinguished one, displaying at this infant stage almost all the more unpleasant facets now accepted as inevitable ingredients of international sport. To begin with most of the European nations who had supported the idea of a World Cup were so displeased when Uruguay was chosen as the venue that they suddenly pleaded lack of funds and refused to take part. Only France, Belgium, Yugoslavia and Romania crossed the Atlantic; seven South American countries took part, and the numbers were made up by Mexico and by the U.S.A., the latter composed chiefly of expatriate English and Scots. If the entries were mediocre, the refereeing was worse (in Argentina's 6–3 victory over Mexico the Bolivian referee awarded them no fewer than five penalties), and the overt nationalism surrounding the latter stages was a clear foretaste of World Cups to come; as Uruguay beat Argentina and Montevideo lapsed into general rejoicing, the firm and fair Belgian referee was reviled in Argentina, the Uruguayan Embassy in Buenos Aires was stormed by furious crowds, and footballing relations between the two countries were broken off.

The political importance of international competition became even more obvious in the other two pre-war World Cups. In 1934 Italy were awarded the privilege of staging the Cup, and turned it into a Fascist carnival not only in their manner of staging it but in their single-minded efficiency in winning it—a triumph, as their national press expressed it, for Il Duce. The entries had been more representative than in 1930, but Uruguay refused to come to defend their title and Argentina pointedly sent a weak team to the country that had lured away many of their best players. The only real threat to the Italians, managed expertly by Vittorio Pozzo, was from the now ageing Austrian team, still managed expertly by his old rival Hugo Meisl. Youth and 'the masculine energies of a bursting vitality in this our Mussolini's Italy' prevailed, Europe's two best teams met in a semi-final in Milan on a pitch that heavy rain had turned into a mud-heap, and which neutralised any superiority in delicate ball-play the Austrians might have had. In the final Italy were taken to extra time by an energetic Czech team, but Pozzo had thoroughly earned his victory.

He earned it again in 1938. More politics affected the entry list; Austria dropped out once their country had been invaded by Hitler; Britain, begged by the French organisers to take part despite the fact that they were still out of FIFA, refused to go; Spain was in the throes of a Civil War. Again Uruguay stayed at home, and Argentina's decision to do likewise provoked a riot in Buenos Aires. But in the results of this Paris tournament we can see the first positive hints of the post-war power structure in international football. Apart from the Italians, whom Pozzo had once again brought to a peak at the right time just as he had done in 1934 and at the 1936 Olympics, the most impressive teams were Hungary and Brazil, the former cool and precise, the latter fiery and brilliant. Italy were able to account for both of them, but enough was seen of both to provide ominous auguries of future domination.

In the 1920s and 1930s Britain's international contribution had been derisory, and the results of their matches largely insignificant. England's last match before the outbreak of the Second World War was a typically sterile affair—a meeting in Milan with Italy organised with bucketfuls of diplomatic tact in an attempt to erase the rancour that remained from Highbury. The game was billed as 'England, Masters of Association Football versus Italy, the World Cup holders . . . and so it will remain whatever the result.' The referee—the time was now May 1939—was a German; the English side received the warmest of welcomes (though they were reported to have been less than happy about giving the Fascist salute to all four sides of the stadium); the Italians scored one good goal and one very dubious one and the game ended in a 2–2 draw. The 'Masters of Association Football', who were still perfectly happy to consider themselves as such, had, in the 30 years or so that they had been playing foreign opposition, never once taken that opposition seriously. They played them on ludicrously exhausting tours, or they played them on Wednesday evenings under dim floodlights in London or Birmingham having barely had time to practise together beforehand. No English club side had played an 'official' match against a foreign club. And England had not played a single game against opposition from South America.

When, at the end of the War, it became clear that the insularity of the British game could not last for ever, it was with condescension rather than trepidation that Britain rejoined FIFA and faced the world. The next ten years were to emphasise that three decades had been squandered.

The first of a whole carillon of rude awakenings came with the grotesquely ill-named 'goodwill tour' of the Moscow Dynamo club in 1945, within months of the victory over Hitler. Britain's football programme had come to a near standstill during the war, though some of the teams raised to play wartime internationals against Scotland are recalled with awe by anyone who saw them, and the visit of an exotic team from an Allied power was to be the gilt on the somewhat tatty gingerbread of the first post-war season.

Dynamo—who later turned out to be the entire Russian national squad masquerading as a Moscow club—were to play no representative games, just four club fixtures: Chelsea and a reinforced Arsenal side in London, Cardiff in Wales and Rangers in Scotland. They arrived with a fearsome camp-following of propagandists and security men and all the stone-faced trappings of Stalinist xenophobia; they wore enormous shorts that would have looked ludicrous even in the days of enormous shorts; they gave their opponents bouquets of flowers before the game, and they were written off by a *Sunday Express* man, who had watched them at practice, as 'not nearly good enough to play our class professionals . . . They are so slow that you can almost hear them think.'

It turned out that they were so fast that you didn't have time to think yourself; they played a creditable draw with Chelsea, who had lately been reinforced by the great Tommy Lawton from Everton; they overwhelmed Cardiff's third division defence and scored ten goals; at White Hart Lane (Highbury was still in the hands of the Civil Defence) they beat Arsenal 4–3 in thick fog with the help of some extremely suspect refereeing by an official they had brought with them on the tour. In Glasgow they held the mighty Rangers to a 2–2 draw. And scorning a hastily arranged fixture with an F.A. XI, set up for them at Wembley, they packed their bags, gathered their commissars around them, and went home unbeaten, closing the door on Western Europe for seven years.

Britain gulped, swapped stories of how rude the Russians had been, and settled down to the serious business of League football again. The next year a Swedish club, Norrköping, toured England unbeaten; in 1947 the full Swedish team were unlucky to lose 4–2 at Wembley; a year later virtually the same team romped away with the Olympic title in the same stadium, whereupon Swedish football was decimated by the cheque books of the Italian clubs. It flowered again only sporadically, once to hold the great Hungarians to a 2–2 draw in Budapest, once to stamp the 1958 World Cup with some exquisite ball-play in Stockholm, but generally to decline into the mediocrity of part-time professional football.

But still English football lived happy in its cocoon. In 1947 England lost away to Switzerland and Scotland away to Belgium, but to mark Britain's return to FIFA a combined British side crushed a scratch Rest of Europe team at Hampden Park 6–1. And the following year, with Matthews, Mortensen, Lawton, Mannion and Finney in the forward line, England celebrated one of the country's finest international victories; they faced Italy in Turin on the fiftieth anniversary of the founding of the Italian F.A. It was a turning point in both countries' footballing fortunes. Finney scored twice, Mortenson and Lawton once each; Matthews lay deep and sprayed passes about like a magician; the defence soaked up all the fury that a talented Italian side were driven to by a roaring, swaying crowd. Frank Swift, captain and goalkeeper, played the game of his life. England won 4–0. They didn't know it, but it was the last time for eighteen years that England would be looked upon as a match for the world.

For Italy it was also the start of a traumatic decline. Their side in Turin was based on the tremendously talented and superbly managed Torino team. The next year the whole Club—players, trainer, manager and all— were to die in the appalling Superga air disaster. And for Pozzo, the man who had founded Italy's international greatness virtually single-handed, the defeat by England was a blow from which neither he nor his national side ever recovered. 'Death to Pozzo' screamed a merciless headline the next day; Pozzo's brave stand against the third-back strictures of 1930s and 1940s football had already been defeated. Now, over the next two decades, Italian club football was to become enslaved by the five-back defensive neck-lock, *catenaccio*, a lovely name for an unspeakable system, against which some of the most attractive forwards in the game would batter away their careers, and where a 0–0 draw had a symmetric satisfaction, and 2–1 win was considered a rather vulgar goal bonanza.

The British come-uppance, so inevitable in retrospect, so unexpected at the time, spanned the first three years of the 1950s. A little earlier, in 1948, England lost at home to foreign opposition for the first time—a match that is generally forgotten. This is partly because it took place not at Wembley, but at Goodison Park, Everton, which is not a very chic place to surrender a proud record, and partly because it was against the Republic of Ireland, who didn't really count as foreigners anyway, particularly as nine of the players belonged to Football League clubs. As England won their next seven matches on the run, the momentary embarrassment was forgotten; what England was not prepared for—and what no Englishman who saw it or wrote about it or read about it can begin to explain—was the utter disaster of England's World Cup defeat in 1950.

The World Cup Committee had been very nice to the British. With the home countries as members of FIFA for the first time since the Cup had been in contention, the British international championship was designated as one of the qualifying groups, with, generously, a place in the finals in Brazil for the top two teams. Scotland, whose administrators in both codes of the football game have managed unerringly over the years to maintain reputations for reactionary stubbornness, for some reason announced before the International Championship that unless they were the champions that year they would not go to Brazil. They beat Northern Ireland 8–2 and Wales 2–0, to make certain of either first or second place; they then went down only unluckily to England, 1–0 at Hampden Park; and as the offer of a finals place was still open, it was only reasonable to expect the Scottish F.A. to change their mind—indeed, their much respected and long-serving captain George Young begged them to do so. But the officials stuck their heels in, refused the experience of a World Cup tournament, and kept the team at home—Cowan and Young, Woodburn and Forbes, Steel, Reilly and Liddell and the rest; and later that year *they* lost their home record against foreign opposition—the Austrians came to Hampden Park and beat them 1–0.

Austria had refused to go to Brazil, too. Hungary and Russia were not yet ready to open any chink in the Iron Curtain. India, though qualifying in a weak Asian group, declined to make the journey. Turkey also qualified and cried off. France, who had been eliminated, were offered a consolation place, but said it was too far to go to play football anyway. The organisation was a shambles; but, never mind, England put on their blue blazers and prepared to lay nearly a century's footballing heritage before the world.

Their 1–0 defeat at the hands of the United States of America, at Belo Horizonte, Brazil, on 28 June 1950, did not actually eliminate England from anything. They had won the first game in their pool, against Chile; they might confidently be expected to win the last—against Spain, to qualify for the competition's final pool. But defeat against the U.S.A.! The match had been such a foregone conclusion that no one had taken any bets. Hadn't the Americans said they had only come for the ride? Hadn't they sat up late at a night club the previous evening? Weren't people predicting a 20–0 win for England? The result, when it first came through, was literally unbelievable. 'England 0 U.S.A. 1' . . . surely it should read 'England 10 U.S.A. 1'. But it was all too true. England had done everything but score, and an immigrant from Haiti headed a chance goal for the States just before half-time. Stranger things have happened in football, but hardly in a World Cup match. The players were stunned as completely as their fellow countrymen at home; they certainly had not recovered in time for the Spain match, which they also lost by a single goal. They left for England without staying to watch the fast, fit, skilful Brazilians and Uruguayans make their way to the final pool.

The Americans in 1950 were a fluke. The Hungarians of the 1950s were not. In 1952 they poked their heads round the Iron Curtain to walk off with the Olympic title at Helsinki. A year later, the first Communist national team to challenge Western Europe, they started ominously enough by meeting Italy in the new Olympic Stadium at Rome and strolling to a 3–0 win in the effortless, accomplished style which was to mark them as one of history's most attractive footballing sides. On their way to England and Scotland in the late autumn they stopped off in France for a warm-up game against a French amateur team and scored 18 goals.

In England, 1953 had so far been a good year. The Coronation and its attendant extravagances had come and gone; Everest had been conquered; Stanley Matthews had, in a dazzling and unforgettable twenty minutes of genius, snatched his long-awaited Cup-winner's medal out of looming defeat. And then came the Hungarians—Hidegkuti and Puskas, Kocsis and Boszik—the brilliant stars of a wonderfully skilful team. They were faster and stronger than England. They seemed to be lighter on their feet. They had all the skills that the England players had and were anxious to show them off. They were so superbly drilled that they could switch at will into each other's roles and still feel at home. Their defenders were solid; and their forwards could take goals as well as make them.

England had, for some 20 years, been used to an exhibition of first-half fireworks from continental opposition, who had then been worn down to straggling desperation by the sheer professional discipline of England's defence and midfield. Hungary produced fireworks from first to last; at the crucial stage of the match—the first quarter of an hour of the second half after England had reduced Hungary's lead to 4–2 and were pressing hard —they delivered a blow from which no side could be expected to recover. Boszik scored one goal, Hidegkuti another to complete his hat-trick, and England's humiliation was complete. A late penalty by Alf Ramsey made the final score England 3 Hungary 6.

It was a display of cool, unhurried brilliance that overwhelmed the spectators (they could not, throughout the second half, make up their minds whether to jeer England's discomfiture or roar appreciation at the Hungarians), sent the British press into mourning, provided the spur for a barrage of F.A. coaching schemes that were to pay their dividends in the next decade, and quite eclipsed a gritty and courageous performance by England who did, when all is said, score three goals against the best team in the world.

To label a single Soccer match as a 'turning point', a 'watershed', 'the end of an era', is as a rule so barren an exercise as to be positively misleading. Eras do not begin with matches, they begin with the fusion of the talents of great players, which are not themselves born one afternoon in a roaring stadium but over months—seasons—of practice and trial and error and inspired guidance. Alternatively, they begin with impersonal decisions made in committee rooms, decisions to launch a competition that might capture the imagination of a continent; or to change a rule that might just coincide with a tactical experiment by a keen-witted manager. And they end with the ageing or the injuring of players and the fatigue of managers, and sometimes, tragically, with plane crashes.

English domination of world football had ended long before the Hungarian triumph at Wembley. The game did not change overnight from 'British' football to 'Hungarian' football; people did not at a stroke stop playing dour football and start playing exciting football. But something did end at Wembley in 1953. Since 1863 the English had, whether winning or losing, been the 'Masters of Football'. They had at first patronised, then ignored or discounted the advances of continental and South American football; they had disdained foreign competitions; they had believed, blindly but sincerely, in their own superiority. In 1953 they stopped being the Masters of Football. And despite Manchester United and Tottenham Hotspur, despite the World Cup of 1966, despite Sir Alf Ramsey and Bobby Charlton and Gordon Banks, they have not been the Masters of Football since.

7

the long divorce

Rugby Union and Rugby League Football: 1896 to 1940

Association Football entered the 20th century on a wave of public support that had increased unabated since the establishment of professionalism in the North and Midlands some fifteen years before. The crowds grew bigger year by year. The South and Scotland had both succumbed to the attractions of professional competition, the F.A. Cup was as compulsive as ever; even the amateur game was still providing important players for international matches. And abroad, with British expatriates and hired British coaches to the fore, the game was taking root in slavish, yet grateful, imitation of the British pattern.

The same should have been true of Rugby. The Union's early attitude to overseas Rugby had been admirable, and the exchange of prolonged tours with South African and Antipodean opposition had proved a valuable and unselfish contribution to the spread of the game. But Rugby, perhaps because of innate attitudes implanted from the very inception of the code, perhaps merely because of intransigence and self-deception among its administrators, had managed to make the 1890s a decade of rancour and recrimination which split the game in two, threatened almost to kill it altogether, and eventually brought two separate Rugby Unions into the 20th century in considerable doubt as to whether either version of the code could survive to 1910. Yet, ironically, out of that ill-tempered decade have emerged two games where there had been only one before, and both games have flourished while moving further and further apart from each other, established their own mystique, and given equal pleasure in their own separate ways.

The trouble began, of course, with money. The Football Association, in the person of Charles Alcock, had realised long before the rest of football's establishment, that a game played by all sorts and conditions of Englishmen, from University undergraduates to coal-miners, and a game enjoyed and passionately followed by increasing numbers of fee-paying customers, could not possibly confine itself to pure amateurism. Winning football not only demanded loyalty and skill from its players, it began to demand time. And time, even with the concessions given to a shorter working week in Victorian times, meant money.

Alcock had both the foresight and the strength of will to guide the Football Association, and its member clubs, from an amateur game to a game which accepted both amateurism and professionalism with a good grace. Rugby did not have an Alcock, but it did have a keen following in the industrial north of England, in pockets of support set at random amongst the Soccer-minded towns of Lancashire, and Yorkshire's West and East Riding. Like the Football Association, the Rugby Union was run from London, and run by the same sort of leisured upper-middle-class ex-player; but the clubs outside London and the South of England, though keen in those isolated areas where the game had been introduced into an industrial setting by men returning home from public school and university, had nothing like the numerical strength, or the record of achievement, that their counterparts in the northern Soccer clubs attained in the 1870s and 1880s.

The unrest in the North grew as it had grown in Soccer. The miners and factory workers, anxious to remain in their successful, well-supported teams, were forced to miss a shift here, a day's work there, to fulfil their commitments to the club. There is no doubt that in some cases under-the-counter payments were made by the more prosperous clubs to recompense players, but the establishment of efficiently organised professional Soccer, sometimes even in the same town as the Rugby club, increased the agitation for official recognition of broken-time payment. The Rugby Union held up its hands in horror (as, indeed, the Football Association had originally done) and refused to hear of it. A diplomat of Alcock's calibre might have foreseen the coming collision, and might even have done something to prevent it. Rowland Hill, the then Secretary of the Rugby Union and certainly the most powerful figure in the game, was not a diplomat. By all rights, his role in the dispute—as an officer of the Union—should have been as objective conciliator; in fact he acted as chief prosecuting counsel, and the split in the game must be placed quite as firmly at his door as it has always been placed at that of the Northern dissidents.

Immediately the clubs of Yorkshire and Lancashire had organised their delegates for the A.G.M. of the Rugby Football Union in 1893, and had given notice of their intention to press for broken-time payment, the southern opposition machine sprang into action with all the fury of a hotel chain resisting a takeover bid. They issued leaflets, printed circulars, wrote letters to all their clubs, organised their own delegates to the A.G.M.—and found as their champion the Honorary Secretary himself. The motion of the Northern Clubs asked 'That players be allowed payment for *bona fide* loss of time.' Rowland Hill moved the amendment 'That this meeting, believing that the above principle is contrary to the true interest of the game and its spirit, declines to sanction the same.'

Rowland Hill was bound to win—and he did, by 282 votes to the Northern Clubs' 136. But 120 of Hill's 282 votes were proxies gathered in before the meeting, and the Northern Clubs could feel encouraged by the size of their minority. Their solidarity was cemented over the next two years by the complete refusal of Rowland Hill and the Rugby Union to make any sort of concession over the matter (indeed, the Union passed a number of minor regulations tightening the anti-payment rules). Since the 1893 meeting the clubs had kept in touch at intervals, and in August 1895 a special meeting of the principal Northern Clubs was called at the George Hotel, Huddersfield.

Twenty-one clubs were represented. Twenty of them voted for the momentous step of resigning from the Rugby Football Union and forming the Northern Union, which would pay broken-time expenses. (The one club reluctant to endorse the split with the Rugby Union was Dewsbury, who voted against it. After three more years of amateurism, they too joined the Northern Union.) The twenty rebels were joined for the first full season by Runcorn and Stockport, who had not been represented at the meeting, and their first matches were played—just to emphasise their new-found independence—a week before the opening of the Rugby Union calendar.

The gulf that now separated Rugby Union from Northern Union was a mere 6s. a day in compensation for work lost—a reasonable wage in those days, but certainly no more than a tentative step on the road to professionalism; what is even more significant about the breakaway of 1895, and what has generally been obscured by the emotional question of playing for money, is that immediately on the formation of the Northern Union the new organisation was geared to *competition*. Until 1895, in the best traditions of the Rugby Union, all matches except inter-county fixtures and internationals were 'friendly' matches. Club secretaries organised their own fixture lists; there was never any persuasion from the top for strong teams to play strong, weak teams to play weak, or results of matches between teams with common sets of opponents to be collated in any way.

In the North of England, where the F.A. Cup had caught the public imagination and where the first seasons of the Football League had almost exclusively been staged, the character of the people demanded a 'winner'. Since 1889 competitive league cricket had been played among the clubs of Birmingham, Staffordshire, Lancashire and Yorkshire, and had grown fast in influence and popularity. It was inevitable that Rugby football organised from a Northern base should look to the same type of competition to attract its first spectators; and it was equally inevitable that this should create even more distrust among the staunch Rugby Union loyalists; whatever they might think when they got onto a football field themselves, a system in which winning had become necessarily more important than taking part was unacceptable.

The attitude of the Rugby Union to the breakaway of the Northern clubs was predictable enough. They forbade any member club to play fixtures with any Northern Union club; and they further tightened their own rules against payment to players. The Northern Union had made their gesture on the question of paying players out-of-pocket expenses, and it was their proposed intention at the outset to avoid going the whole hog—their financial affairs were in no state to start establishing paid staffs of players. The Northern Union was far from being a caucus of shrewd businessmen eager to buy and sell players and reap the gate profits. The members were very much the same sort of people who ran clubs in the South of England—dedicated ex-players with a love for the game; but they knew better than the majority of the Union that Rugby could not maintain high club standards in the North if working-class men were expected to lose money while playing it. Their intentions were thoroughly honourable, but Rowland Hill and his committee were convinced (and so was at least one Northern newspaper at the time of the split) that once the non-payment principle was broken, nothing could stop the next step— a system of full professionalism.

After the measures taken by the Rugby Union, who had certainly acted more in anger than in sorrow, the only alternative was that the Northern Union would fade away. After a year's well supported competition this became very unlikely. The gates had been good and the two initial competitions had produced attractive Rugby. When Manningham won the Yorkshire Senior Competition they were greeted in Bradford by crowds lining the streets. Their fellow-winners in the Lancashire group, Runcorn, were met at the station by a torchlight procession and drawn in a coach through the town. The fervour of the partisan Soccer following had, in the space of a single season, been inherited by the Northern Union. It was a sensation quite alien to Rugby, and it underlined more firmly than ever the parting of the ways.

At the first annual meeting of the Northern Union it was clear that there would be no return to the fold. Far from being cowed by the strictures of the R.F.U., the clubs were flocking to join the Northern Union. And in his annual speech the chairman, H. H. Waller of Brighouse, while emphasising that it was lost work, not playing skill, that the new Union was playing for, pointedly made no conciliatory expressions of regret at the breakaway.

Instead, the new game capitalised on its popularity. In its first year it had proved that its spectators would warm to competition; in its second it introduced a straight imitation of the Football Association's most triumphant money-spinner, the knock-out cup. The first Northern Union Challenge Cup Final drew 14,000 spectators to the luxurious new stadium at Headingley, Leeds, to see Batley beat St Helen's. This further early triumph for the rebels gave them the necessary confidence to take their most controversial step yet—to change the rules of the game. In its first two seasons the Northern Union played perfectly normal fifteen-man Rugby with line-outs and the eight-man scrummage and so on; the weekly expenses chit was the sole difference, apart from a new awareness of competition and a noticeable increase in support from the touchline.

By the end of Victoria's reign, all the frustrations with the Rugby Union rule-book (and there were many of these, both in the North and the South of England, and would be for a long time to come), were brought into open discussion; there was no longer any reason to keep to the dictates of a body from whom they had severed links, and no need to remain loyal to a set of rules which, they felt, hindered the game that they and their fellows in the North wanted to play. Revolutionaries incline to radical law-changing out of a sheer sense of freedom, and the Northern Union felt that, in a sense, they were revolutionaries; they abolished the line-out, which had proved and still proves difficult to control, and substituted the punt-out from touch, which was a shambles. (The punt-out was abolished by 1902, and a scrummage ordered instead; it has proved less time-wasting, but otherwise barely more satisfactory than the old line-out.) All kicked goals were reduced in value to two points—whether conversions, penalties or drop goals, which can be seen in retrospect as a distinct improvement on Rugby Union rules, and which, in various roundabout ways, Rugby Union has itself resorted to over the last seventy years.

In 1901 the Northern Union abandoned the R.F.U.'s strict definitions of 'knocking-on' and instead allowed more than one attempt to catch the ball so long as it did not touch the ground. (A similar rule, introduced by the Rugby Union as late as 1971, was met by the purists with dire warnings about decline in standards of skill; in fact the new law meant that fewer three-quarter movements broke down because of minor fumbles by cold fingers, and the game seemed to benefit.)

Most important of all, the Northern Union, in only their third season of existence, began to talk about possession: there is no evidence that the

early administrators of the new Union had made any sort of contact with
the now well-established game of American Football; indeed, the mid
1890 era of American Football, both among the college amateurs and the
embryo professionals of the mining towns of Pennsylvania and Ohio, was
of such an uncompromising and notorious violence that any sort of fact-
finding mission would have returned with little more than nightmares.
But the fact is that, with just the same arguments put forward by Walter
Camp to revolutionise the Rugby game in America in the 1880s, the
Northern Union determined to revise the essential free-flow principle of
Rugby football. When a man was tackled with the ball, they said, he
should not, as the Rugby Union rules had it, be required to release the
ball, thus opening a new opportunity of attack to whichever side might
grab it first; he should, instead, be allowed to keep possession, the teams
be given a chance to re-form, and he should then restart play by passing
the ball back to one of his own side.

It was a radical measure, at once reducing the premium on inspired,
fast-running counter-attack and increasing emphasis on strength, on hard
individual pounding and on rock-hard discipline. It created, in fact, a new
game. And it seemed to suit the spectators; not only were many more
clubs anxious to part company with the Rugby Union in order to play this
new competitive form of Rugby—they now had the incentive of a genuine
'national' league table to aim for. In the early years of the Lancashire and
Yorkshire competitions, after the initial doubts about gate-money had
been allayed and clubs had a certain amount of money to spend on travel,
there had been talk of amalgamating Yorkshire and Lancashire competitions into some form of super-league. By 1901—and a further factor in the
remarkable early success in Rugby League was the sheer speed and
energy with which they tackled the administration of the game—the
Northern Rugby League had been establishecd.

It would be gratifying, while admiring the spirit of the clubs in these
early years of the Northern Union, to report that this Northern Rugby
League, then as now the game's premier competition, was a product of
democratic agreement prompted by selfless ground-roots planning. In
fact, the formation of the League was a thoroughly autocratic one that
could never have been countenanced in a sporting organisation more
firmly established than the Northern Union was at that time. The League
was formed by twelve clubs, who met at Huddersfield without telling
anyone else, elected themselves to it, and vested in themselves the power
of adding other clubs to it as they thought fit.

It was not exactly a diplomatic move, and those clubs that had been
left out were understandably furious. They had opposed the idea of a

super-league all along, fearing that such a concentration of talent would cream away gate-money from the smaller clubs, who would consequently fade away, deprived of their money-spinning fixtures with the glamorous senior clubs. But the Northern Union Management Committee accepted the new proposal after acrimonious argument and a final tense vote of 12 to 11, and, with resentment on all sides, the Northern League was born.

As might have been expected, this degree of sophisticated organisation among the hard industrial settings of industrial Yorkshire and Lancashire had not been reached by players willing to cover themselves in mud every weekend for a mere 6s. to cover the loss of Saturday's wages. By 1898 it was clear that the early predictions of the Northern Union's critics were coming true; it was impossible to stick to Waller's 'expenses only' principle. Players realised, once the popular appeal of the new game had been established, that they were worth money to their clubs as crowd-pullers, and began demanding more than a mere broken-time payment for their services. Soon the wealthier clubs were paying, more or less openly, well above the agreed rate to their stars. The Northern Union had no option but to bow to the inevitable and draw up regulations accepting full professionalism into the game. The charter (thrashed out, as so much of the Northern Union's early business, in the George Hotel, Huddersfield) was strict and demanding. It required all professional players to be officially registered as such; it stipulated that every player must have legitimate employment outside football, and it laid down heavy penalties for any breach of these regulations.

In theory, the clause about 'legitimate employment' was a doubly shrewd piece of legislation. In the first place, it was good for the fairly grubby image of the game that all its players were seen to be respectable working men during the week who took off their overalls to turn an honest penny on Saturday afternoons. And more important to the survival of the game, it made it perfectly clear that the clubs were not proposing to pay their players very much money—any question of cocooning their stars in idle luxury living would have meant financial death to ninety per cent of the clubs in the Union, and the new game could not afford to lose the clubs it had risked so much to attract. In practice, however, the rule was a troublesome one. It gave no precise definition to the vague term 'legitimate employment' and the Northern Union assumed a pose of unaccustomed puritanism when faced with questions of eligibility. Bookie's runner or billiard marker was not a job, in their eyes, for a professional footballer. A Ratcliffe player had his registration suspended for having taken employment as a waiter in a pub, and an unfortunate Batley player couldn't get registered because he just couldn't find a job anywhere.

But for those who could assume the acceptable veneer of respectability, the pickings were good. It was reported that certain Northern Union men were getting as much as £4 a week for their playing services, which even some Soccer professionals would have envied. And stories of this smoky El Dorado in the North soon filtered down to the still untainted Rugby talents of the South of England and, particularly, Wales—a vast storehouse of Rugby genius waiting unawares for the Northern scouts and their fat, tempting bankrolls. The Northern Rugby managers had been accused even before the North-South split of 'petty trickery, mean cheating and espionage which almost passes belief' in their attempts to pay their 'amateur' players illegally. Now that their professional game was established beyond doubt, they had become poachers, signing on any young prospect they could get their hands on. The activities of the scouts, and the undoubted skill of the players they lured away, did nothing to heal the rift between the two Unions. When a scout from Wigan was discovered in Penarth, he was hurled bodily into the sea and rolled in the sand.

For all the talk of big money, however, and the satisfaction of seeing their rebellion justified by the survival of the new game, the Rugby League clubs knew well in the early years of the century that their success was a desperately precarious one. The adoption of possession play had cut down on the number of time-consuming scrummages, but it had also made the fast, open half-back and three-quarter attacks, Rugby's most exciting asset since their development in the 1880s, no more than a memory; the game was once again played by the forwards, with backs becoming little more than last-ditch defenders and fielders of high kicks. The ball could stay for a whole afternoon hidden in a steaming wave of forwards— the play-the-ball, the charge, the smothering tackle, the next play-the-ball and so on. The spectators were consequently not pouring in with their initial enthusiasm, and it is significant that while the game had kept its hold on Lancashire and Yorkshire, attempts to form other pockets of Northern Union football had met with little success.

The mining and industrial areas of the North-East would seem the ideal background for professional Rugby, but the short-lived career of South Shields in the Northern Union was a financial disaster. Other clubs in Northumberland, Durham and Cheshire were forced to leave the league, and the two-division scheme devised by the Northern Union in 1902 to give League status to thirty-six clubs, with promotion and relegation for two of them each season, had meant such a calamitous fall in the gates of the Second Division clubs that it had to be abandoned after only three years.

Something more fundamental was needed if the Northern Union was to hang on to the existing spectators—let alone attract new ones. And by 1906 the big clubs were beginning to press officially for a reduction in the size of the teams. Plans to restrict the domination of the forwards had been in the air since a particularly ponderous Cup Final in 1903, and since then a lot of junior Rugby had been played with the connivance of the Union between twelve-man teams; a full change-over to smaller sides, however, had been baulked by the Northern Union's own constitution, which required a three-quarter majority to sanction any rule change; and even the Northern Union was not without its share of conservatives. (In 1904 this 'three-fourths' clause, as well as the 'working clause', demanding alternative employment for players, came under attack at the Northern Union's A.G.M. The first was altered to require only a two-thirds majority; the 'working' clause survived until 1905 when for the first time in this country or anywhere in the world it was acceptable for a player to make his living by playing Rugby.)

In 1906 the annual meeting faced a barrage of proposals for what was to prove the game's last radical departure from the laws of Rugby Union. St Helen's proposed fourteen-a-side Rugby; Warrington proposed thirteen-a-side; Whitehaven twelve-a-side. Warrington, supported by a number of the other big guns, won the argument, and from the start of the 1906 season professional Rugby has been a thirteen-a-side game with the pack of eight forwards reduced to six.

The novelty was an immediate success; the crowds came back, at least for the early matches, and the newly admitted Liverpool City, whose first season in the Northern League coincided with the reduction of the teams, proved the scoring potential of the new system by conceding 100 points in their first three matches, and an all-time dismal record of 1,398 points in the season, during which they achieved the not inconsiderable feat of losing every one of their thirty matches. (They actually failed to complete their programme, and never played another season.)

By the end of the 1906–7 season, *pace* Liverpool City, the Northern Union had more reason for optimism than at any time since its inception. The first excitement over the thirteen-man innovation had died down somewhat, but another experiment, the organising of the four top league teams into a championship play-off of two semi-finals and a final, brought a welcome £1,300 in gate money, and bad weather could not deter 18,500 people from watching Warrington beat Oldham in the Challenge Cup Final. And that summer it seemed that the word had been received overseas for the first time. A syndicate of New Zealand businessmen had seen some professional matches while following the 1905–6 All-Blacks tour of Britain, and were now proposing to sponsor a New Zealand tour of the Northern Union. The much-needed expansion was apparently within reach.

In 1896, a year after the rebel Northern Union had broken away from the parent Rugby Union, the second tour of South Africa by the British Isles culminated in the Test Match at Newlands, Capetown, in which South Africa, led with power and flair by Barry Heatlie, won their first ever victory 5–0; the winning try was scored by a fly-half called Alf Larard of Transvaal. The significance of the victory was that after twenty-five years the Masters had been overtaken by the flair and the dedication of the pupils, just as, in the coming thirty years or so, the Masters of Soccer were to see their game transformed by the countries to which they had so zealously carried the message.

The significance of the try-scorer, however, was of a more domestic, but nonetheless far-reaching nature. This match took place a full year after sanctions had been laid down by the Rugby Union following the Northern clubs' declaration of independence: no member of a club belonging to the Rugby Union, they had ordered, should play with or against any man who had played with the Northern Union. And Alf Larard, now fly-half for the Transvaal, had done just that. There is no doubt that both sides knew of his background in Northern Rugby; it is equally evident that no one made the slightest objection to his playing in the South African team. So far, so gentlemanly. But within the next year or two, the Rugby Union so fortified the wall between the two games that such contact would be impossible.

The consequences were inevitable: the tinkering with Union rules in the North in an attempt to attract crowds; the one-way traffic of talented players from the Rugby Union strongholds to cash in on their skill; and the sad 'No Entry' signs facing anyone even considering a return from the North to the amateur game. Without the Rugby Union's intransigence, of course, there would have been no Rugby League football, and the sporting world would be the poorer for that. But both games have suffered from the distrust of those first years of the Northern Union.

The Rugby Union, in the best traditions of the English, took pains to forget that the Northern Union even existed. In some ways it succeeded: the development of the individual skills and the first glorious flowering of the devastating threequarter teamwork, both of which have made Rugby Union one of the greatest of all games to watch, were both coming into their own at the end of the 19th century, and by the First World War Rugby Union had established for itself a character and a popularity comparable, in dedication, if not in numbers, to that of the Association Game.

By the turn of the century, while Rugby League's rule-changes were tending to make it a battle of forwards—a defensive struggle when the opposition were in possession of the ball, a grim, battering advance when you were—Rugby Union had become an authentic attacking game. The forwards, traditionally the focal point of a game of Rugby, without whose surge in the tight scrums and mauls no ground could be gained, suddenly found that they were no longer the stars. The attention switched to the halves and the men behind them, who used the forwards as a shield and as providers of the ball, and who then ran and passed and side-stepped and dummied and chased high kicks and generally ran the heavy boilermen in the pack off their feet.

It was seventy years ago and more; they called it the Golden Age of cricket, and it was also Soccer's Golden Age, the age of the Corinthians and the professional brilliance of Billy Meredith and Steve Bloomer; they were the culminating years of the Victorian development of sport as a mass preoccupation when the youth of the nation, for the first time in the country's history, could become heroes in something other than soldiering. We are aware, looking back, that the half-remembered euphoria that clings to the reminiscences of men who watched Jessop and Ranji bat, or G. O. Smith and C. B. Fry play Soccer, or Gwyn Nicholls and Adrian Stoop on the Rugby field, was to last, at the very longest, only to 1914. Rugby was very probably not all clean heels, snap passing and threequarter movements from 1895 to 1905; but it was a time when the theory of attack held temporary sway over the theory of defence, and we can, on the evidence, envy the spectators who were there to see it.

The great tradition of attacking threequarter play had been weaned at Oxford University and brought to a heady maturity in Wales. It reached its perfection, and by so doing bred its own inevitable downfall, 12,000 miles away. The farmers and the traders of New Zealand, then as now the most British of the British nations overseas, had taken to Rugby with a single-mindedness matched only in the Cape Colony and the mining valleys of Wales. By the turn of the century it had become overwhelmingly the most important game in that country, and in consequence the New Zealand Rugby Union, set up in 1892 to keep the peace between the influential provincial unions, was an extremely prestigious body, running the game in New Zealand without any great deference to the conventions as practised among Rugby men in London or Edinburgh or Cardiff.

One rule of the game that the New Zealanders had passed for domestic use, with the permission of the R.F.U., was a somewhat esoteric ban on

players moving up the side of a scrum while the ball was still in it; while
the ball was in amongst the forwards' feet, the opposing scrum half and
forwards had to keep on their own side of the tunnel. This had two consequences. One meant that in New Zealand a scrum-half had all the time in
the world to pass to the man outside him (which is why for years New
Zealanders had no need to develop the 'dive' pass from the scrum); the
other meant that any of the forwards could detach himself from the scrum
while the ball was in play without being considered either off-side or a
potential obstructor of the opposing scrum-half. And these, in turn, led
to the all-powerful New Zealand formation of the seven-man scrum and
the roving wing forward who, in time, never even packed down with the
forwards but put the ball into the scrum while the scrum-half waited for it
to emerge at the back; the marauding British tours of the First and Second
All-Blacks, in 1905–6 and 1924–5, sprung these tactics on the innocent
British fifteens, and left them gasping.

The New Zealand touring team of 1905 arrived in Britain with none of
the awed expectations that their successors provoke today. Their previous
tour—an exhausting trek by a keen young Rugby nation—had been
successful but hardly world-shattering, and had in any case taken place
fifteen years before; nevertheless, their seven-man pack, and their use of
the five-eighth system of distribution which had been developed at the
turn of the century by the tactical genius of Jimmy Duncan, had earned
them victory over a British Isles team in New Zealand the year before,
and Britain really should have been better prepared for the battering to
come.

Jimmy Duncan, now retired as a player, came with them as coach;
Dave Gallaher came as captain and roving wing forward; their seven-
forward scrum system came with them as their most potent weapon.
As they practised in the West Country for their first match, they were
cheerily told by a Devonian official that they hadn't a chance (Devon
were at that time the champions of the South-West), and that with their
superior passing and kicking 'Devon will be all over you at the finish.'
The New Zealanders won that first game 55–4, scoring 12 tries in the
process; of their next 30 games they won 29; they scored 868 points, and
their opponents scored just 47.

Apart from making everyone in Britain feel slightly foolish, the First
All-Blacks left three lasting impressions. The first was the view held by
all British journalists and most British officials, that the use of the roving
wing forward at the side of the set scrum was illegal by the rules as ob-
served here (though it was never seriously used as an excuse to explain
away the New Zealanders' superior stamina and tremendous capacity for

supporting whichever of their side might be holding the ball); the second was that British Rugby could no longer play top-class football without properly planned strategy among the forwards as well as the halves and backs; and the third was the International match against Wales—the all-conquering All-Blacks against the Triple Crown winners.

Forty-five thousand Welshmen sang as Cardiff had probably never sung before, the Welsh adopted the seven-man scrum and determined to run the New Zealanders off their feet, to spoil the eight-man attacking moves before they had started, and never to give the All-Blacks time to draw breath. For the first time on the tour the New Zealand backs were rattled; they dropped passes and failed to find any of the cohesion that had taken them to double figures against the other three home countries. Wales scored the only try of the game towards the end of the first half; the New Zealanders, who had, up to that point in their tour, averaged three points every five minutes, tore into the Welsh pack in the second half. One despairing rush as the game neared its end saw Bob Deans go over the Welsh line for what many of even the Welsh players considered a perfectly good try; by the time the referee reached the scene Deans was lying, ball grounded, six inches the wrong side of the line. The try was disallowed and no New Zealander has ever forgiven any Welshman since.

Wales's achievement had been a triumph of planning, and Gwyn Nicholls, the victorious captain, told the *Daily Mail* after the match that the system of seven forwards and eight backs was a better formation than the conventional eight-forward pack. It was perhaps understandable that this was not immediately pounced upon by the British Unions as the panacea for all the game's ills; nevertheless, it was entirely characteristic of British Rugby's conservatism that only a handful of clubs gave any serious time to experimenting with the new formation.

When 'Cherry' Pillman, England's great pre-First World War wing forward, tried to get Blackheath to use him as a 'rover', he was given no encouragement at all. It was to Pillman's credit that he devised for himself the British equivalent—the role of 'breakaway' forward, detaching himself from the scrum at the earliest possible moment after the ball had been put in, ready to join the backs in attack or defence as soon as it was heeled. He played for England while still in his teens, astonished the South Africans with his versatility on the British Isles tour of 1910 (he virtually won the second Test on his own playing in the unaccustomed position of fly-half), and sowed the seed for both the South African forward play speciality, the breakaway number 8, and for the more destructive, but nontheless effective, disciplines of the English pack under Wavell Wakefield in the 1920s.

But still no one had a real answer to the All-Blacks. If Gallaher's team in 1905 had been a surprise, C. G. Porter's Second All-Blacks of 1924 were a revelation. Their record in the British Isles and France read: played 30; won 30; lost 0; drawn 0; points for 721; points against 112. A squabble within the International Board prevented their playing Scotland—at that time, with a formidable three-quarter line, the best team in Britain—and it was the England match at Twickenham that was billed as the clash of giants to emulate the drama of the Wales match fourteen years before.

England, though they had dominated the International tournament in the early 1920s, were in a state of transition. Since 1906 two prolonged and magisterial reigns had held their back division together from fly-half—Adrian Stoop, profound tactical thinker, up till 1912; W. J. A. Davies, mercurial open-field runner and, with C. A. Kershaw, the major half of a masterly half-back partnership, spanning the War. But since 1924 the succession had not been assumed by any worthy claimant, and under Wavell Wakefield the emphasis had moved to the pack, particularly the back row, where England had taken well-disciplined initiative both in attack and defence. So even though the All-Blacks had rampaged through their early matches and arrived at Twickenham unbeaten, a lot of people were prepared to back Wakefield's eight-man pack against the seven men and roving wing forward of Porter's New Zealanders.

The formation of the All-Black teams of 1905 and 1924 has been admirably chronicled by Denzil Batchelor in *Days without Sunset*:

They whittled down their threequarters from four to three, one on each wing and one in the middle. They invented and breathed life into two five-eighths. They gave their scrum-half two duties only: the snatching of the ball from the scrum (easy), and the stopping of a forward rush (impossible for anybody but a New Zealander: moderately easy for him). They played a gigantic outrider of the scrum known as a loose forward, who could bullock about in the mauls, but was chiefly employed as a trusty with the job of wrecking opposing tactics and reslanting thrusts for his own team.

But the hinges of the whole New Zealand game were the five-eighths. The first of these was something more than a stand-off half as we know him. The second was (ideally) something more than all the rest of the attack put together. By inventing the very name, five-eighths, the New Zealand authorities gave footballers a fresh conception of a newly discovered function in the game. Halves, threequarters and backs—there was a logical chain linking them into a striking force. But the five-eighth was an unnatural fraction *outside* this straightforward arithmetical progression. They gave him the name, and invited him to develop himself into the thing. They had chosen the right men for the job. The New Zealand five-eighths went to work as shock troops with the task of probing and piercing the defence. The threequarters had only to exploit the bridge-head they gained.

With these tactics, with tremendous team discipline and with five or six members of it quite outstanding at their respective positions, The Second All-Blacks gave England a trouncing—not a humiliating trounc-ing, considering the scores they ran up against some teams, but a sharp and decisive lesson in teamwork that proved their methods beyond any doubt. They did it, too, despite the unprecedented shock in the opening twenty minutes, before there was any score, of having their star forward, Cyril Brownlie, sent off for allegedly kicking an opponent.

It was the first time that a man had been sent off in an International, things like this just didn't happen in top-class Rugby; for it to happen at Twickenham in front of the Prince of Wales was a sensation that so shook the game's comfortable hierarchy that it had barely stopped talking about it in 1967 when Colin Meads—an even greater New Zealand forward—became the first man to emulate Brownlie. He was sent off against Scotland at Murrayfield for 'dangerous play' after a previous warning. It is abso-lutely characteristic of the aura of good sportsmanship that Rugby Union enthusiasts have wrapped themselves in ever since the first split with the Northern Union that they have never quite decided whether it was the New Zealand forwards or the referees who were the villains of the piece. Kevin Kelleher, the Irish referee of the 1967 game, was called a bloody fool by a Rugby Union official for his action. A. E. Freethy, the referee in 1925, was called that and much more. To kick a fellow was damned bad form, the argument seemed to go. But to send a fellow off with his tail between his legs—to brand him publicly as a bounder—was even worse form. Rugby was a game for gentlemen and should be seen to be gentle-manly; single a man out and send him off the field is to imply he is not fit to remain among gentlemen. Next thing we know, we'll be having punch-ups in the scrum like they do in the Rugby League every week.

Shocked though they must have been, the fourteen remaining All-Blacks fell three points behind, equalised, and went ahead before half-time; they eventually led 17–3 and then hung on to win 17–11 as England attacked their exhausted lines in the last quarter of the game.

They hung on, as they hung on in every tight spot during that trium-phant tour, principally through the genius of their full-back. Denzil Batchelor's assessment of the All-Black tactics midly criticises the use of the full-back as a defender rather than an extra three-quarter. That All-Black full-back was more than a defender—he was a whole defence in himself. He was a nineteen-year-old called George Nepia, a Maori of medium height and impressive build. With astonishing confidence in his skill and resilience, the New Zealand Rugby Union had elected to send him as the only full-back of the party. He played, alone of the tourists, in every one of the thirty games. He tackled like a bull and kicked for touch like a computerised howitzer; he would catch a high kick with an opposing pack charging down on him, and turning to face his own goal would charge backwards at them, winning yards rather than feet as his own forwards remobilised around him; and he gained a reputation for being able to tackle two players at once, smothering the ball at the same time, as he squeezed an attacking three-quarter line between touch and the corner flag.

Nepia is still rated by people who saw him as the greatest Rugby player of all time, even though the New Zealand strategies of the day did not give him any real freedom to run with the ball and thus test his powers of attack as well as his incomparable genius for defence. In 1928 the All-Blacks just failed to beat South Africa in South Africa (they would even today be the only New Zealand team to have won a series there); if Nepia had been in the party there is a very good chance that they would have won the Test series rather than draw it two games apiece. But Nepia, a Maori, was left behind. He was back in the New Zealand team for all four tests against the British Lions in 1930, but then came the depression; it hit New Zealand as it hit everywhere, and it hit Maoris harder than most. George Nepia, in financial difficulties, in his late twenties but eager to carry on playing Rugby, turned to the professional game. He signed in 1935 for Streatham-Mitcham during the League's abortive attempt to get the thirteen-a-side game going in London.

In the thirty years since the Northern Union had completed its breakaway from Rugby Union with its rule changes and its establishment of competitions, the gulf between the two Unions had widened rather than narrowed. The biggest blow, as far as the Rugby Union was concerned, was the interest taken in the new game outside the North of England. In 1907 G. W. Smith, who had toured Britain with Gallaher's 1905 All-Blacks, persuaded a Wellington businessman, A. H. Baskerville, that the Northern Union game was even more impressive than the fifteen-a-side code; Baskerville took up the challenge, collected a team together, and prepared to take on the Northern Union at Rugby and the New Zealand Rugby Union at politics.

While preparations were still under way, a group of sportsmen in Sydney, disgruntled over the New South Wales Union's refusal to grant recompense to a prominent Rugby Union international who had broken his shoulder in a match and lost time from work, invited the New Zealand tourists to play in Sydney on their way to England—offering them £500 for the three games. The offer was accepted and the three games were played (under Rugby Union rules, incidentally), with the profits going not to the players but towards the formation of a Northern Union League in New South Wales.

So, within months, the Rugby Union was put under tremendous pressure on two new fronts. The New Zealand R.U. behaved in the now time-honoured manner by declaring the tourists professionals and suspending them from the Union. In Australia the outcome was very different. With the casting vote of their Chairman, Harry Hoyle, the New South Wales Rugby Union voted to abandon the Rugby Union altogether, and to play to Northern Union Rules, and in 1908 they followed New Zealand on a tour to England. After both tours the Northern clubs dipped their hands into their pockets and signed on the best of the tourists—Lance Todd of New Zealand was bought by Wigan; Albert Rosenfeld of Australia, four years later to score a record eighty tries in a season, signed for Huddersfield.

The same year, 1908, saw a real attempt to expand Northern Union to Wales. Rugby Union's grip there had never been stronger—the triumph over the All-Blacks in 1905 had made Welshmen even more proud of their Rugby prowess, and the trinity of Rugby club, coal-mine and chapel in the Welsh valleys was well-nigh impossible to break. Merthyr Tydfil and Ebbw Vale had both bravely attempted to do so by joining the Northern Union in 1907, and despite a financially disappointing season they were joined the next year by four more Welsh clubs—Barry, Aberdare, Mid-Rhondda and Treherbert. But spectators were hard to come by, and the allegiance to the amateur game too deep-seated to tempt many clubs into risking banishment from their traditional Rugby Union fixtures. An attempt to set up a chain of Methodist missions in the Vatican would have attracted much of the frustration and local hostility experienced by those early thirteen-a-side match-pay pioneers of industrial Wales. There was sympathy in the North, but not much at home, over the fact that by 1914 every one of the Welsh clubs had died.

But as Wales flopped, Australia and New Zealand flourished. Between 1908 and the First World War the decks of the P. and O. liners were rarely free of touring teams going one way or the other. The Australians followed the New Zealanders in 1908–9; Britain went to Australia and New Zealand on a triumphantly successful tour—in terms of both the quality of the play and the profits accumulated—in 1910. Australia came back to Britain in 1911 (winning the test series by two wins and one draw to nothing), and the British went back in 1914, sailing home with another highly popular series of matches behind them into the outbreak of the Kaiser's War.

At home Britain, Australia and New Zealand had played flag-waving representative matches in London, Liverpool, Glasgow, Edinburgh, Birmingham, Leeds and—strange to relate—Cheltenham, without ever succeeding in establishing Northern Union as an acceptable alternative to Rugby Union outside the North. And with one match, at Sydney in 1914, they established beyond a doubt that the two forms of Rugby were as different in temperament as they were in organisation and background. The last of the three test matches against Australia was played, on the terms of a hastily rearranged schedule and against the pleas of the exhausted British party, only a week after the Second Test. Britain had won the first and drawn the second—and were badly hit by injuries. A complaint to the Northern Union received a cabled reply ordering the party to fall in with the Australians' new schedule, and adding the well-worn call to arms about England expecting every man to do his duty—a sentiment worthy in its stiff-upper-lip, bite-the-bullet attitude of the Rugby Union at its stuffiest.

They took the field, anyway, with their full-back playing with a patched-up broken nose, and two minutes after the start Frank Williams twisted a knee and was a passenger from then on. The tourists played enough good football to lead 9–3 at half-time, soon after which Clark, the Huddersfield forward, broke a collarbone and had to leave the field. Williams then taxed his gammy leg once too often, and was forced to go off; then Hall, the Oldham centre, was concussed falling on a loose ball, and was carried off. There was half an hour to go: Britain leading 9–3 with ten men facing thirteen. Not only did they survive, not only did the four-man pack hold its own against the Australian six; but they even increased their lead with a breakaway try, and ended up winners by 14–6. The match has gone down in Rugby League history as the Rorke's Drift test, and it proved that no matter what the Northern Union had sacrificed in open play, in tactical slickness, in 'sportsmanship' and in 'good clean fun'—all qualities which the fifteen-man game claimed to retain for itself—it had in no way lost the ability to stir the blood.

In common with other sporting bodies, the Northern Union virtually ceased to exist during the 1914–18 war, and there was some doubt as to whether the four-year lay-off might not damage the loyalty of the fans in even the most staunch strongholds of the game. There was no need to worry; in common with both Soccer and Rugby Union the game was revived with a great resurgence of popularity—the public throughout the country were starved of entertainment, and gates were surprisingly high. (The unexpected post-war success proved something of an embarrassment to the clubs themselves; in an effort to get the game back on a profitable footing in 1918–19, they persuaded the players to appear for just 10s. broken time payment plus 2s. 6d. tea money; with the enormous crowds passing through the turnstiles in the first part of the season the players began to agitate for a return to a professional rate of pay; the dispute became so heated on both sides that both at Oldham and Wakefield Trinity the players struck for full wages, and when in February 1919 other clubs were similarly threatened the Northern Union Council agreed a return to full-time professionalism.)

With the survival of the game assured, the 1920s and 1930s was for professional Rugby a time of consolidation rather than one of expansion. The Northern Union had, in 1922, changed its name to the less parochial Rugby Football League, and a number of minor rule changes were to make goal-kicking less frequent and mauls at the play-the-ball less stulti- fying. In 1927 the first post-war tour by the New Zealanders proved a disaster in every way: they lost money; they quarrelled internally, result- ing in a strike by some of the tourists who were suspended for life on their return home; and they lost all three Tests, as well as eleven of their twenty-seven club matches. They had disappointed as keenly as the Rugby Union New Zealanders of 1924–5 had inspired—an indication that a country of such limited size could not realistically support two similar but entirely independent games. Their plight was further emphasised by a League ruling that year that ended the two-year qualification previously required before an overseas player could appear for an English club. The lifting of this restriction invited a wholesale poaching of Australian and New Zealand players—a further boost for the well-off Northern clubs, but a considerable blow in the Antipodes, where they could ill afford to lose their best players when the game was struggling hard against the popularity of the fifteen-man code.

The mid 1920s also saw another of those suicidal attempts from Wales to swim in the rough waters of professional Rugby; this time it was Pontypridd—and this time the experiment lasted two seasons before lack of support, success, and consequently gate money caused their demise. But from Wales in that decade did come one genuine piece of Rugby League greatness—the first home-grown authentic hero that the game had produced, Jim Sullivan of Wigan.

Sullivan was born in Cardiff in 1903, and signed for Wigan at the age of eighteen in the close season of 1921. He was a huge bull of a man with slicked-back hair, a bullet-head, legs like tree trunks and a mouth that looked as if it were just about to break into a grin. As a storming, battering forward he was invaluable to Britain in twenty-five test matches and to Wigan in every season from 1921 to 1945. But as a kicker of the ball he was unique. He kicked 100 goals or more in every season from 1921 to the outbreak of the Second World War; his total of 2,959 goals for a career will quite possibly never be beaten, and it will take something of a miracle to surpass his 22 goals kicked in a single afternoon in a Cup match against a team of unfortunates from Flimby and Fothergill in 1925. He was supreme in an era when the game was at its most uncompromising, when the life of a forward was a hard slog over bad pitches for small reward, and when injuries were something to be shrugged off and forgotten rather than rested and pampered. It is characteristic of the game that it was a forward who became the game's first undisputed immortal.

The 1930s saw further expansion, some successful and some, pre-dictably, not. In 1930 the French Rugby Union, who had been playing regularly in the international championship since 1910 (though without any great measure of success), were rent by domestic disputes that resulted in the formation of a breakaway Union. This in itself would not have caused too much excitement abroad—the Home Unions' attitude to French Rugby was thoroughly patronising, and the clichés about 'brilliant but unstable' and 'mercurial continental temperaments' would have been as readily applied to the French administrators as to their wayward and inconsistent players. But this row was about money, about transfer fees being paid under the counter when supposedly amateur players moved from one supposedly amateur club to another. Just as the Northern Union had broken away in 1895 in order to get payments for their players, so the French group of clubs broke away in protest against payment to players—and rather pointedly called itself the French Amateur Rugby Union. At the mention of money, the Home Unions sharply drew in their breaths and in 1931 severed relations with the French until the French Union could show that they had successfully sorted the trouble out.

This meant that France was effectively banned from international Rugby—the South African, New Zealand and Australian Unions echoed the decision of the Home Unions—and the reaction in France inevitably led to the development of the Rugby League game. After prolonged negotiations between French officials and the Rugby League Council, a British XIII played Australia—at the end of Australia's 1933 tour—in Paris, and three months later a French side, captained by the much-capped Rugby Union player, Jean Galia, made a successful tour of the

Northern clubs in England. A British side went across to beat France in a
Paris cycling stadium the following April—a match that attracted a crowd
of 20,000—and by that autumn, in the characteristic flurry of high-speed
organisation that officials of Rugby League have shown ever since the
game's inception, a French *Ligue de Rugby à Treize* was formed with
twelve teams, most of them from the traditional Rugby country of the
South and South-West.

With one previously solid Rugby Union area changing allegiance overnight, there seemed no real reason why other equally entrenched strongholds should not be stormed. (In fairness to the Rugby League enthusiasts,
it would probably be true to say that they did not think in quite those
terms; the attitude of the Rugby Union still mystified and hurt them, and
there was no doubt a certain self-satisfied glee when a convert was lured
from one code to the other. But in general they were typical sports enthusiasts, very like the men who carried the Rugby code across the world in
the 19th century, who were convinced that the game played partly for
money in the North was better sport and better entertainment than the
game played purely for pleasure in the South, and who were delighted
whenever they could persuade an unbeliever to agree with them.) At any
rate, the League, and especially exiled Northerners, turned their eyes on
London.

The capital had already been given the opportunity of adopting Rugby
League. Both Australia and New Zealand had played test matches in
London during their first tours; in 1922 England had played Wales in
London, and a search in the late 1920s for a permanent home for the
increasingly compulsive Challenge Cup Final had ended, amid a good
deal of controversy, at Wembley Stadium. The internationals had attracted
only meagre crowds, but the Wembley Cup Final, which had pulled in
some 41,000 spectators in 1929, the first year, had persuaded some ever-
optimistic enthusiasts that the game might find a public even in the midst
of England's greatest concentration of both Rugby Union clubs and
professional Soccer grounds.

The first step was a curious one. The proprietors of the White City
stadium, in West London, proposed to base a team there to play under
floodlights in midweek—and they set about it in a fashion derived piece-
meal from the franchise-selling antics of the American Football owners.
They picked out Wigan Highfield, an ailing team without a future,
renamed them London Highfield, and began the 1933–4 season before a
crowd of 6,000. The crowd dwindled away as the weeks went by and
despite a reasonable run of results, London Highfield and their White
City backers lasted only a season. But no sooner had they given up the

struggle than two other London combines applied for a place in the League—in West London Acton and Willesden, in South London Streatham and Mitcham.

Both teams bought extensively in the North and began their seasons with high hopes and some impressive results. But Acton and Willesden, failing where so many others had failed in the face of apathy, died after a season; Streatham and Mitcham who had taken the trouble to sign no less than five New Zealand players including an older but still incomparable George Nepia, at least felt that they had the potential support to start a second season in the League. But that was all—in mid-season they too collapsed (as did, soon afterwards, another set of gallant outsiders from Newcastle upon Tyne), sending George Nepia, a sad figure amid such failure, home to end his career back among the Rugby Union men whom he should never have been forced to leave.

New Zealand, despite having initiated the overseas spread of Rugby League, had never developed it to the extent of its becoming a truly professional game. Players might receive free equipment and full expenses, but none could earn his living from Rugby; and the New Zealand Rugby Union, after their predictable reactions against the initial breakaway, had come to adopt a creditably realistic attitude towards the League game. They had long since abandoned the sort of witchhunt that could in England or Scotland, say, have a man banned for life from Rugby Union for playing a single game of Rugby League, and they were happy to turn a blind eye to George Nepia's wanderings. The story is, indeed, that when he was over the age of fifty, at a Rugby Union charity match he received the ball thirty yards out, charged his way through and touched down under the posts to the roars of a delighted crowd. He was referee at the time.

New Zealand had suffered something of a decline since the start of the 1930s. An international ruling had forced them to abandon their highly effective seven-men pack, and their wing forward now had to get down and shove with the rest of the scrum. Then, in Great Britain in 1935 they were managed by an autocrat, Vincent Meredith, whose ideas of both tactics on the field and man-management off it were as dictatorial as they were bizarre; early in the tour they were defeated by Swansea—the first club side in Britain to beat them in the 20th century; and on top of that they lost two test matches, unluckily to Wales by 13–12, resoundingly to England by 13–0 and two unforgettable tries by Alexander Obolensky. And at home the New Zealanders had the humiliation of losing a test series to a touring side—the 1937 Springboks, a name still used by New Zealand mothers to strike terror into the hearts of disobedient children, a team of tremendous forward power, of all-round efficiency among the backs, and a unique Rugby brain in Danie Craven, the 1937 scrum half destined to coach so many invincible South African sides after the War.

The British expatriates in South Africa had taken to the game with the same fervour that the New Zealanders had shown, but by 1940 it had achieved the status that it still holds today—the national sport of the Afrikaaner. The British clubs of the Cape and Natal had gradually given way in importance to the former Boer strongholds of Transvaal and the Orange Free State, and the Anglo-Saxon names in South Africa's remarkable pre-war teams had become far outweighed by the Dutch, just as the British tactics and techniques had been progressively outgunned by the power and preparation of the South African teams.

The development of Rugby—both Union and League—in the first half of the century can be summarised not so much as in rule-changes and championships and match results, and not even in the place of money in sport, but as the consolidation and entrenchment of attitudes. The most professional Rugby players, in the widest sense of the term, were the South Africans and the New Zealanders—two countries where ability at Rugby Football ensured immediate support and help from a Rugby-mad community. It was in these countries where Rugby could remain for weeks and months on end the most important single driving force in a man's make-up; where coaching and club competition were long established; where the schools dedicated themselves to include tackling, drop-kicking, and passing among the Maths and the Scripture classes. Here the games were organised on a complex national scale, from intensive coaching in the schools, though junior and club Rugby with their ever-increasing competitive pressure, to the heights of provincial and national competition.

Yet these were amateurs. Professional Rugby in Britain could claim none of this organisation. There was only the merest smattering of Rugby League in schools, and there was virtually none in the influential colleges and universities. The game was no doubt played out of enjoyment, but principally it was played for entertainment and, consequently, for the attraction of money. The game had found a formula for itself—not very different from Rugby Union, but enough for there to be no mistaking the one game from the other. It pleased crowds who had grown up with it —in Lancashire, Yorkshire and certain other points North; it commanded, as far as gate receipts can be an indication, a bigger following than Rugby Union. But Rugby League was always to suffer from financial worries, never being fully certain that the wolf threatening at every door might not finally decide to pounce during the coming close season.

The League was becoming more and more resigned, as the seasons went by, to the fact that outside the North of England the game simply would not catch on, despite the staging of internationals and demonstration matches well outside Rugby League's traditional catchment area. Rugby League men were professionals, but only in the most haphazard way, with clubs coming and going from season to season, paying their players what they could and frequently seeking out local jobs for him if, as was very common, they couldn't pay him enough just to play Rugby.

The Rugby Union, conversely, had become almost belligerent in its amateurism. The Union had been taken by surprise when the Northern Clubs broke away in 1895 after what can have seemed little more than a little local difficulty—a stormy meeting followed by a satisfactory, pro-Union vote. Their reaction was two-fold; first, the Union were never to be caught napping again, and strict laws against the erosion of the amateur spirit were drafted, passed and consolidated over the years; secondly, they developed a sincere and unfailing belief in the superiority of their brand of Rugby over any other game—an attitude that seems innocent enough, if a little naïve, but which gripped the hierarchy of the Union in what amounted to an obsession.

The sentiments occur again and again in the literature of Rugby produced in the first half of the century: that Rugger is a 'man's game'; that, because thirty men spend eighty minutes manhandling each other without launching a full-scale vendetta of violence, the game is somehow the perfect developer of character. 'It is something more than a game, this Man-maker', wrote E. H. D. Sewell in his entertaining farago of Rugby writings characteristically entitled *Rugger, the Man's Game.* '. . . No other game if it is played seriously in the highest company, equals Rugger in its combined call on its players for Courage, Self-Control, Stamina and Sticking-it. Why should this be so? Mainly, nay almost wholly, because of the Man-to-Man element in Rugger. To play Rugger well you must play it fiercely, and at the same time, and all the time, remember that while doing so that you are a gentleman.'

The Creed tended to continue with the re-statement of the amateur line: 'Large crowds watch our games nowadays,' wrote England's great fly-half W. J. A. Davies on his retirement in 1924, 'and generally return home with thoroughly agreeable recollections, because Rugby Football (thanks to the foresight of Rowland Hill and others) is, and will always remain, a sport and not a business.' And it would generally end with a reminder that victory on the Rugby field is a team triumph striven for with unselfish vigour by each member regardless of his own glory, and with a claim of utter confidence in the game's superiority: 'Rugby football is assuredly a game where the higher mental faculties are employed more than in any other' (Davies again).

The trouble lies not with the sentiments themselves—most keen sports-men are thoroughly convinced that their game is better than anyone else's —but a concomitant attitude among the Rugby Union men of the great amateur era that their faith in the game gave it some kind of moral superiority—that because they didn't get paid, because they weren't competing for a cup, because they weren't coached, then the game achieved an essential purity which, by inference, Soccer and Rugby League and the rest could never aspire to.

The maintenance of this purity had been the sworn mission of the Home Unions, under strong and dedicated leadership, ever since the first scandals over payment broke in Wales in the early 1890s, and the Rugby Union Committee were forced to 'professionalise' (i.e., brand as a professional) David and Evan James, Welsh international half-backs from poor families who accepted payment for playing Rugby for Broughton Rangers (this was two years before the breakaway, when Broughton became a founder-member of the Northern Union). The real test case had come in early 1896 as, still somewhat shell-shocked from the Northern breakaway, the Union decided that the supporters of Newport Rugby Club should not be allowed to organise a testimonial for their distinguished international three-quarter, A. J. Gould. All right, said Gould's well-wishers, if we can't collect money for him, we can at least buy him a house. 'No you can't,' said the Union, 'the giving of a house is tantamount to giving money.'

The people of Newport were determined to show their appreciation of Gould's talents (and Gould, let it be admitted, was by no means reluctant to receive it), so the row continued. But the Welsh Union were forced to take back their £50 donation to the cause—the conflict in Wales over the issue was such that Wales withdrew from all international competition for two seasons—and the whole business was brought before the International Committee. They put their collective foot down firmly: all clubs and players belonging to the Rugby Union were forbidden to play against Gould. And later a further ruling forbade any English club to select Gould to play for them. Oddly enough, after Gould had understandably accepted his testimonial, the Rugby Union met again and, trotting out such time-honoured bromides as 'special circumstances' and 'isolated case', allowed Gould back into the game.

Such compromise was rare, and over the years the Union's attitude hardened not only against payment to players, but against anything that could be construed as a professional attitude. In 1932, soon after the break with France, the Rugby Union, having been 'officially' informed that substitutions were allowed in New Zealand under certain circumstances (in fact the system of replacements had been used in New Zealand for some time, and the Rugby Union must have been perfectly well aware of it), made it clear that there would be no question of allowing replacements in matches in which teams from the British Isles were engaged. In the same year the International Board turned down a request from New Zealand for teams to be allowed to leave the field at half-time. And another decree deemed that football played by floodlights for gate money 'was not in the best interests of the game', though why it should be any different from playing football in daylight for gate money, which the clubs did every Saturday, was not explained.

In 1933 the Union asserted that 'the competitive system' was responsible for breaches of amateurism and unnecessarily rough play, an unmistakable dig at the French but also clear notice that knock-out and league competitions in the home countries would not be allowed. In 1939 an American undergraduate who had played professional gridiron football in the U.S.A. was declared ineligible to play Rugby at Oxford.

It was the same attitude that deplored the idea of squad training or of intensive coaching before important games, and at the same time made the Oxford and Cambridge match at Twickenham each December the high point of the Rugby season in England, partly because it represented everything fine and gentlemanly about the game and partly—did they but realise it—because it was the one game of the season for which the teams had been in intensive squad training for months. It was this attitude that virtually handed the playing domination between the wars to the South Africans and the New Zealanders, and that led to a decline in the standards in British Rugby—or at least an unsatisfactory advance—that was not to be overcome until well into the 1960s.

the entry of the gladiators

American Football: 1900 to 1940

After the revolt among the colleges in the 1890s against the increasing brutality of American College Football, it would be logical to assume that the game entered the 20th century in more settled state than it had known for some time. In fact, it was in a sorrier state than ever before. The mass momentum plays and the interlocked interference had been watered down, but the game was still one demanding courage, strength, unscrupulousness and good doctors. Play was still as tight as ever, with close marking by the heavy men in the line; without the threat, yet, of a forward pass, ten of the eleven defenders could stand within a yard of the line of scrimmage (the other one covering the possibility of a punt); and the man receiving the snap could not run himself—he had to pass or hand the ball off—which virtually dictated that play progressed in short, violent, bruising rushes relieved only by the occasional liberating kick.

A handful of coaches were able to devise running plays to beat the deadlock. The most successful of them was Fielding Yost at Michigan, whose team scored their fabled 600 points in 600 minutes' play in 1901, and went four seasons without losing. But even Yost, with a whole encyclopaedia of running plays at his command, described the game as 'a man-to-man fight! It was part of football to be rough, to batter up or batter down the opposition, to rough and knock down the kicker, to do about everything except slug with the closed fist—and even that wasn't always penalised.'

It was in 1905 that Football once again decided it had got too rough for itself. The Mid-Western universities were first to take note of the growing public dissatisfaction with the game, and they reacted by limiting the season to a maximum of five matches; the players were limited to three years' participation only; and freshmen were barred from the game. The one thing they could not do was change the rules of the game itself, which was a power given, in the reforms of the 1890s, to the Rules Committee alone; and though it had been suggested as early as 1903 to Walter Camp that the forward pass might relieve some of the hard pounding, the Rules Committee had failed to take the hint. For the first time in the game's short history the rules had been stable for some years, and the Committee were clearly reluctant to monkey with them purely for the sake of change.

It took the President of the United States himself to wield a stick big enough to make college football change course. It is said that Theodore Roosevelt's mind was finally made up by a gory news photograph of Bob Maxwell, a huge Swarthmore tackle of some repute, being led from the field after rough treatment at the hands—and probably the feet as well—of Pennsylvania. Presumably with the quaint assumption that he would be talking to the right sort of people, Roosevelt summoned the old aristocrats of the game—the representatives of Yale, Harvard and Princeton—to the White House and told them to do something about Football or else. They in turn contacted other colleges, formed a large Intercollegiate Football Rules Committee, and within a few months had made the one decision that drove American Football into the modern era.

The forward pass was not everybody's choice for opening up the game; certain vestiges of Rugby instinct must have remained in a few ageing minds. Rugby games—and after all was said and done, American Football remained at root a Rugby game—had set themselves a number of restrictions in order to make things more difficult, or more demanding, or more distinctive. Just as Association Football, while allowing one member of each team to throw the ball forward if he wanted to, had restricted itself by forbidding the rest of the team to touch it with their hands at all, so the Rugby-based games had initially restricted themselves in two ways—firstly by manhandling only the man with the ball and secondly by throwing the ball sideways or backwards, but never forwards. American Football had dispensed with the former many years earlier in the days before it had found any real identity for itself. But the principle of passing backwards was integral to the game—part of its very being. It was not, clearly, as important as it was by this time to Rugby itself, where so many movements in attack or defence, so many patterns of the open game, depended on the ball moving backwards from hand to hand as play moved forwards; American Football was by now so tight that long lateral passing was virtually unknown, and most passes were made by 'handing off'—one player slapping the ball into the hands of a colleague just a pace away—or by lobbing it to a player twenty yards or so behind the scrimmage. But the idea of abandoning the principle clearly seemed to some an unnecessarily radical move.

One widely lobbied proposal to open the game out, and therefore dilute the force of the mass attacks and defences, was the not unreasonable one of widening the field of play. When Walter Camp had been giving all possible emphasis to the scrimmage line and the tactics of the possession game in the late 1870s, he had purposely narrowed the field to a mere 160 ft.; it seemed logical that now the Rules Committee had been ordered to take some of the emphasis away from the line of scrimmage, a wider field would encourage more wide running by the backs. There is every reason to suppose that this might have been accepted—and consequently that the game might never have legislated for the forward pass—had it not been for Harvard. At Harvard, they had just completed Soldier Field, the first concrete stadium built in the United States to house football, and it had been built to accommodate a football pitch of the regulation size. To tack another 20 yards on the width of the playing area would mean chipping lumps off the concrete wonder of Cambridge, Mass., and this Harvard would not countenance at any price.

Some of the Rules Committee's reforms were technical: the playing time was cut by ten minutes to the sixty minutes it remains today; the scrimmage lines were separated by the length of the ball, and, more importantly, emphasis was placed on forward movement by increasing the ground to be gained in three downs from five to ten yards. But most revolutionary of all was the introduction of the forward pass.

Revolutionary but, at the start, both counter-productive and chaotic. In the first place, the original rules placed so many restrictions on the pass that hardly any quarterback dared attempt it; the forward pass, said the 1906 rules, had to be thrown five yards behind the line of scrimmage, and cross the scrimmage line five yards, laterally, from where it had been snapped—i.e., the ball had to go across the field as well as forward. Only one forward pass could be thrown during a single play. There was a fifteen-yard penalty (and the loss of a down) for failing to complete a forward pass, whether the ball were dropped by the receiver or intercepted by a defender.

One immediate effect was that for the officials to manage an extra dimension with their measuring eye to determine the longitudinal *and* latitudinal distances of a pass play, a five-yard grid had to be painted down the field as well as across it—the gridiron became, for a few years, a chess-board, and the quarterback with an aptitude for trigonometry and navigation would be at a premium; this particular ruling—an almost perfect example of how to harm an essentially free-ranging game by wrapping on it a network of arbitrary mathematical barbed wire—was dropped within four years. The penalty for failing to complete the pass—another powerful deterrent to opening up the game—lasted no longer than 1907.

In time teams did learn to use the forward pass as an exciting ground-gaining, even match-winning, gimmick. The lore of American Football is littered with claims as to who completed the first legal forward pass; the verdict at present seems to rest with Eddie Cochems, the coach of the St Louis University team of 1906. In the summer of that year he took the whole team from St Louis to Lake Beulah, a training camp north of Chicago, perfecting the forward pass with Bradbury Robinson throwing and Jack Schneider receiving, for 'a wonderful two months' (only twenty years beforehand, in the north of England, Blackburn Olympic had had serious questions asked about their amateur status after training for a few days at Blackpool before the F.A. Cup Final!). The training worked. Robinson has claimed throwing the first legal forward pass for St Louis against Carroll College, Waukesha, Wisconsin, in the first couple of weeks of September 1906; in the following months St Louis won all their games, scored 402 points and conceded 11; and this in an era when 0–0 ties were by no means rare.

The conservative Eastern Universities did not take easily to the forward pass, though it caused a major sensation when Yale gained 30 yards with one which led to a touchdown, and another flutter of eyebrow-raising the following year when Yale flung two long passes to defeat a ten-point lead by Princeton. But in the Mid-West such wily coaches as Alonzo Stagg and Glenn 'Pop' Warner, though out of sight of the sophisticated sports-writers, were far from slow on the uptake. Stagg, then still at Chicago, wrote later with a customary lack of modesty 'The first season, 1906, I personally had 64 different forward pass patterns . . .' His team was so good, in fact, that he kept his pass plays up his sleeve for the vital championship game against Minnesota, only to be frustrated by appalling weather which dissuaded him from risking any of them. They lost the match and the Championship, but resurrected the forward pass the following week against Illinois and won 63–0.

Warner was then in charge of some of the most amazing raw athletic talent that had, up to that time, ever been gathered in one college. The Carlisle School for Indians was just what it sounded, a small and not particularly well-endowed university for students of pure or mixed American Indian blood in a small town in Pennsylvania, which had the luck or foresight to have, during the first decade of the new century, one of the most inventive and effective coaches ever to emerge in college football. In those dozen years, picking his teams from an eligible student population of a bare 250, touring from college to college with only three substitutes for his tired and badly mauled linemen, matching the giants of Columbia and Harvard and Pennsylvania with guards and tackles weighing a bare twelve stone, Warner managed to produce winning teams playing entertaining football, coaching to national prominence the Sioux Gardner, the Arapahoe Exendine, the brilliant Cheyenne Pete Hauser; and to introduce to football and track athletics the Sac and Fox Indian Jim Thorpe, whom America, with its unbounded love of a hero and its compulsive habit of making lists, has successively chosen as Number One football player of the age, Number One male athlete of the half-century and Number One football player of the century, as well as selecting him on every all-time All-America team.

— No one with the strategic foresight of Pop Warner would ignore the value of the forward pass—and he went one better: the football in those days was fatter, more melon-shaped than the narrow, compact bullet now in use, and although quarterbacks and halves had managed on occasions to throw a spiral pass, rather than an end-over-end lob, the torpedo fired overarm from the quarterback's shoulder was virtually unknown. But Frank Mount Pleasant, another of Warner's Carlisle Indians, was using it effectively by 1907, and was proving too fast and accurate with it for the opposing defences.

Though it was not used universally, the forward pass was enough of a threat to force the reorganisation of defence. The defensive half-backs had now to withdraw from the backsides of their linemen in order to guard against a pass play over their heads; this was roughly what the Rules Committee had imagined would happen, and they assumed that this would guarantee more open play. What they failed to grasp was that it would fatally weaken the defence while imposing no restrictions at all on the attacking line; with the half-backs on watch elsewhere, the defence linemen were left to cope on their own with mass offensives. Instead of the forward pass legislation reducing the number of injuries, they actually increased, and in 1909 at least six college linemen were killed or fatally injured on the field of play.

So, in desperation, the Rules Committee undertook another burst of legislation, banned all interlocked interference and required the defence to have seven men on the line of scrimmage; the pendulum immediately swung the other way—defences were now so powerful that scoreless draws returned to fashion, and matches were often decided by the odd field goal. In 1912, finally, the committee allowed a forward pass of any length to be thrown, gave an extra, fourth, down in which to make the ten ֪ ards, and increased the value of a touchdown to six points.

At last the game achieved the equilibrium it was seeking and at last the conservative easterners began looking for points with the scorned forward pass. The day that it became respectable, the date, perhaps, on which the modern era of Football can be said to have begun, and the date when it was proved once and for all that a small team with skill and tactics could expect to beat a big team with none, was 1 November 1913. Not only did it see the forward pass make its mark among the Eastern colleges; it also introduced to the public a star who, as player and coach over the next twenty years, was to form a vital link between the golden era of college football and the foundation years of the professional game.

His name was Knute Rockne, the son of a Norwegian immigrant, and in 1913 he was in his third year on the football team at the unremarkable Notre Dame University at South Bend, Indiana. In the summer of 1913 Rockne, the left end, and 'Gus' Dorais, Notre Dame's quarterback, spent the summer working in casual jobs at Lake Erie and spending every minute of their spare time throwing and receiving forward passes; by the start of the season Dorais's accuracy with the pass was matched only by Rockne's newly developed ability to catch a ball looping high over his right shoulder while running full tilt. It was something of a coincidence that, at the start of the next term, Notre Dame had engaged a new football coach, Jesse Harper, a man who had learned his football at Chicago under Alonzo Stagg and who had for three years been using the (rule-restricted) forward pass with some success at another minor college in Indiana; and even more of a coincidence that, for the first time, Notre Dame had been granted a plum fixture with one of the major colleges of the East—the Army cadet university at West Point.

Both Rockne and Dorais have since written about the momentous meeting with the Army; about the humble way in which they travelled on the trains to Virginia, about the courteous way the boys from the backwoods were received by the well-bred young officers—and about the superb game itself. The Army led 13–7 at half-time, with two touchdowns smashed through the lighter Notre Dame line to one classic forward pass loosed by Dorais to the high-stepping Rockne. Another 35-yard pass to Rockne after half-time laid the way open to another touchdown for Notre Dame, a series of short passes and powerful runs won them another, and two more series of long passes splitting the now thoroughly bemused Army defence carried their line twice more, leaving Notre Dame winners by 35–13. The result was achieved—almost incredibly by today's standards—with one single substitution, when the running back, Joe Pliska, left the field for two minutes to repair a broken shoelace.

When the team returned to South Bend virtually the whole town, accompanied by several bands, were there to greet them, but the fact that Notre Dame had overnight become a major force in the game was only part of the story. Following that match, the Army immediately adopted a forward pass routine for themselves, and in the season's climactic battle they in turn crushed a talented Navy team 22–9. From having been a mere threat, opening up defences for powerful running charges, the forward pass had become an integral part of attack.

From 1905 to 1925, college football was the biggest news—and made big money for successful teams. Notre Dame's success over the following years meant big gate receipts and, subsequently, new buildings and academic improvements for the University; Harvard, whose Soldier Field Stadium had played its part in the introduction of the forward pass, added more hardware to its concrete to seat an eventual 50,000. Walter Camp, far-sighted and dramatic as ever, persuaded Yale in 1913 to build the Yale Bowl, a 28-acre giant holding 80,000 fans, the biggest of its time. Other colleges followed suit. Some of them could not afford it, particularly where the student body was small and the local townspeople, fickle as football crowds anywhere, would pay only to watch a winning team. Abuses to the amateur, academic code found some colleges recruiting talented footballers for financial inducements, though as a rule even these desperate measures were not enough to help a college in economic difficulties. The truth was universal and unchanging—the size of the college did not matter; even the capabilities of the players could vary enormously. But the right coach, with a team he could mould and ideas they could exploit for him, could bring an unknown university into the national headlines in a couple of seasons. It happened at Notre Dame under Jesse Harper. It happened, at the close of the First World War at the Centre College, Danville, Kentucky, under 'Uncle Charley' Moran, whose players were nicknamed the 'Praying Colonels' because they were said to kneel in prayer before each game. Centre, invited East in 1920 to play Harvard, the current Rose Bowl winners, scored more touchdowns on Soldier Field in fifteen minutes than Yale had scored in fifteen years.

Rockne had now returned to Notre Dame as coach. As he had started off his career teaching the Football world a lesson, he climaxed it by producing the most famous college team of all time. Their record, though good, had been equalled before. And it has been claimed since, by people who saw the 1924 Notre Dame side play, that Rockne himself had coached better teams; but they went through their season undefeated and overwhelmed a great Stanford team 27–10 in the Rose Bowl in California, and their effectiveness cannot be contested. What lifted this particular team to the ranks of the immortals, however, was not a fine season or any individual hero, or even a single, exceptional victory, but a single newspaper report.

It was written in the prestigious *New York Herald Tribune* by the doyen of football writers of the day, Grantland Rice, on 19 October 1924, the

33 A game for the people: by the turn of the century Soccer in Britain had no rival as a spectator sport—64,000 people watch from the Crystal Palace terraces as Bury beat off a Derby County attack in the 1903 Cup Final. *Radio Times Hulton Picture Library*

34 The rout of Spain, 1931: two years earlier England had lost 4–3 in Madrid, their first defeat by overseas opposition. At Highbury the revenge was emphatic; Ricardo Zamora, Spain's much vaunted goalkeeper (here challenged by Dixie Dean), had a nightmare afternoon, and England won 7–1.   *Radio Times Hulton Picture Library*

35 The Battle of Highbury, 1934: the Italians came to London as the new World Cup winners, and came as close as anyone ever had to beating England at home. Much of the game was a violent brawl, but Italy pulled back from 0–3 to 2–3 in the second half, and England had to fight hard to hang on. Here Ceresoli, the Italian goalkeeper, makes a save, watched by Ted Drake (right).   *Central Press*

36 The Saturday heroes: the idols of the 1930s were the great club players, the men who put their talents on show week after week and commanded the loyalty of the supporters on the terraces; none was more popular than Dixie Dean, Everton's majestic centre-forward, here outjumping the Arsenal defence. *Syndication International*

37 The world champions: on the Continent, glory lay in
international competition, and with Mussolini in the
background and Vittorio Pozzo at the helm, Italy beat all
(non-British) comers in 1934 and 1938. Here, in the
all-important World Cup semi-final of 1934, Italy scramble
the decisive goal against Austria. *Mondadoripress*

38 Arsenal in attack: in the 1930s Arsenal emerged as the best disciplined of all British club teams, but it was individual flair that made their name. Alex James, their star Scottish forward, leaves three Manchester City defenders floundering in his wake in a 1934 league match.   *Topix*

39 Arsenal in defence: after the Second World War some of the genius had gone, but Arsenal's discipline held firm. In this league match in 1950, the defensive pattern is rigid—eight men guard the penalty area against three Derby attackers. *Popperfoto*

40 The end of an era: Ferenc Puskas (number 10) turns in triumph after scoring Hungary's third goal in their 6–3 rout of England in 1953. For the first time in 45 years of international football, England had lost at home to a continental team. *Fox Photos*

41 The making of a legend: the story of the F.A. Cup is littered with heroism, but none more remarkable than that of Bert Trautmann, Manchester City's German-born goalkeeper in the 1956 Final. In this clash with Murphy, of Birmingham City, fifteen minutes before the end of the match, he broke his neck—yet played on to the final whistle to ensure his side's victory. *Central Press*

42 Defence in disarray: the golden age of college
football—fast, furious and physically dangerous.
Steve Philbin of Yale bullocks his way through the
Harvard line in 1907. Despite football's high mortality
rate, few of these players bothered with headgear.
Culver Pictures Inc.

43 Perfection in attack; the lean years of the
professional game—disciplined, hard-working,
unrewarding. With brilliant precision, the 1935
Detroit Lions blockers have thrown open a gap as
wide as a door in the New York Giants' defence.
Glen Presnell (number 3) gratefully charges through.
Pro Football Hall of Fame

44 Grange the idol: Harold 'Red' Grange, first of the popular heroes of pro football, loses his helmet as he crashes over for a touchdown against the Los Angeles Tigers. To launch him as a money-spinner, Chicago Bears played eighteen exhibition games in less than two months, including one run of eight games in twelve days. *United Press International*

45 Grange the legend: the runner at his greatest, outpacing the
defensive cover to the line. But this was autumn 1926, Grange
was playing for New York Yankees against Boston Bulldogs, and
the miserable crowd testified to the disaster of Grange's breakaway American Football League. *United Press International*

46 The magnificent arm: Sam Baugh—'Slingin' Sammy'—in characteristic pose; as defencemen hurl themselves towards him, he lets go yet
another forward pass. A tall, slim, shy Texan, he threw match-winning
passes as quarterback for Washington Redskins for sixteen seasons.
Pro Football Hall of Fame

47 The invincible T: Sid Luckman, a reluctant recruit to pro football, became the classic quarterback, first master of the modern T-formation and, in 1940, architect of Chicago Bears' all-time record 73–0 massacre of Washington Redskins. *Pro Football Hall of Fame*

48 Everybody's favourite: Jim Thorpe, Sac and Fox Indian, Olympic all-rounder, baseball giant, football-player of frightening ferociousness, and automatic choice as first president of the National Football League. *United Press International*

day after Notre Dame had defeated the Army 13–7 (the Army, again; and it is worth noting that this time, far from relying on student support at the stadiums of South Bend or West Point, the game was filling the Polo Grounds stadium in New York City). And it was written with the panache and somewhat syrupy self-indulgence that somehow shared with its readers a knowledge that Rice had witnessed, and the readers were now experiencing, an event of national importance. It took the sort of liberties - English football-writers were confident enough to take after the World Cup victory of 1966, and that Welsh Rugby writers take whenever the New Zealanders get beaten on Welsh soil. It could not have been written years earlier, because college football had not yet become a national preoccupation; and ten years later the feats of college boys were taking very much second second place to the feats of well-paid ex-college boys; in the middle of the Roaring 'Twenties, with college football at a never-to-be-repeated apex of prestige, it was just right.

Outlined against a blue-gray October sky [Rice wrote], the Four Horse-men rode again. In dramatic lore they are known as Famine, Pestilence, Destruction and Death. These are only aliases. Their real names are Stuhldreher, Miller, Crowley and Layden. They formed the crest of the South Bend cyclone before which another fighting Army football team was swept over the precipice yesterday afternoon as 55,000 spectators peered down on the bewildering panorama spread on the green plain below.

The phrase 'Four Horsemen' caught the imagination of the whole country. A local press photographer at South Bend commandeered four horses, sat the four heroes on their backs complete with helmets and footballs under each arm, and made a fortune syndicating it across the Republic. The legends surrounding their prowess on the football field multiplied a thousandfold. Years after they had stopped playing their personalities were news, reminiscences of their playing days treasured. They were certainly very good indeed; as a backfield combination, Harry Stuhldreher, the quarter-back, Don Miller and Jimmy Crowley, the half-backs, and the full-back Elmer Layden, first played together in 1922, and in the three seasons during which they dominated the team at Notre Dame they won every game but two. All were well enough respected to be offered lucrative coaching positions after graduating, and three of them had short and relatively uneventful careers in the pro game.

But even in those heady days, no one would have denied that the triumph was Rockne's. Lucky enough to have four such talented players together at Notre Dame in the same years, he had moulded them into an attacking force of great power. And if the spotlight refused to budge from the four heroes behind the scrimmage line, it was the untiring work of the linemen —lugubriously dubbed The Seven Mules—who gave the Horsemen the room to strike. Captain of this legendary Notre Dame team was one of the Mules, the centre Adam Walsh, a player every bit the match of the Horsemen and placed alongside them in Football's Hall of Fame. He led the charges from the front and is best remembered for breaking a hand against Indiana one week, insisting on playing against the Army the following week in the match that Grantland Rice was to write into legend, breaking the other hand in the first few minutes and passing the ball faultlessly for the rest of the triumphant game. He must have felt slightly piqued that the Bible hadn't provided for Five Horsemen of the Apocalypse.

The winter of 1924–5 was a watershed for more than the emergence of college football's unbeatable legend. Two other entirely unconnected events of that football season in America provide us with a link between the cradle days of American Football and the big-money, all-ticket, TV-spectacular football of the 1970s. First, Walter Camp died. He died, of course, with his boots on, attending, as he always did, the annual Rules Committee meeting in New York, still directing the game he had virtually invented and which had changed out of all recognition since he had first, as a brash young undergraduate, tried to railroad an intercollegiate football convention.

Until his death he had retained a keen interest in football at Yale; it was at his advice—and his advice by the 20th century was virtually a command from the mountain-top—that Yale had built their tremendous bowl; and in the early years of the century he coached them in the successful mould of the Yale steamrollers of the 1880s and 1890s. As a rulemaker he had been indispensable; he had been chairman of the Committee until 1911; he had edited the annual *Football Guide* from the day in 1883 when the intercollegiate convention resolved that 'Mr Camp copyright and print the football rules' until his death, transforming a necessary handbook of the game's baffling and fast-changing laws to an almanack of immense authority.

Perhaps most significantly of all, Camp had become, almost by chance, the prime judge of excellence of American Football. The game's one disadvantage, which has remained a disadvantage and will probably always do so, was that America had no other country to play against on an international basis. So while half-hearted and generally arbitrary methods have been devised for determining the best team in America in any particular season, the question of naming the best possible team picked from every

player in the country has remained a purely academic exercise. Nevertheless, it is an exercise that Camp and Caspar Whitney devised as early as
1889, and which became established in no time as the game's one worthwhile accolade.

Camp and Whitney called their selections—eleven players, four line
substitutes and four backfield substitutes—the All-America team; and
from 1898, when Camp moved to *Collier's* magazine, the oracle spoke forth
every year, all-knowing, all-seeing, evaluating on paper the college
careers of several thousand young footballers, most of whom he had never
seen, and granting just a handful of them, every year, the end-of-season
Christmas present of football imortality. There were, from the earliest
days, dozens of contradictory imitations; but Camp's prestige was such
that there was never any question as to which list was 'official'. (It was
appropriate, and another of the curious quirks of 1924-5, that on Camp's
death the *Collier's* column was handed over to the year's other great
purveyor of immortality, Grantland Rice.)

College football did not, of course, die with Camp, just as it did not die
with the graduation of Notre Dame's Four Horsemen. But the arrival of
Harold Grange in 1924 ensured that college football was to take an increasingly minor role in the headlines, in the stadiums and in the public's
imagination.

The game that made Red Grange the most talked-about individual in
America took place, by a quite monumental coincidence, on the very same
afternoon as the game that made the Four Horsemen the most talked
about quartet in America. The Four Horsemen were at the Polo Grounds
in New York making mincemeat of Army; Grange was some 750 miles
away at the inaugural game of the new stadium at Champaign, Illinois,
playing half-back for the University of Illinois against the University of
Michigan. And in the space of twelve minutes in the first quarter of that
game, Grange turned in the most spectacular piece of individual running
the game had seen: in those twelve minutes he ran for four touchdowns
on the only four occasions he touched the ball, without a single Michigan
hand being laid on him. And these were some touchdowns—not catches
from a quarter-back's pass trotted over from the 1-yard line, but full-
powered gallops of 93 yards, 67 yards, 56 yards and 44 yards respectively.
The blocking of his own linemen was superb, but the way he exploited it
was unprecedented. After the fourth touchdown his coach, Bob Zuppke,
'the Little Dutchman', staggered both Grange and the crowd (and, one
assumes, the red-faced Michigan defence) by taking Grange out of the
game for twenty minutes or so ('No Michigan man laid a hand on you,'
he told Grange 'and I want you to come out unsoiled.') He unbarred the

cage in the third quarter when Grange ran for a fifth touchdown, and again in the final period when Grange, for a change, threw an 18-yard pass for one of his colleagues to score.

From that afternoon to the end of his career he was the most hunted man in the game; writers, spectators, photographers hounded him wherever he went. His blue and orange shirt, with the famous 77 on the back, became so celebrated that Illinois 'retired' the number when Grange left the University; and in his three years on the Illinois team he gained more ground than any other college player in history—3,647 yards.

Great college players had, of course, emerged before; they had briefly captured the imagination of sports writers, earned themselves enough prestige to ensure the offer of a good career when their college days were over and then became accountants and salesmen and real-estate dealers, and occasionally left a piece of the legend behind on college honours boards and year-books and silverware. Over the last few years, it was true, the occasional tough young graduate would follow his three years on the team with a lucrative season or two in the industrial towns of Ohio and Pennsylvania and Michigan, playing football for money in the burgeoning but hardly attractive world of the professional game; but as yet the sports writers and the crowds followed the big college boys, and Pottsville Maroons *v.* Dayton Triangles, hard and exciting though their football might be, caused not a stir when compared to the allure of, say, Cornell *v.* Penn. State.

But in 1925 Red Grange, that winter the biggest single name in the whole of American sport, was signed by Chicago Bears to play pro football. His debut in Chicago against the Cardinals attracted a capacity crowd of 36,000. A week later the Bears travelled to New York to play the Giants, and 68,000 were crammed into the Polo Grounds to see the Galloping Ghost. Grange and the Bears then undertook a coast-to-coast tour that launched the rise of professional football from its small-town, money-grubbing origins to America's most popular spectator sport.

The formative years of the American game, as far as the central organisation was concerned, had differed from the British, Irish and Australian experience in that there was no initial governing body. In Britain the Football Association and the Rugby Union, though to a great extent manned by men who had been at public school or university together, forer formed specifically to govern football clubs, whether they were wemed by stockbrokers, coalminers, weavers or Lancers. In the United States the only bodies empowered to make rules were all appointed by the colleges, from the colleges for the good of the colleges. For this reason alone the heart-searching over the coming of professional games-playing, which had worried the F.A. and, more particularly, the Scottish F.A. for years, and which had completely demoralised the Rugby Union in the 1890s, barely touched America at all. It was understood that if a man was at college reading for a degree he was eligible to play football for that college; he was not, it was also understood, going to receive any sort of salary for playing football for his college, but no inquiry was going to be made into whether or not his academic abilities were up to scratch, or whether his bills were paid by his parents or the football fund, or whether he attended quite so many classes as his less talented fellow students, or even whether or not he had been at a different university altogether the previous term.

But outside the universities there sprang up dozens of clubs, particularly in industrial towns of the northern states, whose players had never been to college and who never would go, and whose desire to play the game that they might possibly have seen played on the local campus stemmed from the same urges that made Lancashire cotton-weavers take to the gentlemanly game of Soccer and Welsh miners make a second religion of the public-school-dominated Rugby. These clubs, organised on the most rough and ready basis but generally formed round a small-town community centre or factory or mine, took their rules and regulations from the Intercollegiate Committee, and formed a number of lasting and fruitful rivalries among the coal tips and the rolling mills. The rivalries produced a desire to win, which in turn promoted the search for star players to bolster the efforts of the local team. And, as they found in Lancashire when the Scots professors came south to teach the English how to play Soccer, the way to employ star players is to offer them a job, find them a house, and slip them a few dollars when the team does well.

These teams, often starting their existence as 'Athletic Clubs', were every bit as keen to entice the young giants away from the Eastern campuses as, in the 20th century, Rugby League scouts were concerned enough to tour the Rugby fields of the Rhondda. And their pull was immense. The fast-growing American college system, coupled with the pride of the immigrant and his determination to give his sons a good education in the New World, meant that many young men were entering their final year at college with no parental money to fall back on. On top of that, the prospect of leaving the game altogether having, within two or three short years, become proficient in its intricacies, can only have made an actual offer to carry on playing football for high wages extremely tempting, even in spite of the prospect of living in an obscure and grubby town in Pennsylvania and receiving none of the adulation that the college hero was becoming accustomed to. Indeed, some of the heroes were not above taking a day off school for a few dollars. In 1892, well before the first documented all-professional football game took place, the Yale guard 'Pudge' Heffelfinger was paid $500 to play in a match between two Pittsburgh athletic clubs.

Some of the toughest of these ex-college players found their way onto the payroll of the first two major Athletic Club teams to emerge as professional sides—the Pennsylvania towns of Latrobe and Greensburg. Latrobe, sponsored by the local Y.M.C.A., are credited with staging the first pro football game in 1895, hiring a college quarterback for $10 plus expenses, sharing out the take among the players themselves, and beating the equally obscure town of Jeanette, Pennsylvania, 12–0.

Throughout the latter part of the 1890s the professional prospered in the hard industrial confines, attracting a modest but gradually increasing share of spectators to what soon became a fiercely competitive series of local derbies. Remember, this was the time when the college game was undergoing a radical transformation, both in its rule-making and its organisation, because of the violence encouraged by the laws and the subsequent crop of serious injuries. In the universities the violence was tempered by a certain good-natured give-and-take spirit among the students. In the professional game violence tended to be met with violence, and the most awe-inspiring tales from the Pennsylvania days concern the blacking of eyes, the ancillary fist-fights, and the legendary viciousness of Lawson Fiscus, ex-Princeton half-back and the first man to admit taking a weekly payment ($20) for playing football for Greensburg. His other claim to immortality is having broken the jaw of an opponent by deliberately kicking him in the face as he lay prostrate on the ground.

The clashes between Latrobe and Greensburg, conducted in a fever of Cup Final proportions, frequently developed into all-in fights involving spectators, umpires and hot-dog salesmen as well as the players themselves. The mêlée was traditionally followed with the aggrieved team breaking off all relations with the other. But there was no doubt that violence was good business, and the following year the fever would be whipped up once more and the battles renewed. And the professional football stage in those days allowed for the kind of involved local support that America cannot provide any more.

Professional football, baseball, ice-hockey and even basketball are now confined primarily to the big cities, and their progress followed largely on television. For those few years before the money became too big to be invested in small towns, the supporters of Latrobe or Greensburg or Massillon, Ohio, or McKeesport, Pennsylvania, could watch their mer-

cenaries plough into those of a rival town, put their money on the result
and dance through the streets in drunken triumph ('Aristocrats embraced
miners and thought nothing of it', wrote an enthusiastic Latrobe editor
after a famous victory over Greensburg, thus shrugging off, in his jubilia-
tion, the scoop of a century—the discovery of an aristocrat in Latrobe).
Greensburg countered such occasional setbacks by hiring, in 1897, the
entire backfield quartet from Lafayette—Best, Barclay, Bray and Wal-
bridge (whom the Latrobe supporters—nudged, could it be, by the class-
conscious editor—renamed Bitch, Bastard, Bugger and Whore), and by
signing the first of the great stars from the Carlisle Indians School,
Isaac Seneca, the first Indian to be named as an All-American by Walter
Camp, and believed by some, who presumably had attempted to tackle
neither of them, to have been faster and stronger than Jim Thorpe.

In the first two decades of the new century, pro football prospered
modestly in the shadow of the college game, kept pace with the rule
changes, squabbled over fees with young college graduates and, in the
uncertain financial climate, flowered, faded and died from year to year.
The spotlight—dim as it then was—passed from Western Pennsylvania
to Philadelphia, to up-State New York, to Chicago and to Ohio. In
Philadelphia Connie Mack organised the Athletics, who travelled throughout the East in 1902 playing a lot of football for very little money, tempting
the crowds with such gimmicks as playing a baseball star, Rube Waddell,
in his line-up, and claiming the championship of the just-born and already
almost dead National Football League by beating Pittsburgh in a decider
in December. In the same year, with the game still starved of spectators,
pro football staged their first indoor game—at Madison Square Garden,
New York—and their first game under lights—at Elimira, New York—
without making any spectacular profits.

In Ohio, Canton's Bulldogs and Massillon's Tigers took up the small-
town rivalry that Latrobe and Greensburg had by now, with neutral
referees, tighter rules and an unnaccountable opposition to twenty-two-
man brawls, allowed to fade. The Bulldogs poached players from the
Tigers, and the Tigers from the Bulldogs, and in 1904, along with the less
famed Akron Club, they both got into a bidding auction for what all
assumed to be the plum of the year, the backfield ace from Michigan,
Willie Heston, star of Yost's point-a-minute team of 1901.

Heston demanded a fee of $1,200 for ball-carrying in the pro game,
a figure that sent the club owners into tears of incredulous laughter, and
consequently he played for no one that year. The following season the
Canton Bulldogs craftily approached Heston and lured him for a mere
$600 (or an astronomical $600, depending on the point of view) to play

in the Massillon game. The result was the sort of nightmare that has haunted high-spending professional football managers throughout the century: the first time Willie Heston touched the ball and began one of his celebrated runs, he tripped on the frozen ground, fell flat on his face, and received the entire complement of the Massillon defence on the back of his neck. His running gained not a single yard for the Bulldogs, who lost the game 14–4. He played again once as a professional, broke his leg, and retired for good. If his college feats and his dramatic, big-money signing had woken the general public up to the growing realities of pro football, his ignominious pro career soon led them to forget it again.

But not for very long. In 1915 Canton Bulldogs bought Jim Thorpe, and paid him to set about building a real football team.

Thorpe's career since he had been discovered by Pop Warner at the Carlisle School had been a sensation. He had officially finished his time at the School in 1909, and had retired, everyone thought, to his home in Oklahoma. Then in 1911 Warner wrote to Thorpe, telling him that if he returned to Carlisle for a year for training there was a very good chance of his making the American team for the Stockholm Olympic Games of 1912. Thorpe accepted, trained most of the winter by playing tremendous football for Carlisle, was persuaded by Warner to continue his athletic training the following summer (Thorpe wanted to give the whole thing up to play professional baseball), trounced the field in the Decathlon at Stockholm by the fantastic margin of 700 points with a total that wasn't matched for fifteen years, and returned to play football at Carlisle.

It was in this season that Dwight D. Eisenhower remembered playing for Army against the Indians; Eisenhower and another linebacker were instructed to follow Thorpe wherever he went; in the third quarter of the game they both hit Thorpe so hard that the pair of them were dazed and were taken out of the game by their coach. Thorpe played on to the end.

Later that winter it was revealed that Thorpe had, indeed, played some very minor baseball for some very modest rewards while home in the South in 1910. His Olympic honours were stripped away, though his impact on the Olympics will never be forgotten, and he was snapped up to play baseball for the New York Giants—the one part of his career that flopped.

But as the playing coach with Canton Bulldogs, Thorpe hit his peak. The Bulldogs of the First World War years not only ran over Massillon, they ran over everyone. Thorpe brought in a star quarter-back, 'Greasy' Neale, and two or three other hard men, and bet whole fortunes—$2,500 a game sometimes—on his ability to win matches with them. Thorpe not only ran fast enough to win Olympic titles, he ran hard enough to steamroller a tackler, like a lorry flattening a Mini, or lightly enough to sidestep and dummy in the traditions of Britain's much more delicate game of Rugby. And in defence he was devastating: the theory that he wore a shoulder pad of lightly padded steel to ram into anyone who tried to pass him was never actually proved, but it was not entirely a product of the imagination of those players who had felt his tackle—'like being hit with the blunt end of a telegraph pole', one of them put it. The alternative story was that Thorpe didn't actually need padding—he just enjoyed felling opponents so that they stayed felled; but he was playing three or four games a week in those days, and a little shoulder protection would have been understandably welcome by the end of the season.

If Thorpe had given pro football a touch of the class that it so desperately needed, the game still lacked an organising genius to create a championship and a fixture card among the best clubs—the only sure way of capturing sustained public interest. The barnstorming pro teams pulled in an occasional good crowd, but too often the best pro footballer aped the hired gun-slinger, selling his skills to the highest bidder and changing teams after every other game. The Columbus Panhandles, from Ohio's State capital and enjoying greater loyalty than most clubs by the clever expedient of having no fewer than seven members of the Nesser family in their 1916 line-up, swore that in that season they played against Knute Rockne six times—and each time he was in a different shirt.

The organising talent emerged at the end of the War. George Halas, son of two Bohemian immigrants, was brought up on Chicago's West Side; a highly promising baseball batter, he had injured himself during his first game for the New York Yankees and turned to football where he played end with the Hammond Pros of Chicago in 1910. The piece of luck that lifted Halas from run-of-the-mill player to great innovator came in March 1920 when a well-heeled factory owner from Decatur, Illinois, who had made his money out of corn by-products, decided that it would do his ego good to own a pro football team. A. E. Staley, the factory owner, proposed to call the team the 'Staley Starchmakers' and to pay Halas to run it, to play baseball for the firm's team in the summer, to be general athletic director at the works, and in his spare time to learn how to make starch.

Staley's deal specified that anyone Halas hired for the team could have a year-round job at the starchworks and, most attractive of all, could practise for two hours a day in company time, this in days when pro players were often having to work overtime to keep themselves in food. This was near-luxury; within weeks he had gathered at the starchworks a formidable nucleus of college graduates eager for a job and a chance to go on playing football, particularly in a situation like this one where the preliminaries for each game did not involve financial bickering with a hard-up club owner. But the lack of a recognised machinery for securing fixtures was something of a handicap for a newly formed team. Halas proposed, in a letter to Ralph Hays, manager of the powerful Canton Bulldogs, that some of the best teams might get together to form a League. (It is a measure of Halas's determination that he included his team among 'some of the best' before they had ever played a match.)

Here the story becomes the subject of some dispute. In Halas's account Hays agreed to the meeting; so did Cofall of the Massillon Tigers, and on 17 September 1920, the managers of eleven professional clubs, assembling in a car showrooms at Canton, Ohio, formed the American Professional Footballers Association, elected as president apparently the first name that came into their heads, which happened to be that of Jim Thorpe, and awarded a total of eleven one-hundred-dollar franchises.

So informal was this initial agreement—no minutes were kept and no records survive—that it is not altogether surprising to find two other quite different accounts of the formation of the Association. Both of these put the meeting in Ralph Hays's car showrooms not in 1920 but in July 1919, about a year before Halas had his first whiff of starch and was still on the books of the Hammond Pros; these accounts list only five teams represented, four from Ohio (Dayton, Canton, Massillon and Columbus) plus Rochester, N.Y.; and they put the initial franchise at $25. One account says Jim Thorpe was at the meeting with Hays, and was elected president on the spot; the other that no president was elected until the following season, when, all are agreed, the franchise *was* $100 and the Association had swelled to eleven clubs. Certainly in 1919 no 'league' as such was organised, and even in the 1920s it was too late to organise a fixture list by which all the members played all the others. Whether or not, as he claims, the idea for an organised league did come from Halas, he certainly did everything to make it a success.

The additional six teams which made up the Association in 1920 also came from the industrial belt below the Great Lakes: from Cleveland, Ohio; Muncie and Hammond, Indiana; from Rock Island, way out West in the geography of pro football, on the western borders of Illinois; plus the Chicago Cardinals and the Staley Starchmakers, whom Halas had saved from total embarrassment by persuading Mr Staley to change the name to the Decatur Staleys.

The Staleys had a highly successful year in 1920; the starch business, however, was feeling the first effects of what was to become the 1921 Depression. Staley had no alternative but to axe the football club from the company's expense sheet, but he was generous enough to give Halas $5,000 and suggested they move the 150 miles or so to the Chicago flesh-pots, and asked only that they should retain his name in the team title for one more season.

Halas, ever with an eye to the main chance, worked out an extremely businesslike deal with the owner of Chicago's most famous baseball ground, Wrigley Field. He had to pay the owner fifteen per cent of the gate receipts, but was charged no regular rent and was even granted the profits on the scorecards. By the end of 1921 the Chicago Staleys were drawing creditable crowds of up to 12,000, winning the first properly organised professional football title, and making George Halas very happy to show a mere $71.63 loss on the season. '(Go back to the railroad, George,' said his mother, 'it's a steady job.') Losses were the rule rather than the exception. Of those original seven franchise holders of the 1920 season only the Chicago Staleys, which Halas renamed the Bears in 1921, now survive in the city where they first competed. The Chicago Cardinals are still living, having undergone major transplant surgery in 1960 to become the St Louis Cardinals. The rest—the great names of Canton and Massillon and Akron and Dayton, the upstart unknowns of Muncie and Rock Island—have faded and died. And many another such small business, for these teams were run with little more economic organisation than a hamburger stall, rose in their place, only to fall away as fast.

There was one exception, a small, insignificant town on the shores of Lake Michigan, a cold, unlovely port open to the winds screaming straight off the Canadian Arctic and subject, towards the end of each football season, to the most awesome of low temperatures. Green Bay, Wisconsin, was little more than a trading post in 1921, with a population of just 30,000 and not much to keep them there apart from some fishing in the cold waters of the Lake and the alternative of a job in the Indian Packing Company. As the little, fly-by-night clubs came, bought a set of jerseys, played a few seasons and faded away, Green Bay followed the pattern. A young local ex-Notre Dame player, who couldn't face the idea of giving the game up, persuaded the president of the Packing Company to sign away $500 for equipment, and acknowledged receipt by naming the club the Green Bay Packers.

In a town of 30,000 souls there was never any likelihood that the team would make ends meet. Curly Lambeau—the Notre Dame player—and his co-founder, a newspaperman with unfailing energy and a florid style called George Calhoun, managed to collect a few dollars as the Packers thrashed what little opposition Wisconsin had to offer, and scraped together enough to buy a franchise in the N.F.L. in 1921. Incredibly, they have been there ever since. From being a remote and unremarked fixture in the season's roster for the giants of Akron and Rochester, the Packers became a better-known name than the town they came from, better-known even than the state that they conquered in their early days.

The Packing Station went out of business within a couple of years of the Club's foundation, but a keen-witted local businessman helped the Club out of its inevitable financial difficulties, and hit on a plan that might have saved a dozen unfortunate clubs in the 1920s; in the certain knowledge that nothing stirred an American more than property, he exploited a nice line in capitalist democracy by selling the Club to the townspeople—five dollars a share with an understanding that there would never be a dividend and a guarantee that the Club would not be sold or transferred without the consent of a two-thirds majority of the shareholders. With the whole town football-crazy since about 1922, the chances of that happening are beyond imagination.

In the subsequent fifty years the Green Bay Packers have maintained the phenomenon. They have won everything that can be won; they have taken more National Football League championships than anyone else; and they have remained since the mid-1920s by far the smallest community in the country to maintain a top-ranking professional football team. There is no equivalent in Britain. Featherstone Rovers, perhaps, one of the more feared of the Yorkshire Rugby League teams, have regularly crashed through to League and Cup honours from a minute mining town. But Featherstone is pitched right in the centre of Rugby League country; surrounded by the might of the thirteen-man game; there is no reputable football team within two hundred miles of Green Bay. Green Bay could have happened in England if a team in St Ives, in the west of Cornwall, had started playing professional football in, say, 1890, had reached the First Division and won a couple of F.A. Cup Finals by 1905; had provided two or three members of the England team for most of the century, and had been a regular competitor in European football since 1960. And, most important of all, pulled in 40,000 gates at every home match from the whole of the Cornish peninsula, sometimes in temperatures thirteen degrees below zero. This is the achievement of the Packers, which without the chaotic and basically unco-ordinated start of the professional football circuit could never have happened.

While the early supporters of Green Bay were contributing to their own small slice of history, back in the real world George Halas and the Chicago Bears were winning a lot of football games—the team finished second in the league three times in a row following their first championship in 1921 —and at the same time failing to make any real money. Like every other team in the business at this time the Bears were playing tremendous, hard-fought football with many of the stars of the college game on show only months—days sometimes—after leaving their passionately supported college squads, turning out in front of tiny crowds and half-empty press-boxes.

Then, in 1924, like everyone else in America who could read a news-paper headline, Halas read about the extraordinary feats of Red Grange. As the adulation grew over the following season, with immense crowds piling into the stadium of the University of Illinois just to catch a glimpse of the fabulous ball-carrier, Halas became increasingly certain that Grange was the one thing to bring the crowds to Wrigley Stadium. During his last year at Illinois, Grange, who had spent most of that summer trying to avoid men with chequebooks and a hungry look in their eyes, had formed a partnership with the manager of a cinema near the Illinois campus, a Mr C. C. Pyle. So astute did Mr Pyle prove in financial matters (he was nicknamed 'Cash and Carry' Pyle within months of his first association with football) that Grange signed for the Chicago Bears in an extraordinary deal: from the day of his joining the Bears, Grange would receive *half* the club's profits. (Halas once recalled that this amazing piece of optimistic profiteering was settled only after twenty-six hours' solid negotiating between him and Pyle; Pyle had sat down at the table demand-ing a full two-thirds.)

For once, the ballyhoo and the build-up were justified by events. Grange's first game was to be the Thanksgiving Day local derby between the Bears and the Chicago Cardinals. And, wonder of wonders, Wrigley Stadium closed its gates—on a capacity crowd of baying fans for whom, until that day, pro football had been a list of scores between reports of Notre Dame and Illinois University games. Immediately Halas threw Grange into a schedule of matches that brought to mind the barnstormings of Jim Thorpe's heyday—eight games in twelve days in which Grange was expected to prove to the entire United States that he was worth all the fuss.

After the Cardinals game, in which Grange was somewhat over-awed by the company and outwitted by the opposing kicker, who rarely let the ball get anywhere near the new star, the Bears beat the Columbus Tigers in front of another 28,000 fans. Next, they travelled to play a scratch team in St Louis where Grange cut through the bitter cold to score four characteristic touchdowns. In Philadelphia he bogged down a little in the mud, but scored both the Bears' touchdowns. And then, the very next day, to New York where the biggest crowd ever to have seen a football game fought to get into the Polo Grounds—73,000 of them, to watch a shattering battle in which the Giants, their pride stung by press jibes that they were just another chopping block for Grange to practise his runs on, gave the new star the roughest time of his whole trip.

Grange was exhausted by this time. Quite apart from the schedule of games, he was expected to be on hand for the reporters and the newsreel cameras at every stop; he was drawn, his eyes bloodshot, his body covered in bruises. But the profits got bigger with every extra fan, and Grange did not need even Mr Pyle to remind him that half those profits were his.

The next day, for the third day running, the Bears played again, a long train ride away in Washington. Grange, virtually at a standstill, collected a wrenched arm, a bloody nose and a badly bruised mouth. A couple of days later he had a poor game in Boston, and in Pittsburgh he collected a blow on the arm that put him out of that game and the next one too, in Detroit, where the announcement that he was not going to take the field caused a mass walk-out and the refund of thousands of dollars. And back in Wrigley Field for a return game against New York Giants Grange, determined to prevent another exodus, played with one good arm throughout the Bears's 9–0 defeat.

It had been one of the most crippling sporting tours ever undertaken; but it had proved that professional football need not necessarily remain a hand-to-mouth business relying on week-to-week turnstile takings to keep the team in hot showers and sticking plaster. There was enough potential in the game to justify the interests of big-money business, a far more stable base for a nationwide sport than a handful of football fanatics, however dedicated. And it had conclusively showed the college footballer that there was more to pro football than long train rides and bruises. From his first game with the Bears, Red Grange took home $12,000 as his share of the take. By the end of his first barnstorming tour, unimpressive though his play had been, he had also accumulated some $40,000 for endorsing various products and $300,000 for starring in a film that Holly-wood was to make when he had a week or two to spare.

The success of this tour, and of an even more successful one that the Bears undertook the following summer, when Grange's arm had mended and he finally came into his own with some of the elusive running and point-scoring that had made his name, may have been the turning point in the professional game, but it was not the end of money troubles. As suddenly as the Bears had discovered their running gold mine, so they lost him. It was possible that Halas had not played his cards as sensibly as he might have done; certainly Grange might have enjoyed his years with Chicago Bears had the blocking, to protect him from the opposing tacklers, been as fanatical, as well organised and as selfless as it had been at the University of Illinois. Had Halas paid these unsung linemen just a little more than the customary pittance while Grange was taking home $3,000 a game, this protection might just have been that much more forth-coming.

Whatever the reasons—and the financial ambitions of Mr C. C. Pyle must have been largely responsible—in 1926 he and Grange broke with the Bears. And instead of inviting a small financial disaster by merely starting their own team (Pyle wanted to do this, in fact, but he was refused a franchise by the N.F.L.), they virtually guaranteed an astronomical disaster by starting a whole new league.

The American Football League of 1926 was one of the biggest organisa-tional shambles in sporting history: Pyle and Grange founded both the New York Yankees and the Chicago Bulls, with Grange playing for the Yankees, and seven other teams contested the new league. There is a superb photograph that survives of a game played during these few chaotic months. It is of an isolated moment in the meeting between Grange's Yankees and the Boston Bulldogs. Racing out of the picture, clearly outpacing all the opposition, is the powerful, high-stepping athlete with the famous '77' on his back, on his way to a 55-yard touchdown—the sort of inspired, elusive running on which the Grange legend was founded, and that a year before would have had 50,000 fans on their feet roaring him on from the bottom of their throats. It is the background of the photograph that tells the pathetic tale; in the vast bank of tiered seats in the huge stands of the stadium there are about fifteen lonely spectators dotted about.

Some of the 1926 A.F.L. teams did not even finish the season; all of them ended 1926 in debt; the league collapsed in confusion, and even the big boys in the National League felt the pinch. In 1926 there were twenty-two teams in the N.F.L.; by 1927 there were just twelve, and only the Yankees had survived from the A.F.L. (They too collapsed after two more seasons; Grange went back to the Bears, and played a useful part as a defenceman for a number of years.)

After all the furious activity in the pro game of the mid 1920s, it is some-what surprising that it took so long to consolidate its hold on the crowds. True, within a couple of years America plunged into the depression and football franchises felt the same pinch as everyone else, but there were years in the mid 1930s when, despite the undoubted talents of the players, the imagination of the franchise-holders and one or two supposedly crowd-pulling rule changes to 'open up' the game, it really looked as though professional football on any officially organised scale might fade away altogether—a fate that would have been quite an extraordinary slap in the face to all American traditions of flamboyant showmanship.

The game still threw up the occasional hero whose name would burn brightly for a season or two, sometimes even longer. The otherwise obscure Duluth Eskimos had bought Ernie Nevers, the Stanford full-back, in the year of the abortive American Football League, and had embarked on a schedule barely less demanding than the Grange barnstorming. Nevers played 29 games in 112 days, missed only 27 minutes of the action and played one game with appendicitis, still managing to throw the running touchdown pass. Three years later he set one of the longest lasting of pro football records in scoring every point for Chicago Cardinals in their 40–6 defeat of their local rivals, the Bears.

The Bears themselves added Bronko Nagurski to their list of stars, an almost unstoppable running back who was equally effective as a tackle and, with an uncanny knack of unloosing the unexpected forward pass just as the defence were massing to resist his charge, he gained a reputation for unequalled all-round excellence. And in the mid 1930s Green Bay, whose early championships, worthy though they were, were often based on percentage points gained at the expense of clubs that played none of the other members of the League, introduced a tall, underfed end from Alabama called Don Hutson, who could apparently catch anything thrown at him however fast he happened to be running at the time, and who kept Green Bay at or near the top of the now much more competitive tree for ten years.

In the 1930s, once again at the instigation of George Halas, the National Football League finally broke with the Intercollegiate Rules Committee; their own rule-changes, they thought, could attract a few more people to fill those empty seats. They finally adopted the unrestricted forward pass—one per play from any point behind the line of scrimmage—which meant a lot more quarterback passing and, theoretically, a lot more touchdowns; they moved the goalposts forward from the back of the end zone to where it stands in every other Rugby-based game—on the goal line—with a resulting rise in kicks at goal; they moved the centre of the scrimmage line away from the touchlines, to open the game up further. And between 1925 and 1935 they reduced the size of the very tool of their trade—the ball itself. Aware that the forward pass was going to be the saviour of the game as a crowd pleaser, and equally aware that only the most talented backs could throw an accurate torpedo pass with the squashed melon that they had played with to date, the ball was slimmed down to a mere $21\frac{1}{4}$ inches round the fatter part; the ends were more pointed, and in the hands of an expert it now behaved like a well-balanced dart.

College football had remained keen, well-disciplined and well supported in the face of the professional game, but the poaching of stars, the constant prowling of scouts for the major league teams, did nothing for the confidence of college players and wrought a lot of harm in the academic results of a disturbing number of students. A rule in the late 1920s, by which the league agreed not to sign any college player before his graduation, had been only partially kept by the pro clubs (a rule that would, a couple of years earlier, have prevented the dramatic entry of Red Grange into the big time was not going to be popular with clubs whose owners spent whole nights dreaming of a similar coup). Then in 1935 Bert Bell, the Commissioner of the N.F.L., proposed a system by which all the League teams sat down together at the start of each season and picked, in turn, the college graduates of the year, with the team with the worst record from the previous season taking first pick. The college students could refuse the draft only if they wanted to give up football altogether; they could not hold out for a better club. (The first man picked by this system in its first year, 1936, was a half-back called Jay Berwanger from the University of Chicago. To the fury of the Philadelphia Eagles, the lowly club who had selected him, he refused to sign and never played football again.) The Draft had the desired effect of stopping the successful clubs becoming even more successful—and richer—by creaming off the talent with their cheque books. It was good for competition, too, and is retained in very much its original form today.

The last few years of the 1930s can be regarded as the last formative era of the professional game, which since the Second World War has, in effect, been reaping what was sown in these early years. Modern pro football was ushered in through these years by the rivalry of two great teams and the emergence of two great quarterbacks, whose jobs, now that the forward pass could be thrown from any position behind the scrimmage, became in every way the most vital on the field.

The first to arrive on the scene was Sam Baugh, a Texan who preferred baseball to football and who was persuaded by the owner of the Washington Redskins to arrive in the city in high-heeled boots and a ten-gallon hat. With football boots and a helmet on, Sammy Baugh showed the crowds just what a game American Football could be. There had never been a ball thrower like Baugh; and any quarterback today whose accuracy and daring and unpredictability make the crowds gasp is only piling up the debt he owes to Baugh. He could not only retreat behind the line, hand held high like the Statue of Liberty, to loose a fifty-yarder over the heads of the whole opposing defence; he could throw long and accurately while sprinting laterally in the opposite direction to the pass; and he would fire four, five or six passes in consecutive plays when the opposition were convinced that he *must* run next time. 'You gotta be able to hit the receiver in the eye every pass', warned the Redskins' coach when Baugh arrived from Texas. 'Which eye?' drawled Baugh.

He threw the Redskins to the top of the Eastern Division of the N.F.L. in 1937, and threw for three touchdowns in the title game to defeat Halas's Bears. And he was still throwing passes when the Korean War ended, fifteen years later—still slim and match-fit, still with the best eye and the strongest right wrist in the business. For those fifteen years the sporting press was littered with football photographs based on a single theme: in the foreground, a Redskin end, running full tilt, hands in an attitude of prayer and the ball looping into them; in the background twenty, thirty, forty yards away, the spare, helmeted figure of Sammy Baugh, throwing hand upraised, impervious to the futile grabbing hands of opposing linemen.

Strangely enough, the most celebrated game that Sammy Baugh played in was one in which he threw no touchdown passes and handed off for no touchdown runs. That was on 8 December 1940, when the Redskins and the Bears met once again in the title game. For some years George Halas had been unsatisfied with the chopping and changing of the formations behind the scrum, the slight variations in the position of the back four men at the snap which, they hoped, would confuse the opposition's defence. Everybody used some sort of variation of the T-formation —the quarterback behind the centre, the full-back behind him, and the half-backs as the arms of the T; but so many complex variations had been devised, complicated by the movements of the 'man in motion' (the one man allowed to be moving at the moment of the snap) that the T was barely recognisable any more.

In 1940 Halas and Clark Shaughnessy, who coached at Stanford University but who also worked with Halas at Wrigley Field, actually reverted to a wide-open, symmetrical, unadulterated T-formation that would have had Walter Camp and the pioneer coaches leaping about in their graves with excitement. The methods were simple. The quarterback took the ball straight from the hands of the centre, and handed it off to one of the backs running at speed. For variations he would throw or punt, but basically he was the calm man in the eye of a whirlwind, with no blocking duties and, if his cover was doing its job, nothing to fear from the opposing line. He was the brains of the attack, calling all the complexities of the play himself, and he was alive to every possible variation of movement in the field in front of him.

It needed a remarkable man to be a quarterback in these circumstances. The Chicago Bears had Sid Luckman, who had not even been a quarterback when he had played football at Columbia University, and who had to be coaxed and coached very carefully by Halas before he would even consider taking on the job at Chicago; by the time he gave the game up in 1950, his quick brain and sleight of hand were as unique to football as Sammy Baugh's right arm.

On that day on which Sammy Baugh failed to score, Sid Luckman never stopped. The Chicago Bears, their new-old T-formation working like clockwork, trampled all over the Washington Redskins in the most convincing drubbing the professional game had seen. Ten Bears went over for touchdowns, one of them twice, and they won by 73 points to nothing. Within five years almost every high school, college and professional team was using the T-formation; more young boys than ever before had given up dreams of home-runs for dreams of throwing touchdown passes, and professional football was suddenly becoming very popular indeed.

9

the television age

The World Game: 1945 to the present

The years since the Second World War, and particularly since the early 1950s, have seen Soccer progressing in two strangely inconsistent directions. As far as the essence of the game is concerned, the rules, the organisation, even the patterns made by footballers on the field of play, have remained virtually static. Football in the 1970s is the same game as football in the 1940s—faster, by all accounts; tactically more sophisticated (and consequently, it is argued, rather less exciting); individually more skilful, certainly in the middle and lower reaches of the professional leagues; but in no way a different game. Yet at the same time football has become, in many otherwise unrelated parts of the world, an obsession, a religion, an unrelenting preoccupation at every level of society.

Twenty-five years ago, it is true, Soccer had its full share of delirious fans; but their delirium was a release, a Saturday-afternoon expression of local loyalty, an experience shared among twenty or thirty thousand other supporters and discussed over the factory bench for the next five-and-a-half days of work. Today football is all-pervasive; it saturates the media, demands loyalties far beyond the Saturday cheering, clothes its young supporters in imitations of their heroes' playing strip and invests them with their heroes' traditional displays of petulance, stirs up hysteria at the merest hint of international competition, maintains as household names not only the local stars but the stars of other clubs, indeed of other nations, and embodies to the envious outsider all that is galmorous, desirable and successful in public life.

The transformation could not have happened without television; nor without the elevation of international competition for both clubs and nations to such a well-organised level that they regularly provide drama and revenue in equally generous shares. It would not be fair to Soccer to say that without television there would be none of this excitement; indeed, both the World and the European Cups were established without the benefits of television (though the latter competition did what it could in its formative months to interest European television networks, and did not have to wait long for the coverage it deserved). But without this interest the competitions could never have achieved the status they now enjoy, nor could the appreciation of the game, nor the wider loyalties dictated by the improved communications, have increased so dramatically.

The expansion of Soccer to an international game—as opposed to a game played in isolation all over the world—had been launched by the Olympic tournament in the early years of the century and by the Jules Rimet Cup since 1930; but the belated recognition of the World Cup by the original footballing nations in 1950 was countered by the boycott by the Iron Curtain countries, and the four-yearly display of nationalistic fervour, by such nations as at that time condescended to play against each other, took football away from, rather than nearer to, genuine international appreciation.

The European Cup was to achieve in time what national championships could clearly not hope to do—provide a regular, exciting insight into the skills, methods and attitudes of other nations' sportsmen, and a genuine extension of the European nations' own domestic competitions. In 1950 it would have been inconceivable that, within 20 years, the football fans of Manchester would know today more about the players of Lisbon or Amsterdam or Munich than they would about the players of, say, Bolton or Bristol. (Yet, conversely, were the footballers of Bolton or Bristol to be drawn against the footballers of Manchester in the course of the F.A. Cup, their faces, their lives, their careers and the astrological proclivities of their nearest and dearest would be the breakfast-reading of the football fans of Manchester for weeks prior to the game. Internationalism may be alive, but parochialism is by no means dead.)

In the early 1950s, while the British nations were learning that they were no longer the masters of Soccer, the European nations were doing what they could to reorganise their disrupted club competitions. A rather woebegone Zentropa Cup was contested in 1951 by those clubs from old Mitropa counties lying outside the Iron Curtain; a Latin Cup, proposed by Spain and Portugal, lost all attraction in its very first year, 1949, when the entire F.C. Torino party, containing a large proportion of the Italian national team and odds-on favourites for the new competition, died in the Superga air crash; the Latin Cup limped on for three more seasons, but was cancelled to make way for the World Cup in 1954, and Europe was again without a major club competition.

In December 1954 Wolverhampton Wanderers, the English champions who had beaten Moscow Spartak a month before at their home ground of Molineux, overcame a 2–0 half-time deficit to beat the touring Czechoslovakian champions, Honved of Budapest, by three goals to two; they were acclaimed by the *Daily Mail* as 'Champions of the World', an accolade only marginally more preposterous than those bestowed by the rest of the popular press. Less hysterical judgements (one had to leave these shores for them) put the match in perspective, pointing out that a visit by Wolves to Moscow and Budapest might give a clearer indication of the team's true qualities. But within days *L'Equipe*, the French sporting daily newspaper, had published details of a project for a European Cup, to be competed for by one representative of each Association, in home and away matches, played under floodlights in midweek. (*L'Equipe* also resurrected the old French proposal for a European League Championship without any real hope of having it accepted.) The European Cup found a lot of support from the Associations, though in the face of high-level fence-sitting by FIFA, by U.E.F.A., and by the French F.A., the Cup found itself without a willing organiser. It took a brilliant piece of bluff by *L'Equipe*, who formed their own executive committee to run the whole competition, to persuade FIFA to act, and U.E.F.A. reluctantly accepted the responsibility.

England's allotted representative for the first European Cup in 1955 was Chelsea, who had somewhat unexpectedly held on to win the English League from Wolves. But with a last characteristic grab at the fast-fading isolationism, the Football League forced the Londoners to withdraw with the excuse that participation would create too much congestion in the home fixture list. Parochialism, clearly, was not confined to the terraces. Scotland, however, not at that time noted for progressive thinking or for international success, entered Hibernian of Edinburgh who had finished only fifth in the Scottish League the previous season, but who exhibited a coolness and resourcefulness in their unaccustomed ambassadorial role in reaching the semi-final of the first European Cup.

So began an era of European competition that has flowered immeasurably in the years since, and which can only be counted a success. It has not, by itself, produced great teams, but it has proved the greatness of a number of teams that might never have received their due from posterity. No outsider, for example, in the 1950s could really claim to know how easy or how difficult it might be to win the Spanish League Championship —indeed, the regularity with which Real Madrid managed to carry off the trophy can only have thrown doubts on the depth of talent in the Spanish game. Yet Real Madrid won the European Cup against all comers for the first five years of the competition's existence, and reached eight of the first eleven European Cup Finals. Other unfamiliar names began to make themselves heard across Europe. Benfica, of Portugal, reached four finals in five years in the early 1960s, winning two of them; two rather better-known Italian clubs, A.C. Milan and Inter-Milan, shared a period of dominance in the mid 1960s; and Holland, a country whose national team had not qualified for the World Cup Finals since the war, produced a European Cup finalist in 1969, and the winner for the next four years.

British clubs can only have entered this competition—and the European Cup Winners Cup which followed in 1960, and the U.E.F.A. Cup, which had expanded from unpromising beginnings in the late 1950s—with considerable optimism. The English League, after all, was the hardest national competition in the world to win; with the English League title under their belts, the argument went, what had they to fear from short-tempered foreigners who had qualified in inferior competitions in the provincial wastelands of Europe?

The answers soon came. The English League, indeed the most taxing competition in Europe by virtue of its size—twenty-two efficient teams, meaning 42 hard league fixtures each season—was an immense task on its own. Such is the fierceness of the domestic competition that since 1950 only two teams have won the English League in successive seasons; none has won it in three successive years since the great Arsenal of the 1930s. To maintain a reasonable level of success in the English League leaves little opportunity for freewheeling to concentrate on the problem of a home-and-away fixture with a well-drilled team of multi-national ball-players from Italy. Another cruel lesson was that same one learnt so humiliatingly by England against the marauding Hungarians in 1953: it was not only the national sides of Europe who had discovered the individual flair and the managerial know-how to revolutionise the old footballing concepts; it was happening in the great clubs, too. Real Madrid were able to create an attacking machine of unbeatable skill round the genius of Alfredo di Stefano, who scored at least one goal in each of his club's five triumphant European finals between 1956 and 1960; the Milan teams built their success on rock-solid defences; Ajax of Amsterdam did it more recently on mid-field inventiveness and sharp striking.

Only one English club had proved its ability to live in this world with any consistency. Matt Busby built up a team—indeed, he built up two teams, one to be swept away, as Torino had been swept away, in an air crash, the other to rise out of the ashes—with the stamina and the intelligence to pace themselves through the rigours of an English League season and an English Cup run, and still have the flair to overcome the best that Europe could offer. Twice Manchester United reached the semi-finals of the European Cup in the 1950s, the second time only after the Munich air disaster. In the 1960s the reconstructed team again lost a semi-final before, finally, sweeping aside Benfica in extra time at the Wembley Final of 1968.

The previous year their fear had been anticipated by a British side in even more devastating form, Jock Stein's Glasgow Celtic; at the start of the 1965–6 season, when Stein took over as manager, Celtic had won only a single Scottish championship since the war, and had been doubly humiliated by the perennial domination of their arch-rivals, Rangers. From 1966 to the time of writing they had won every Scottish championship, and won the Scottish Cup five times; they won the European trophy by proving the only side in the competition capable of putting two goals through the massed defences of Inter-Milan, and increased speculation in Britain about the results they might achieve in a British League, when they would have to do weekly battle against teams of real calibre, rather than in the three-or-four team race into which the Scottish League had usually degenerated by mid December. (The sceptics—and these included large contingents of the rival Rangers fans, who had sat in front of pub television sets in Glasgow during the 1967 final roaring encouragement for Inter-Milan—were partially answered three years later, when Celtic met Leeds United, then with a good chance of the English League and the English Cup, and beat them in both legs of the European Cup semi-final.)

The late 1960s had seen a timely revival in British football; for ten years following England's defeat by the Hungarians the game had been in something of a decline; the very existence of World Cups and European competitions had tended to devalue the Home International competition, and if England beat Scotland 7–2 at Wembley in 1955, or 9–3 in 1961, it created a brief sensation, but it meant far less than it had done when England and Scotland taught the world.

All four home countries had qualified for the 1958 World Cup finals in Sweden—Wales and Northern Ireland both reached the quarter-finals, England and Scotland did not. (Scotland drew one game and lost their other two, a minor improvement on their performance in 1954, when they came away pointless and goalless from their two preliminary matches.) In 1962 England did reach the quarter-finals, as they had done in 1954, only to lose there to the eventual world champions Brazil. But British football had still barely woken up to the new implications of football abroad. Even after a decade of sporadic European club competition, the domestic league and Cup were still of paramount importance: tales of heroism and achievement meant Stanley Matthews's Cup winner's medal with Blackpool in 1952; or Bert Trautmann's display, keeping goal for the victorious Manchester City Cup Finalists in 1956 with a broken neck; or anything achieved or lost by Manchester United in the emotional weeks after Munich; or Tottenham Hotspur's Cup and League double in 1960–1961, the 'impossible' feat that had not been performed since 1897. But no talk of stirring deeds to show that Britain was holding her own against Europe; European Cup ties were games that happened in midweek under dim lights somewhere behind the Iron Curtain—games that we might see snatches of on television if the networks could come to some agreement and if the programme schedules could find a space for it. And they were also games that British clubs tended to lose.

Then, in the early 1960s, attitudes began to change. In 1961 the Professional Footballers' Association, having banged their heads for years against the Football League without success, at last achieved their long-standing objective, the abolition of the 'maximum wage'. Footballers could now, it was whispered, earn £100 a week, and their transfer fees—which had been escalating at a comparable rate to football-pool jackpots since the early years of the century—could soon top the £100,000 mark (five per cent of which went to the man who actually did the work); players tempted to follow such fortune-seekers as John Charles, Gerry Hitchens, Denis Law and Jimmy Greaves to the fleshpots of continental football could think again. Indeed, Greaves and Law came back to add their Italian experience to the prospering giants of the First Division; and the Finneys and Mortensens and Lawtons and Mannions smiled wry smiles and reflected on the meagre rewards that a career of crowd-pleasing had left them.

In 1963 Bill Nicholson's Tottenham Hotspur at last broke the European barrier by winning the European Cup-winners Cup with an overwhelming defeat of the holders, Atletico Madrid. And in the same year Alf Ramsey, a shy, withdrawn manager whose international career as a full back had included the chastening double experience of losing 1–0 to the United States at Belo Horizonte and 6–3 to the Hungarians at Wembley, but who had performed managerial miracles with Ipswich Town, was appointed England Team Manager in succession to Walter Winterbottom. The only thing that anyone can remember him saying on his appointment was that England were going to win the next World Cup.

Ramsey's 1966 achievement has been called unexciting, though few Englishmen remained unmoved during the last climactic week. It has also been called a cold, analytical victory, which it was, though coolness and analysis are the only way to triumph over teams with greater flair and equal skill. The World Cup of 1966, and many of the English League championships since, have been won by work rather than by brilliance. The Brazilians had dominated world football since the mid 1950s with a system that relied on a team geared to the thrust and the ball-playing genius of one or two stars; in 1966 they were kicked, brutally and un-ceremoniously, out of the competition before it really got under way, and

England took the world title by sheer running, by winning the ball ruthlessly in the middle of the field, and by the energy that could instantly convert an eight-man defence into a seven-man attack. It was a system that could afford to use Bobby Charlton, one of the world's great striking forwards since the late 1950s, as a decoy just as often as he was required as the key finisher, and it was good enough to beat the uncompromising defence methods of Argentina, the brilliant forward play of Portugal and the all-round talents—albeit slightly misdirected—of West Germany.

Hard on this World Cup victory, which put a temporary brake on the disturbing fall-off in attendance figures for English League matches, came Celtic's European Cup win in 1967 and Manchester United's European Cup in 1968. The same year an English team, Leeds United, won the European Fairs Cup (later renamed the U.E.F.A. Cup) for the first time, to be followed in successive years by Newcastle United, Arsenal, Leeds United again, Tottenham Hotspur and Liverpool without a continental side getting a look-in; from 1970 Manchester City, Chelsea, and Glasgow Rangers won the European Cup-winners Cup in successive seasons. The British clubs were impressively managed, in the main, by former footballers who had finished their playing days well before the abolition of the maximum wage, but who had been able to instil into this much more prosperous existence a hungry will to win; and in spite of an undistinguished 1970 World Cup (Scotland again failed to qualify, England went out disappointingly in the quarter-finals) when the individual flair of the Brazilians reasserted itself, and even less distinguished performances in two European Nations Cups in 1968 and 1972 and the elimination of England in the preliminary rounds of the 1974 World Cup it was clear that, on a general level, club football in Britain was the best organised in Europe, and demand for British managers among continental clubs, and British professional coaches all over the world, indicated that the original masters might not have lost all their know-how.

The 1966 World Cup had not, it must be repeated, been considered an exciting tournament. But throughout the world it had attracted, through advanced systems of communication, a television audience of unprecedented size, and had produced a tremendous popular reaction. The enthusiasm stemmed not only from the battles of the giants for the major honours, but from the performances of such outsiders as North Korea and Mexico. Soccer was given its biggest popular boost since the War—creating enormous interest among the less developed nations of the world, and at the same time touching off in the United States an experiment in sports promotion at once ambitious, well-intentioned and hilariously ineffective.

Soccer was not, of course, entirely new to the United States. There had been one sort of Association Football organisation or another since 1884, but attempts in the 1920s to promote professional Soccer had encountered even more apathy than the early professional American Football leagues, lacked the staying power and the vital college support of the home-grown game, and eventually died in the Depression. Even the sensational victory over England by a team of immigrant Americans in the 1950 World Cup—the ideal springboard for a domestic Soccer boom if ever there was one—failed to excite more than passing interest.

But after 1966 not one, but two rival groups began to battle, on good old capitalist principles, for the crowds they were convinced would clamour at the turnstiles and the television audience they believed would soon be demanding Soccer in prime time. The United Soccer Association, who were the official nominees of the U.S. National Football Association, would begin the summer of 1967 season with each club in the Association being represented, initially, by a European or South American club playing under the local colours—so Aberdeen became the Washington Whips, Dundee United the Dallas Tornados, Cerro of Montevideo was to be New York's home club; Sunderland were to represent Vancouver, Bangu, of Rio de Janeiro, were to play in the amazing indoor Houston Astrodome, Chicago were allotted Cagliari, the talented Italian League team, and so on.

The rival National Professional Soccer League, on the other hand, formed their own teams, usually with commercial backing and in many cases linked to baseball clubs, and signed a vast job lot of players from Europe—many of them dissatisfied with their present clubs or on the point of retirement—and lumped them together as best they could. There was a sprinkling of highly talented players among the dross—the Czech Kubala, Szimaniak of West Germany, Kostic of Yugoslavia, Phil Woosnam of Wales, Bill Brown of Scotland; but in the lower reaches the franchise-holders were forced to dig around the uncharted areas of West Indian and African football to make up the numbers.

The N.P.S.L. also caused comment by the radical rejection of the normal league points system; instead of the time-honoured 'two for a win, one for a draw, none for a loss', they decided they would award six points for a win, three for a draw, and a point for every goal scored up to a maximum of three. The decision, as Brian Glanville has indicated in his irreverent account of the American experiment in *Soccer: A Panorama*, was absurd. Far from promoting attacking football, as the promoters promised, it would positively demand defensive tactics from a team holding a one-nil lead, and thereby sitting on a potential seven points.

On almost every level both leagues were failures—even in that first heady season of 1967. The N.P.S.L., badly coached and unimaginatively recruited, was dull, dirty, ill-co-ordinated (there were insurmountable language difficulties within most of the hastily organised teams) and atrociously refereed. The U.S.A. League, where at least the teams were co-ordinated within themselves, promoted riots, ill-feeling and crippling fatigue for sides playing in the height of an American summer and flying hundreds of miles between every fixture.

American Football itself was plundered for some of the fringe absurdities. The leagues went mad on statistics, crediting players who passed the ball for scoring shots with 'assists', and totting up the 'saves' made by the goalkeepers. And much was made in the more conservative Soccer countries of the alleged collusion between players, referees and the TV men so that Soccer might have pauses for injury long enough to slip in the odd commercial.

Crowds remained desperately small. In the following year the two leagues, both of which had lost frightening sums of money on the venture, merged into the same organisation (while keeping their two distinct leagues); the franchise-buying of the early (and not so early) days of American Pro Football was rife: Golden Gate Gales of San Francisco merged with a Vancouver club; Kansas City took over Chicago Spurs, Los Angeles Toros became the San Diego Toros and so on. The standard improved: Santos, of Brazil, and Manchester City, the English champions, both lost matches on respective North American tours. But there was no saving the experiment. Even in New York it was rare for more than 3,000 to watch a game; in Detroit and Boston the clubs went into liquidation; one estimate was that every club in the Association had lost something between a million and three-quarters of a million dollars. At the end of the 1968 season the League was disbanded.

It had proved that in an era in which Soccer had become a highly successful branch of the entertainment business, even the very cradle of entertainment business know-how could not foist such a pre-packaged show on an unwilling public. A community, even in America where communities tend to be socially and racially more diverse than anywhere in Europe, can always learn to support its local team, to rejoice in local success, even to band together in local sporting adversity. But an alien game played by alien teams of alien players could never have excited real participation—imagine a determined promoter of Australian Rules Football dictating that, for the summer months of the next two years, eight Victoria State Clubs would represent Aberdeen, Dundee, Newcastle, Blackpool, Coventry, Cardiff, Southampton and Chelsea, would adapt local cricket grounds for their new league every Sunday, and would show matches on television. Financial disaster would be inevitable.

Perhaps the American Soccer experiment's one real success was to foster an already growing interest in the game in American schools where the qualities that have made it so attractive throughout the rest of the world—its adaptability, its simplicity and its independence of a strict organisation —have begun to make it an extremely popular game, with six hundred colleges already fielding major teams.

The professional game is not entirely dead, either. When everyone else had listened to their bank managers, packed up and gone home, three people hung on: Lamar Hunt, the millionaire of the tennis circuits, whose coffers were bottomless; and two Britons whose determination and optimism were boundless: Clive Toye, former sportswriter on London's *Daily Express* and Phil Woosnam, first player-manager (at 20,000 dollars a year) of the Atlanta Braves, enthusiastic football coach of the schoolchildren of Atlanta, and by the 1970s—still with the crew-cut he sported as a starved-looking schemer with Aston Villa—Commissioner of the North American Soccer League. The League's members were few and far between, their gates still ludicrously small; there was in 1973 still no league team west of St Louis, and of every twenty professional players, seventeen were still non-Americans.

But Woosnam was confident that a company investing in Soccer today would be showing fat profits by the 1980s. Soccer's American doldrums were not unlike the troughs from which pro football pulled itself in the industrial states in the 1920s. If the youth programmes begun by the existing clubs and the interest aroused in the high schools and colleges could make young Americans want to play football, it would not be long, as England and Wales saw in the 1860s and 1870s, before people would be paying to watch it being played well.

It was bad luck or bad management to mount the Soccer experiment in America at the precise time when American Pro Football was unified, confident, booming and more popular than it had ever been.

Twenty years before it was a different story; the old sequences of the 1920s were being repeated once again by businessmen who should have known better. In 1945 the professional Football clubs were battling for what, to a European, would have seemed a derisory public. The stands may not have been as empty as they had been when Red Grange ran in the ill-fated American Football League, but the whole of the N.F.L. had to be satisfied with a total attendance of about a million spectators; when we

realise that a million spectators per season would barely have been adequate to sustain a single First Division club in England in those days, it
seems scarcely credible that businessmen found the courage, the backers
and the confidence actually to start a rival pro Football league, the All-
American Football Conference, in 1946. Once again attention switched
from deeds on the football field to deals in the boardrooms. New York
and Chicago had now three pro Football teams each—far too much for the
patronage available. Miami lasted just one year in the A.A.F.C., and money
was scarce even though attendances were rising satisfactorily. Clearly the
clubs could not go on losing money—only one A.A.F.C. side in 1947
actually made a profit—and in 1949 the Conference went out of business,
and the four franchises that still remained intact merged with the senior
organisation to produce an expanded National Football League.

Principal among these four survivors were the Cleveland Browns—the
one indisputable benefit to accrue to the game from that short-lived
organisation. For each of the four years of the A.A.F.C. Cleveland were
the title winners (they continued their success the following year by beating Los Angeles Rams 30–28 in the title game to celebrate their first
season in the N.F.L.) and in that period had lost only four of their fifty-one
games. They were run by slender, balding, diffident ex-law student called
Paul Brown, who did more than anyone since the war to establish the
present pattern of American Football. Though he brought his team to
prominence through the ailing A.A.F.C., his methods there were so
sound, so direct and yet so original that they would soon become a text-
book system for virtually every coach in the game.

Brown was a dictatorial coach, but an extremely shrewd one, and one
with an unusual regard for the intellects as well as the physical skills of his
players. It had long been practice for every member of a Football team
to know off pat every move he might be called to make by his quarterback;
under Brown, the Cleveland players were expected to know not only their
own tasks, but the tasks of every other member of the team. Improvisation
was out; once the quarterback had called the play, everything followed
computer-like in its allotted place. This 'blueprinting' was not particularly
popular, particularly as it meant hours of compulsory and concentrated
note-taking in front of blackboard diagrams, something less than welcome
to football players used to a rather more cosseted existence. The squads
were regimented, living together, eating together, travelling together,
dressing alike, obeying a curfew on pain of a fine, both during the playing
season and, unkindest of all, during the long, muscle-hardening summer
training camps.

Brown revolutionised the recruiting system, too. Far from picking his players from the much publicised All-American lists or relying on the words of amateur scouts from the big-name colleges, he developed and trained a full-time professional scouting staff to cover, as far as possible, the whole of the United States. On the field—or, at least, on the touch-lines—Brown was as dictatorial as in the classroom; his meticulous planning was based largely on the forward pass, which Cleveland used with far greater frequency than other contemporary teams, and on the strong and accurate right arm of his quarterback, Otto Graham. But with his observers high in the stands and his own seat on the sidelines, Brown would insist on calling every play himself, allowing Graham to use virtually none of his own initiative, but sending out a lumbering replacement lineman after every play to pass on the coach's instructions in the huddle.

It was effective; it produced surprise plays in unheard-of situations, such as one celebrated forward pass thrown by Graham from inside his own end-zone to Mac Speedie on the line of scrimmage, who then ran ninety-nine yards for a touchdown; it gave Brown the ultimate in control over a game in which he was not actually playing. It made Cleveland the only profitable club in the old A.A.F.C. and the most successful in the enlarged N.F.L.—so successful, in fact, that the rival Cleveland Rams had been forced to sell their franchise to Los Angeles. But it also marked the closest point that American Football has come to chess and the farthest it has strayed from the other football games where teams' tactics can only be subordinate to individual skills and initiative, and where even the most regimented sides are made up of individuals rather than pawns.

No team since has been quite so shackled to the brain of its coach, but since the days of Paul Brown at Cleveland, no matter what skills the great individual players have displayed and no matter how they have been idolised from the stands, the coach's name has always been spoken in the same breath; team victory since Paul Brown has invariably been a coach's victory, and the victory of his subordinate staff—his offence coach, his defence coach, his special squad coaches, his masseurs and trainers, his tactical intelligence scouts, his talent scouts, his match observers and the communications team relaying strategic advice from various parts of the stadium.

The coach, however, has still had to find the crowd-pleasing individuals to spearhead his teams—heroes of the backfield willing and able to charge through opposing lines, to throw dramatic passes or to make a blistering end run. It is significant how great a proportion of those particular heroes since the war have been Negroes.

Football in America never went the blatantly bigoted way of major league baseball, which persistently refused in the 1920s and 1930s to sign coloured players to their clubs, and in the very early days of the pro game a number of strong, heavy Negroes played alongside white linemen as peaceably as anyone could play in a pro-football line in the hard, raw days of barnstorming professionalism. (One particular black lineman from Rutgers played three seasons of professional football in the early 1920s in Milwaukee, Akron and Hammond before deciding on a less punishing career as a cabaret singer—that was Paul Robeson's first job.) But from the mid 1920s until the end of the Second World War, though there was no official colour bar and though a number of gifted coloured college players were signed on by big clubs, there was a general feeling the coloured players didn't 'fit in'; they generally sat at different tables for meals, were housed in separate rooms from the white players; and, given the undeniable athletic strength of the American Negro, there were surprisingly few of them.

There was a thoroughly unprincipled (and unwritten) agreement on the foundation of the All-American Football Conference, that Negro players would not be employed; to his considerable credit Paul Brown took absolutely no notice of that ruling; from the start the Browns were liberally stacked with blacks, and Paul Brown's well-publicised insistence on his team living together as closely as they played together, as well as his team's apparent invincibility, went some way towards proving that integration was somewhat less disturbing to the squad than it was to the opposition, who discovered that having black linemen leaping at them was very similar to having white linemen doing the same thing—except that the black linemen tended to come a bit faster.

The black players' cause took its biggest boost in 1957, when Paul Brown signed a vast 6 ft. 2 inch, 16½ stone Negro with an 18-inch collar who could have become a heavyweight boxer, wanted to become a champion track athlete, and in fact emerged as the greatest of all football-carriers —Jim Brown, now a movie actor of some repute, in 1957 a full-back out of Syracuse University, New York State. He was as near unstoppable as any runner has been—and he ran and ran and ran, fearlessly, often painfully, but very successfully. Paul Brown would see that he was fed by the quarterback time after time; he would charge into the opposing cover and either be submerged or succeed in slashing through. He is said to have resented the punishment that his coach forced him to take in the line of duty, but in his first five seasons with the Browns he led the whole league in total yardage gained; in his career from 1957 to 1965 he gained 12,312 yards with the ball in his hands—his nearest rival is nearly 4,000 yards behind. By the time he retired he had become football's first black superstar, a term generally used to mean that the media were as obsessed with what he did off the field as with what he did on it, and the Negro's place in the game had been fully assured.

By now, too, Football was receiving the attention it had long threatened to claim. The crowds were coming at least within a respectable distance of filling the stadiums, and the power of television, tightening its grip on the most TV-conscious nation in the world, had finally been harnessed for the selling, rather than the exploitation, of football. Since the end of the War television had realised its potential ability to enhance a game rather than merely save a viewer the trouble of going to it. Over the years America had developed some of the best informed and best presented sports coverage, and Football was an ideal subject, particularly as a high camera position could embrace as much of the play as all of a coach's grandstand spotters put together. It had been ruled very early that live TV coverage should not be allowed in the catchment area of the home team—frustrating for those who could not make the journey, but an essential for clubs still relying to a great extent on gate receipts. (The one club to defy this convention, in 1950, was the Los Angeles Rams, who sold the full TV rights of all their home games. Their total attendance dropped from 205,000 in 1949 to 105,000 in 1950; coming to their senses the following season and conforming to the local 'blackout', they attracted 234,000 to their stadium.)

Later, in the 1950s and throughout the 1960s, television effectiveness increased with its technological advances—play-backs, slow-motion replays and supplementary camera points, abetted by the experience and expertise of the commentaries gave the game an even greater meaning to the fan and succeeded in teaching the finer points of an otherwise confusingly fast game to an ever-increasing public. In 1958 the play-off for the N.F.L. title, between the Baltimore Colts and the New York Giants, tied 17–17 at full time, provided a nail-biting eight minutes of sudden-death extra time that convinced both public and television executives in New York in a way that no amount of boardroom public relations could convince that it was football, and not baseball, that was to be the great television sport; and with this realisation, and the inevitable talk of big money that accompanied it, came yet another Football League after a slice of the cake.

This time the American Football League, as it was called, with franchises in Boston, Buffalo, Los Angeles, Denver, Houston, Dallas, Oakland and New York, had more cause than ever before to expect a return for their money. In their first year, 1960, despite a gate average of only 16,500 a game, a television contract netted each club 200,000 dollars, and with increasing interest in the game they were confident of much more to come.

What followed was a protracted series of financial and political squabbling; the new A.F.L. accused the N.F.L. of monopoloy and conspiracy in various areas of league expansion, player signing and television coverage—and lost their case. Meanwhile the Commissioner of the N.F.L., Pete Rozelle, had taken the game into the more rarified realms of politics by hustling through Congress a bill exempting football from possible monopoly charges (a well-founded fear, apparently, under the unfathomable anti-trust laws of the United States). The N.F.L. were winning all the way, the A.F.L. were running second best in press and television coverage, in receipts, in crowds, and in prestige. But the money rolled in. By 1964 the N.F.L. was collecting a little over 14 million dollars from C.B.S. for rights to televise all regular season games in 1964 and 1965; at the same time the A.F.L. signed away five years' games—1965–1969—for 36 million dollars.

Not until the mid 1960s did things begin to go right for the American Football League. In their early years, the attention paid to their exploits in the nation's newspapers was derisory. Promising young players were reluctant to sign with A.F.L. clubs, afraid that the league was too rocky to last; to mention their names in the same breath as the N.F.L. super-teams was sacrilege. But in 1963, the most derisory, shakiest and most despised of the A.F.L. teams began its transition from ugly duckling to swan.

The New York Titans were a national joke. They once had to withstand a players' strike because they couldn't pay the wages, and their playing record, in a city where success is everything and mere competence is counted as failure, was not even competent. In 1963, however, they were taken over by Sonny Werblin and renamed the Jets. Within two years Werblin had moved his team into the vastness of Shea Stadium, to share it with the baseballing New York Mets (and, for one screaming afternoon, the Beatles) and to set a new A.F.L. attendance record; and he paid a much-publicised 400,000 dollars to a brash young extrovert from Alabama called Joe Willie Namath, to come to New York and throw passes as quarterback for the Jets. Namath threw passes brilliantly (Werblin had found a Texan called Don Maynard who caught passes brilliantly, too) but also he made as much extra-curricular news in the big bad city as the whole of the American Football League had done for years.

By 1966 the two leagues had stopped tearing at each other's throats and decided, instead, to share Football's by now considerable spoils; the leagues were still to keep their old fixtures, but the coalition government introduced what was initially called the 'A.F.L.–N.F.L. World Championship Game' and which everybody now calls the Superbowl, American

Football's first comparable occasion to the then ninety-four-year-old F.A. Challenge Cup—to be played after the end of the season by the champions of the respective leagues on a neutral ground.

For the first two years of the Superbowl the N.F.L. champions were Green Bay Packers, whose return to their proprietary position at the top of the National Football League had been engineered in the mid 1960s by the inspired coaching of Vince Lombardi and the power-house running of the handsome, mountainous Paul Hornung. Each year they overran the A.F.L. champions, and the newspapers aired once more their tired dismissals of the junior league as a second rate collection of has-beens and never-will-bes, the 'losers' league'. Then, in 1968, the mighty Baltimore Colts stormed to the N.F.L. championship with ease and started to lay large sums of money on themselves to destroy the New York Jets in the Superbowl. The only man who was prepared to give the Jets a chance was the 400,000-dollar quarterback, who spent the short period before the Miami showdown bragging, as loudly as Cassius Clay had done before his first fight against Sonny Liston, of what he was going to do to the Colts' fearsome defence.

The storybook endings to such tales come as rarely in football as anywhere else in life; but Joe Willie Namath threw pass after pass into free space, his runners had nothing to do but catch them, and the Jets had run up a 16–0 lead by half-time that the Colts never looked like catching.

The victory, celebrated notoriously, vulgarly and mercilessly by Namath and the Jets, altered the whole American attitude to the Leagues. At last the writers and the television men treated the A.F.L. and the N.F.L. on a par; at last they realised that the country had, instead of sixteen first class teams and 10 triers lagging along behind, a full twenty-six top-class teams —good enough, when the N.F.L. and the A.F.L. re-aligned into a single National Football League in 1970, for it to be immaterial, and very quickly forgettable, which teams had once been part of the losers' league and which had been the aristocrats.

By the start of the 1970s, American Football had become quite the most compulsive entertainment that the country had seen. Every National League game was carried each week by one of the television networks, and there was an evening game televised every Monday throughout the season. The Superbowl, which had achieved a full house every year since the first one—a feat by no means common in a game that had been forced to fight for its spectators for fifty years—was now a hotter property than the baseball World Series. And the game was receiving all that popular attention of the press on and off the field, factual and frivolous, analytical

and absurd, that America had been missing since the heyday of Holly-
wood.

Combined with the new popularity, perhaps even the cause of it, was the
single-minded and quite unique search for perfection; it may be an unduly
harsh criticism of what has become the first vicarious love of millions of
Americans, but American Football does seem to have become, certainly
in its professional arena, a game that no one plays for pleasure—money,
fame, exhilaration, certainly; perhaps even pride in achievement and
comradeship and the satisfaction gained from a ritual trial of strength.
But not pleasure—the stakes are too high, the margin for relaxation too
low. The meticulous blackboard planning of Paul Brown has spilt into
every corner of the game; a quarterback will refuse to catch a ball thrown
to him in practice in case he stubs a finger on the pigskin—his throwing
hand is too valuable to risk that; a professional end, whose ability to
catch a forward pass at full tilt is vital, wears specially made distorting
contact lenses so that he can focus more quickly on a ball floating down
over his shoulder; a back will dab shoeblack on his cheekbones to
minimise the glare of the afternoon sun.

   With the search for efficiency has come the extremes of specialisation:
specially coached squads of players merely to receive kick-offs—and to
return them with all the drilled ferocity of a flight of kami-kazes; men
who dress up in the full fighting gear of an eighteen-stone lineman just to
kick field goals and tap over the extra points after a touchdown; two
virtually separate units—separately coached, separately disciplined with
separate philosophies—who change places on the field when possession
passes from one team to another. While increasing the game's efficiency,
intense specialisation has undoubtedly reduced the chances of one seeing
anything unexpected happen.

   The ridicule poured on to the head of Garo Yepremian, the Miami
Dolphins' specialist kicker, who had the rare experience during the 1973
Superbowl of having to catch a charged-down kick in open play and then,
presumably, to do something with it, demonstrates how tight a hold
specialisation has taken. A parallel in any other branch of football is
difficult to find, simply because specialisation in the other games has to be
extremely adaptable, but a fair analogy—and about as likely—would be
if the Leeds United goalkeeper were to find himself on the halfway line,
the ball at his feet, only one man to beat to score a Cup Final goal, but
with the whole of the opposition thundering up behind him. Yepremian
did what the goalkeeper would probably do—he made an almighty hash
of things (after all, he had been imported from Cyprus to kick balls over

goalposts; no one had thought of teaching him how to catch one), and gave away a touchdown which, had Miami not been winning handsomely at the time, would have been received less than favourably by his team-mates and their supporters.

Efficiency, of course, has had a far more worthy role in the popularising of the game. As a spectacle—both before, during and after a game—American Football is unparalleled; television coverage is superb; the reams of facts and figures kept on every aspect of the game, underlining the staccato nature of play that makes such detailed measurement possible, allows the game a literature of statistics surpassed in sport only by cricket (and in its ability to recall the number of fumbles per one hundred passes per individual, no less cruel to the indifferent player); the control of the game, by six separate officials with real responsibility, is rigid and rarely fallible. And its efficiency at self-promotion, at providing an entertainment package for both spectator and TV viewer, has brought the game the reward that efficiency will bring in a society of business executives—success.

The football game that has evolved in Canada over the last century provides little more than a footnote to the American game it so closely resembles, but a number of fundamental differences in the laws have given Canadian Football a flavour of its own, and in a huge country beset for so long by the difficulties of communication—a country, moreover, permanently addicted to ice-hockey—the game has made an immense advance in popularity.

It was Canada, of course, who converted the American universities from round-ball Soccer to oval-ball Rugby in the very early days. Rugby had been introduced into Canada in the 1860s, and by the time McGill University and Harvard played to Rugby rules in 1874 the game was well established at a number of colleges in the East and in Vancouver. The pure British Rugby game preserved its original form in Canada much longer than it did in the United States (one Walter Camp was quite enough for any continent), and in British Columbia and the Eastern Maritime States the game was still played in its original form until after the Second World War—and, indeed, still has a sufficiently buoyant network of clubs to exchange short tours with the major Rugby countries.

But inevitably the game that grew so fast in the colleges of the United States was bound to filter north. In Ontario and Quebec the Rugby rules were gradually modified towards the American pattern. Canada kept as many as fourteen players to each team until 1921, when sides were reduced

to twelve, but the principle of possession was already part of the game—
at that time called, somewhat confusingly, Canadian Rugby; running
interference was allowed, and, in 1931, the forward pass was introduced.

As the game's rules had followed the American pattern, so did its
administration. The control had been in the hands of various inter-collegiate bodies ever since the 1880s, but in 1912 they first faced intense American salesmanship in the form of Frank 'Shag' Shaughnessy, a Notre Dame
college player who turned to coaching after graduation; in 1912 he got a
job at Ottawa coaching baseball, and that autumn he became Canada's
first paid football coach. Under his badgering the Unions adopted American tactics, which during the next two decades removed the last traces of
Rugby influence (apart from the name; Canadian Rugby did not officially
become Canadian Football until the professional Canadian Football
League took over the administration of the major competitions as late as
1958).

The first influx of American Football players arrived soon after the
War. Some relatively unambitious football had been played in the 1930s,
but crowds, as in American Football's early professional days, had been
small; after the War, however, a new rule allowed blocking up to ten yards
beyond the line of scrimmage, and Canadian players, whose football
education had omitted this particular refinement, needed American
experience as fast as they could hire it. To protect the domestic interest,
the Canadian League set the import quota at four players per team.
With increasingly large squads, trained in specialist offence or defence
skills as in America, the quota rose inexorably, to eight per team by 1954,
and, by the 1970s, a maximum of twelve American-trained players on
any thirty-two-man team.

The Canadian pitch is the main key to the difference in the style of the
games. It is about 12 yards wider than the American field, which allows
proportionately far more chance of successful running and passing plays
down the flanks. This advantage is increased by the two scrimmage lines
facing up a yard from each other rather than faceguard to faceguard—a
further split second for the quarterback to launch the play—and by the
attacking team having only three downs, instead of four, to gain their
ten yards. These are only partly balanced by the 12th man on the Canadian
teams—a 'flanker' or 'flying wing' in attack, an extra linebacker in defence
—who do not in practice clutter up the tight moves of a game as an extra
man in an American Football team would tend to do. Canadian Football
has followed the scoring values of the American game, with the addition
of a *rouge*, an extra point either for kicking the ball over the opposing
end zone, or for tackling the kick receiver within the end zone.

The economic state of Canadian Football is healthy, and improving with the continued prosperity of the game. It has had its own 'Superbowl' for more than sixty years, since the Governor-General of Canada in 1909, Earl Grey, presented the Grey Cup for annual competition between the amateur Rugby teams. In time the Cup became an open competition, after 1924 no intercollegiate team was strong enough to win, and by 1937 they had dropped out—very much the story of the amateurs' eclipse in the F.A. Cup in England and Scotland—leaving the field open to the professionals.

These operate in two Conferences—British Columbia, Calgary, Edmonton, Saskatchewan and Winnipeg in the West, and Hamilton, Ontario, Toronto and Montreal in the East, playing, to avoid the Canadian winter, twice a week between July and late November when the two Conference winners meet in an American-orientated play-off to decide the Grey Cup.

The game looks like American Football, the players train and dress like American Footballers, they throw passes and block linemen and earn big money ($20,000 a year for some of the bigger stars) like American Footballers. The crowds, partly because of the small stadiums, are not yet as big as American Football crowds, but the package is every bit as exciting as the one the Americans have sold to their spectators (some would say the few rule differences make it an even more attractive game), and it is not surprising that Canadian Football is closing fast on ice-hockey in the battle for spectators.

As Britain's two Rugby codes re-opened business after the War, both were anxious for signs of a spectator resurgence—the League game because it had needed them to survive, the Union game to prove to itself that as well as being the most purely amateur game of all the popular team sports, it was at the same time the most attractive.

Rugby had enjoyed what in the terminology of the time might have been called 'a good war'. Even before it started, there was a real hope that there might be some closing of the breach between the two codes. French Rugby's flirtation with money, which had resulted in their exile from the International Championship in the early 1930s, was magnanimously forgotten by the Home Unions in 1939—while Britain and France faced a common foe, the logic went, it might look rather better if they were prepared to play against each other at the same games. Thus France returned to the Rugby-playing world, and when mobilisation started on a major scale the Rugby Union went even closer to a compromise with the powers of darkness: they gave permission for soldiers who had played Rugby League in civilian life to play Rugby Union in the services.

At the same time, while such unseemly hobnobbing was going on between Harlequin three-quarters and Wakefield hookers, Rugby League earned itself the major distinction of being banned by Hitler—not Rugby Union, the bastion of the middle-class; nor Soccer, the new opiate of the British masses, but Rugby League, a desperately hard and uncompromising war-game on its own account, which, it seems, had impressed the Germans by maintaining strong links with its French counterparts in the 1930s despite the breaking off of relations between the French Rugby Union and its British equivalent. Accordingly the Vichy Government, on 29 December 1941, dissolved the French Ligue de Rugby à Treize, confiscated its money and property under the name of Marshal Pétain, and thus bestowed on the game a pride and a purpose which saw it back with redoubled vigour after the War.

The mutual respect and tolerance dictated by the conditions of war did not last; beyond a resolution by the Rugby Union to grant National Servicemen, as well as regulars, permission to play services Rugby whether or not they had played Rugby League in civilian life, the two codes were off speaking terms and back in their own self-imposed corners almost before the ink was dry on the Surrender papers—Rugby League to rebuild a chain of precarious businesses that had been lying neglected for six years, Rugby Union to re-establish its comfortable place in sport and society.

Rugby Union had, it could reasonably believe, a stable position. Its spectators, in the South of England, the West Country, Scotland and Northern Ireland, were the same spectators that the game had always attracted—the club's ex-players, their wives and their friends, swollen at internationals by even more ex-players and their wives, and reaching a well-established exclusiveness for the University Match in December when wives were left at home but other members of the board were asked in their place. Rugby Union spectators—and in all such generalisations we must exclude South Wales, where Rugby is their Soccer and Soccer their perennial shame—did not constitute 'crowds', they were the members of a club, people who knew what the people on the field were going through and who were willing, huddled on un-terraced touchlines and unroofed stands, to share some of the discomfort.

Rugby's administrators in the British Isles deserve credit for realising that their game, which they had barely changed since the split from the Northern Union for fear of being accused of Radicalism, was not beyond improvement; what could not conceivably have been imagined by the players and the administrators of the late 1940s was that within twenty-five years it was to emerge almost entirely from its middle-class hiding places and—once again with the powerful influence of television prodding from behind—capture for itself a following of millions.

The process took time; the early post-war years began to imitate the patterns of old—honours even between England and Wales in the international championship (with a fine but uncharacteristic peak of dominance by Jack Kyle and Ireland in the late 1940s); the traditional flatter-only-to-deceive performances by Scotland; the traditional mercurial display by France, feeding every Briton's store of xenophobic misconception by invariably, it seemed, playing brilliant Rugby for three-quarters of a game and losing their heads and the match in the last ten minutes; and the traditional thrashings by New Zealanders in Britain, New Zealanders in New Zealand, South Africa at home and abroad and even, still in our post-war confusion in 1947, by Australians in Britain.

It was through such lessons learnt from overseas that British Rugby found the impetus for change. By 1950 Rugby on the highest level, despite what might be seen at Twickenham and the schools and the traditional strongholds of the amateur game, no longer held to the Vassall ideal of heavy, pounding forwards winning the ball, heeling to the scrum-half and letting the half-backs and three-quarters have the fun. Disciplined coaching in New Zealand and South Africa by hard-faced students of tactics now saw the Rugby forward as a creator rather than a provider; they saw that the ball was safer in the heart of a ruck or a maul than it was bobbing about between centres; and they saw that broken play caused by marauding, short-passing forwards could launch far more effective, unexpected attacks than could scrum-half and stand-off half from a set-piece scrum or line-out.

Nine-man Rugby had been born, so-called from the practice of the pack ploughing forward in attack keeping the ball amongst themselves, releasing it to their scrum-half only when stopped, and allowing him two options only—to kick it over their heads for touch or to continue the charge afresh, passing the ball back inside to his own forwards once he, in turn, was stopped. Sometimes the fly-half was brought into the act by the scrum-half in order to provide a better kicking angle, but this ten-man Rugby was little more exciting than the nine-man version. To say that this emphasis on forward-play made the backs redundant would be an exaggeration; but the celebrated South African teams of the 1950s and 1960s, rich as they were in fast and talented three-quarters, rarely let these greyhounds off the leash except in the final, beautifully co-ordinated 10-yard dash for the line after the great machine-like pack had forced a defensive error by sheer, pummelling persistence.

One of the additional features of this style of Rugby was its legitimate, but in the long run stultifying, exploitation of Rugby's imperfect scoring system. Since 1948, when the International Board reduced the value of the drop-goal to three points from its disproportionately valued four, no single Rugby score was worth more than three points—penalty goal, drop-goal and try—no matter what the effort expended. And the 'better' the try from the spectators' point of view—a dramatic three-quarter move culminating in a chase for the corner-flag—the less likely the scoring side were to benefit from the two-point conversion. Penalty kicks, conversely, were beginning to assume an unwelcome importance in the first-class game. The Rugby penalty had been included in the rules as a deterrent to foul play, particularly foul play indulged in to prevent the scoring of a try; over the years, however, a whole range of offences, some of them technical, others more mistakes than wilful misdemeanours, had been blanketed as unfair play and subject to a penalty kick against the offender—offside, unfair use of the hands, failure to roll off the ball, entering the ruck from the wrong direction, dangerous play—the referee had only to take his pick and blow his whistle. And in the opponents' half of the field that meant a very fair chance of three points—far less trouble than running the ball across their line.

To exploit the increasing number of penalty kicks came yet a new breed of Rugby player—the place-kick specialist. He came gradually upon our awareness, it seemed, in the 1950s; previously one of the backs, usually the full-back because he was often required to kick to touch, would lope up for the conversions and generally take one or two pots at goal from penalties in the course of a match; goals were sometimes kicked and sometimes missed—the kicker's name was rarely recorded except by the most meticulous statistician; teams were picked to score tries, and the place-kicker, as a rule, was then appointed from among the fifteen chosen men.

On 18 July 1959, British Rugby received one of its most brutal initiations into the facts of modern Rugby life. If the cavalier reputation of British Rugby had lasted into the late 1950s—and the skills of some of the game's most delightful runners then on display argues that it had—that test match in Dunedin, New Zealand versus the Lions—triggered a reaction in the Home Countries that overshadowed top-class Rugby for a decade. The final score of that match was New Zealand 18, Lions 17. The Lions scored four tries, one conversion and one penalty goal; New Zealand scored six penalty goals. The Lions ran everywhere and displayed the sort of Rugby skills that people recall in memoirs; the New Zealanders disciplined and compact as ever, surged forward with their expertly drilled pack, forced the Lions to concede penalties, and gave the ball to Don Clarke, the deadliest and most prolific points kicker in Rugby's history.

In New Zealand and South Africa, where innocence on the field had died long before, such traumas of Rugby were not new; ten years before the Dunedin Test the All-Blacks themselves had suffered in much the same way when the South African prop forward, Okey Geffin, who had honed his kicking to perfection by daily practice in a prisoner of war camp, kicked five penalties to beat New Zealand 15–11. But in the British Isles there were grim demands for and promises of greater discipline, tighter control, stricter training, surer method. (There were also calls for an increase in the value of a try and the corresponding reduction in the value of a penalty goal—an oft-repeated plea that took years to get a sympathetic hearing.)

What the Home Countries did produce was no more than a half-hearted imitation of the New Zealand and South African tactics at their worst. Because of the inborn mistrust of everything that could be construed as methodical coaching, there was still considerable reluctance to allow more than token squad training before internationals and representative games. The result was slow, steamroller-like advances by the stronger of two packs, trundling up the opponents' touchline by means of infuriating touch kicks over their heads by their own scrum-halves. It was a method perfected by Wales under Clive Rowlands—scrum-half and captain—in the mid 1960s, followed by the other countries with rather less effectiveness but with the same basic result of smothering enterprise both in their opponents and themselves, and in all cases backed up by a growing breed of specialist place-kickers.

A reaction against these methods was inevitable, and much of the credit for the subsequent improvements in the game must go to television. Rugby had been televised in England since 1937, when the first live broadcast of an international was shown from Twickenham, and since the war the Home Unions had enjoyed reasonable relations with the B.B.C., so that by the mid 1950s a good proportion of all Home Internationals, as well as a number of tour matches and the University Match at Twickenham, were broadcast live; in 1955, there was some criticism that television was having an adverse effect on the clubs' attendances. But the revenue from the contracts, the publicity the game received from these broadcasts, together with the intelligent and unemotional way the game was covered by the B.B.C., all persuaded the Board to leave the situation as it was.

As a result, by the early and mid 1960s the great majority of Rugby spectators were television viewers who had never paid to see a Rugby match in their lives; they were seeing perhaps half-a-dozen top-class games live every season, and those games, in the years of forward domination, were becoming extremely boring. They were years when memories were made not of whole games, or whole halves, but of isolated incidents in a welter of unmemorable gloom—of Richard Sharp's triple-dummy and try against Scotland in the 1963 Calcutta Cup, and Andy Hancock's ninety-yard, match-saving score in the corresponding match two years later. And they were years when Rugby commentators looked back almost to another age to recall the great running backs of the early 1950s, to Lewis Jones or Cliff Morgan, whose brilliance might well have been snuffed out by fast-breaking forward power in the 1960s just as, after two or three seasons of unforgettable speed and grace, Richard Sharp was in his turn snuffed out. Only the French were not subdued by the times: their advances since the post-war resumption had been dramatic, and inspired first by the gigantic Jean Prat and then by the studious-looking Lucien Mias, they brought to attacking forward play a control and a deftness reminiscent of the Harlem Globetrotters in full flow.

The airing of Rugby's ills on television in international after tedious international, interspersed with a number of December afternoons when the one-time showpiece of cavalier amateur Rugby, the University Match, degenerated into an equally sterile exchange of penalty kicks, was compounded by a series of triumphant tours by New Zealand in 1963–4, and 1967, by South Africa in 1960–61, and even in 1966–7 by Australia. It is to the credit of the Unions in Britain and France that within five years of the lowest ebb in these series of defeats, Rugby in the British Isles had become not only faster, more skilful and more enjoyable to watch—it had become good enough to beat the all-powerful New Zealanders in New Zealand and give them a very frightening tour in Europe.

The Unions not only changed their laws to improve the game, they changed their attitudes as well. Coaching ceased to become a dirty word. In 1965 the Rugby Union (while with the same breath giving assurance that Radicalism had not entirely taken over by banning a proposal for a floodlit league in the West Country) agreed to set up a coaching panel 'in hope of betterment of the game's standards at all levels'. Two years later, in 1967, the Welsh Rugby Union announced the appointment of a paid director of their coaching scheme, an honorary coach to the Welsh national fifteen, and the establishment of a national squad of players who would meet, practise and talk to each other from time to time during each season.

In 1969 Wales, with an established team of players possibly unsurpassed in Britain at any time, won the Championship; they shared it in 1970, won it outright in 1971, would almost certainly have done so again if the 1972 series hadn't been disrupted by the Irish troubles, and only surrendered their superiority in 1973 when they were overtaken by the coaching schemes of the other Home Countries. These were imitative, slightly more reluctant (the Scottish Union referred to their national coach as an 'adviser', a somewhat unfortunate echo of the early American military commanders in Vietnam, who didn't like to be called soldiers), but with an effectiveness proved for all time in 1971 when the British Lions, based largely on the triumphant Welsh squad and their half-back pairing of Gareth Edwards and Barry John, and expertly coached by another Welshman, the remarkable Carwyn James, carved a swathe through New Zealand Rugby causing consternation unknown there since the 1937 South Africans and proving that winning Rugby is not necessarily learned in the cradle.

Until the 1960s training had consisted largely of running round Rugby fields in the evening to keep fit; tactics had all too often depended on the scrum-half saying to the fly-half at half-time 'How about a dummy scissors at our next scrum in their half?' Coaching had brought system to the game; if a 'dummy scissors' was to be tried, it was no longer to be a spontaneous piece of conjuring as it had been since Onllwyn Brace and Mike Smith had first used the move tactically in 1955. Now a dummy scissors was to be an exercise recognised, followed and supported by the whole team. Team practice under the old dispensation had meant teaching the forwards to ruck together; squad coaching meant effective experimentation with more sophisticated forward play; of using the centres as extra forwards, charging 'on the burst' into the opposing pack much like an American Football half-back, in the knowledge that his own forwards would be behind him to continue the forward momentum, secure 'second-phase' possession, and re-launch the attack.

With the increased team skills came the life-saving changes in the laws of Rugby. For players as well as spectators, the Rugby Union method of returning a ball to play from touch had long been unsatisfactory, line-outs were rough and frequently indecisive and the practice of advancing up the field by a series of short but sure kicks to touch merely ensured more and more indecisive, scrappy line-outs. In 1958 the International Board, confronted by 93 separate proposals for changes to the laws—ranging from knock-ons, heeling and playing the ball after a tackle, penalty kicks and line-outs—momentously decided to change absolutely nothing. They relented somewhat in 1961 by ordering the gap of at least a yard between the two lines at a throw-in. And in 1968, again reacting to the bad press the game had been receiving, they introduced as an experiment the 'Australian dispensation', a law the Australian Union had used successfully for some years by which a side gained no advantage by kicking for touch except when kicking from inside its own 25-yard line; thus, while defensive touch-kicking would rightly remain as important as ever, the attacking side would have to think of something more constructive than a hopeful belt into touch in an attempt to gain ground. The experiment worked impressively. In a questionnaire circulated to clubs at the end of the first season of the '25 yard rule', the Rugby Union received 726 replies of which 585 recommended that the rule be retained on the books; it was.

In 1971, too, the long awaited change in scoring values was implemented, with the try at last being given greater reward than the penalty goal. A converted try was now worth six points—twice as much as a drop-goal or a penalty goal; again response was favourable—matches were won by try-scoring that before could have been lost or drawn through penalty goals; the International Championship—perhaps fortuitously, more probably as a result of the scoring changes and the coaching method—gained a new excitement and provided a new compulsiveness for Rugby's millions of television viewers. The game, it seemed, had been saved from introspection and conservatism and given a new lease of life.

Other concessions to the so-called 'professional' approach began to gain ground. The County Championship, which had evolved round the annual Yorkshire–Lancashire battle in the 1880s, and which had provided the only major competition in England below full international level, had lost a lot of appeal for players and spectators alike. But the call for more competition was widespread. Already in the other Home Countries, and, of course, in New Zealand and South Africa, local and regional competitions were being contested with the fervour of the Soccer leagues. In England the argument was that Rugby was a game for the clubs, that the clubs arranged their own fixture lists and played against exactly whom they wished, and consequently none of the major Rugby clubs had a common fixture schedule; a league on any national, or even regional basis, would mean clubs dropping long-standing fixtures to make room on their cards for new, keenly contested ones, and this was not the spirit of the game.

What did appear to be in line with the spirit of the game was the idea of a Knock-out Cup open to all clubs affiliated to the Rugby Union. The Union had vetoed the idea themselves in 1968, in the long-held belief that formal competition was liable to bring out the worst in players and teams alike; but in 1971 they relented, and English Rugby Union's first Cup Final was played in 1972 (seventy-four years, incidentally, after Rugby League's first, and exactly one hundred after Soccer's). It was a quiet enough affair, with a crowd of 15,000 hardly straining at Twickenham's facilities, and proved something of a sop to the sceptics in that one of Moseley's forwards was sent off for foul play within minutes of the start— the first man to be sent off at headquarters since 1925; but the Cup, with Gloucester's name occupying first place on its roll of honour, was almost certainly set for a romantic and passionate role in the further popularisation of Rugby.

The spread of Rugby outside the English-speaking parts of the old Empire is a phenomenon that appears somewhat curious to the British. Team sport, as it evolved in the 19th century, was an exclusively Anglo-Saxon-cum-Celtic preserve; the very simplicity of Association Football made it an inevitable choice for foreign countries once the spread of sport and leisure reached them, but Rugby was essentially different, Rugby was and remains, a violent sport of bodily contact, and team violence for fun is far from being a universal idea of an afternoon's pleasure. True, the French had taken to the British game with relish, but they were alone for many years in their enthusiasm, which makes the present upsurge of interest in the game both a mystery to the ethnologist and a feather in the cap of both Rugby missionaries and to the attractiveness of the game itself.

In most parts of the world the original influence was inevitably British or British colonial. In Canada the game flourishes modestly, despite the glamour, the headlines and much of the support going to Canadian Football. The New Zealanders introduced the game into the Polynesian cultures—first, of course, through their own highly adaptable Maoris, and, as early as 1905, through the lithe, fast and cheerful Fijians, who loved the game from the outset, formed a Union of their own in 1913 and now have more than seven hundred and fifty clubs serving a population of barely half a million. The Fijians' first prolonged tour to Britain in 1969, during which they scored more dramatic and unlikely tries before television audiences than had been seen in internationals for years, made them immensely popular (despite the disturbing tendency of some of their number, in their enthusiasm, to leap into rucks feet first) and conjured up visions of the kind of Rugby that might be seen if the schoolboys of Black Africa were to be converted to the game.

Argentina, too, home of the most uncompromising Soccer players in the world, saw Englishmen playing Rugby at the end of the last century, caught the bug, formed a River Plate Championship, founded a River Plate Rugby Union, and learned enough in the first half of this century, with help from tours by British Lions and Junior Springboks, to beat Wales in 1968, Scotland in 1969 and Ireland in 1970.

In Japan, on the other hand, where Soccer has never taken a significant

hold, there are some 1,900 Rugby clubs. The celebrated print purporting
to show a Rugby match at Yokohama in 1874 is being played before an
exclusively European audience and, such was the state of the rules of the
respective games at that date, could just as easily be Soccer, but the
driving force for Rugby's development came not from the merchants or
the military but from a Cambridge graduate called Ginnosuke Tanaka
who returned to Keio University in 1889 with Rugby in his blood, and
engendered enough enthusiasm to have a Union formed there at the height
of Imperial Rule in 1926. The Japanese now play the game with the same
dedication they give to golf, and despite their disadvantage in height they
run fast and elusively with the ball, have given considerable trouble to a
number of touring sides, and in 1968 and 1973 won much respect during
short tours of New Zealand and Britain.

   In Europe, much of Rugby's spread must be credited to the French;
they took the game to Italy quite early in the century, where it was
adopted enthusiastically by the Fascist regime and appeared on the State-
run football pool alongside the great Soccer names of Italy; Spain and
Portugal, too, took to the game with a certain interest between the wars—
indeed, at the 'Mediterranean Games' in 1956, France, Spain and Italy
took part in a Rugby competition. Today the game in Italy, after a post-
war decline, began in the 1970s to return to a more reasonable competitive
standard with a number of British and South African players playing
important roles in the senior teams.

   Leaving aside Chile and the United States, Poland and Belgium,
Morocco and Malaysia, where more and more Rugby is being played
independent of outside help, Romania—extraordinary, isolated Romania—
completes the world picture. In 1954 a crowd of 95,000, then the biggest
Rugby gate of all time, watched a match in Bucharest between Swansea
and the local Locomatavia. The fact that a Soccer international began a
minute or two after the final whistle might have had something to do with
the attraction, but Romania's ethnic, cultural and linguistic links with
France had meant that throughout this century Romanian graduates from
Paris University had been returning home converted to the 15-a-side
game, and the following, as well as the standard, had become impressive.
The next year Locomatavia toured four British clubs, beating Swansea and
Bristol, drawing with Harlequins and losing to Cardiff, then the most
awesome club in Britain, by a mere three points. In 1957, before another
95,000 crowd (and just before another Soccer match) Romania narrowly
lost to the full French XV, in 1960 they beat France 11–5, in 1961 drew
with them 6–6 and in 1962 beat them again. In each of those three years
France won or shared top place in the International Championship.

49 Match-winner: goalkeepers in Gaelic Football have less of an aura about them than their Soccer counterparts, but this vital save by the Kerry captain John Culloty in the 1969 All-Ireland Final against Offaly shows just how impressive they can be. *Irish Press*

50, 51 A world apart: running, handling, high-kicking, desperate blocking—only the shape of the ball distinguishes the games. A Gaelic Football match between Galway and Cork in London, 1972; and an Australian Football Grand Final between Carlton and Richmond in Melbourne, 1973. *Colorsport/Australian Information Service*

52 Crowd-appeal: the greatest of all the Victorian League
Grand Finals, with Carlton overhauling Collingwood in
the last quarter to beat them 111–101, watched
by a record attendance of more than 121,000.
Australian News & Information Bureau

53 Catch and carry: the great drama of Australian Football lies not so much in the goals as in the all-important 'marking'—catching from long kicks—which gives possession. A crucial mark, as in this incident from the 1973 Grand Final, is worth all the physical danger.
Australian Information Service

54 The great tradition: England *v*. Scotland at Rugby, the oldest international event in world football. Scotland's Peter Brown crashes towards the England line during their victory in the centenary match at Edinburgh, 1971.   *Colorsport*

55 The new intruders: the spread of Rugby Union has been slow but surprisingly wide, and it now seems in no way incongruous for the Japanese international XV to face a full Welsh side at Cardiff Arms Park, as they did in 1973. *Western Mail*

56 Thinking small: though all football codes have developed miniature versions of the parent game, only Soccer has successfully adapted itself to the indoor arena. In the five-a-side game even such long-retired veterans as Stanley Matthews can briefly recapture the old magic. *Syndication International*

57 Going hard: South American Soccer is arguably more courageous, more passionate, more committed than anywhere in the world. It can also be highly skilled and very dangerous, though Joria Aendro of Penarol, Uruguay, made contact with neither ball nor opponent with this piece of acrobatics in a South American Cup tie. *Syndication International*

58 High stakes: since the early 1960s European Soccer has
flourished on its three international club competitions—
Champions' Cup, Cup-winners' Cup and Inter-Cities Fairs Cup
(now the UEFA Cup). Leeds United have contested one or
other of these every year since 1965; here, their long-serving
defender Jack Charlton commanding the air, they hold on to
win the last Fairs Cup final from Juventus of Turin, 1971.
United Press International

59 High tension: the physical stress—and the high rewards—
of top-class Soccer have made it the most difficult of all games to
control. Here British referee Norman Burtenshaw is quickly on
hand to mediate in a difference of opinion between two Scotsmen
in the English League, Dave Mackay (Tottenham Hotspur,
left) and Billy Bremner (Leeds United). *Syndication International*

60 Without frills: the powerhouse of a Rugby League pack—the front-row forwards—face a penalty kick during a Challenge Cup tie, for Wigan against Wakefield Trinity, 1962.   *Ray Green*

61 Without compromise: at its most basic, the job of a Rugby League forward is that of a battering ram, charging again and again into the opposition to soften it up for the assault troops; Frank Collier of Widnes takes on the Swinton defence, 1964. *Ray Green*

62 The man they couldn't stop: in an unprecedented day for American Football, in December 1965, Gale Sayers scored six touchdowns for Chicago Bears in the 61–20 drubbing of San Francisco 49ers; here he dives over for the fifth of them.
United Press International

63 The man they couldn't gag: Joe Willie Namath wide open to a charge by Bubba Smith in the 1969 Superbowl; he was rarely so vulnerable, and having boasted for days that the unfancied New York Jets would destroy Baltimore Colts, he defied all odds to make the boast come true *Vernon J. Biever*

64 After all, it's only a game: climax of a thriller—Bart Starr (number 15) burrows his way through a mass of bodies to win the classic National Football League championship game on New Year's Day, 1967. His touchdown, thirteen seconds from time, gave Green Bay Packers a dramatic 21–17 victory over Dallas Cowboys. *United Press International*

There is little reason why the Home Countries should not soon emulate France in their willingness to meet Romania, for example, on equal terms; in 1973 a full Welsh touring team played Canada; Japan and Argentina could soon deserve a major tour, with official test matches. As recently as 1956 the Rugby Union, while encouraging the spread of the game as far as possible, said there was 'no question of engaging in further international matches'. Clearly now this pronouncement has been overtaken by events: foreign tours by British teams have frequently included matches which the local sides, at any rate, have entered into in the full spirit of an international. It remains only for the younger Rugby nations—from Eastern and Southern Europe, from North and South America, and from the Far East and Africa—to be awarded some legislative status among the Rugby giants for the game to achieve the cosmopolitan status now enjoyed only by Soccer.

Rugby League, in the years following the end of the Second World War, was to enjoy the greatest period in its history. When the war began the game was popular enough on its own stamping ground, but there was still the uncomfortable knowledge that the fickleness of a crowd for just a season or two or the temporary loss of form for a leading club could lead to financial trouble—and the game was a business as well as a sport. After the war, as their business tentatively resumed trading, it was clear that a spectator boom was on the way. Not just in Rugby, of course; the American professional Footballers had their first taste of regular money-spinning matches at this time; for each of the three seasons up to 1950, League Soccer in Britain was watched by more than 40 million people (in the last season before the war the figure had been some 28 million; by 1972–3 it was down to $25\frac{1}{2}$ million); other sports, too, enjoyed euphoric times as cricket attendances shot up for a few seasons, and speedway racing cashed in on a short-lived boom that it never experienced before or since.

This post-war spectator glut astonished Rugby League football. Only a few months after the guns had stopped firing there were 30,000 spectators to see a test trial in Swansea—deep in the heart of Rugby Union territory; in Sydney 50,000 watched New South Wales play Queensland. The French, spurred by the still remarkable energy of Jean Galia, and feeling none the worse for the effects of either Hitler's ban or the complete destruction of their Federation's headquarters, arranged for an immediate tour of their club sides by Castleford. In 1946 Great Britain, despite the priorities faced by post-war shipping, were persuaded to send a touring team to Australia and New Zealand; they went by aircraft carrier, attracted vast crowds and took more than £21,000 in receipts in Australia alone.

The boom had its less happy side-effects; the unexpected inflow of money set the bigger clubs back searching for better players; not only were they recruited from the Rugby Union clubs, a not unexpected return to the contentious practices of pre-war days, but there was a busy spate of overseas signings—particularly from Australia and New Zealand. Such were the depredations suffered by overseas clubs, in fact, that the Rugby League Council were forced in 1947 to place a temporary ban on overseas signings. And still attendances rose; in 1949, for the first time, the Challenge Cup Final at Wembley between Bradford Northern and Halifax brought a capacity crowd down from Yorkshire, and the Final gate topped 90,000 for the next two years as well.

These successes fired all branches of the game with optimism; in 1949 eight Welsh clubs formed a league of their own, and a year later two of them, Cardiff and Llanelli, applied to join the full League (Llanelli was unable to give satisfactory ground assurances, and was voted out, but Cardiff were accepted into the League for the 1950–1 season). That year, too, an all-amateur Rugby League team arrived from Italy with little experience behind it but with requests for tours and coaching from Britain. In 1951 the game emphasised its confidence in the future by agreeing a minimum wage guarantee for all professional players; and the showmen, whose recognition of the crowds' love for trophies and competitions and knock-out finals have done so much to keep Rugby League alive, began talking about a Rugby League World Cup.

It is ironic perhaps, that what should have become the game's greatest showpiece was inaugurated just as the game itself was beginning a slow decline. The suggestion had come from France, ever the fountainhead of grandiose sporting schemes, where a businessman called Paul Barrière guaranteed £25,000 to sponsor the competition in France in 1954, and where enthusiasm for the game since the war had built an organisation, virtually from scratch, to rival the best that Australia, New Zealand or Great Britain could muster against them.

In Britain, however, enthusiasm was perceptibly on the wane; the brave attempts of Cardiff to live with the giants of Lancashire and Yorkshire had brought a series of comprehensive defeats and no small resentment from the big clubs at having to travel all the way to South Wales to play them. At the end of the 1951–2 season the Welsh once again gave in to the inevitable; since 1952, despite the Welsh continuing to provide a large proportion of the League's stars, the Union code has reigned unchallenged.

There were rumblings, too, that the players were being asked to do rather too much in the cause of crowd-pulling. In the 1950s, even more than today, the game was uncompromisingly hard; those were the days when there was no rule requiring the acting scrum-half to pass the ball after a play-the-ball. Long periods of a close game could be spent in an ever-repeating pattern of play-the-ball, charge and tackle, play-the-ball, charge and tackle—a punishing, exhausting and frustrating exercise for the defending side, and certainly one which took its toll of nerves and strength over the course of a season. Added to this, rigorous tours of Australia and New Zealand were undertaken every three or four years.

Now, in 1954, the tourists left New Zealand after a long tour with the prospect of a bare couple of weeks' rest before the first World Cup competition in France that October. A number of players had been injured on tour, others were disgusted at the terms offered to them to play in the World Cup—three weeks' duty for £26 plus expenses was not the sort of money to make tired players raise themselves in preparation for yet another foreign trip—and the team of eighteen players that were finally selected included several who had never played international football at all. The fact that Britain beat New Zealand and Australia, drew with France at Toulouse and finally won the play-off and the first World Cup by beating them 16–12 in Paris, said a lot for the depths of talent in the British League.

That World Cup Final was televised live in Britain—and caused a considerable slump in the home League gates that afternoon, ammunition, no doubt, for the arguments that were soon to rage over the proposals for live coverage of League matches. But another phenomenon of crowd unpredictability had already been experienced early that year. English Soccer will always remember the shambles of the first Wembley Cup Final in 1923. Rugby League had its counterpart at Odsal Stadium, Bradford, in 1954. Warrington and Halifax had drawn their Challenge Cup Final in a dull game at Wembley; for the replay a totally unprepared Bradford police force stood helpless as well over 100,000 spectators were crammed on to Odsal's vast slopes. Half an hour after the game started people were still pouring in as those who realised they would see no more than a fraction of the pitch were leaving in disgust. It proved—and at the time in the 1950s this proof was very welcome to the game's authorities—that for the big occasion, the Cup Match, the International, the prestige competition, Lancashire and Yorkshire were still eager to watch Rugby League.

It was the Saturday afternoon, week-in and week-out, bread-and-butter Rugby that was beginning to cause concern; the game had become bogged down by its own efficiency—and when efficiency in Rugby League is not matched by flair, when infallibility in defence is not countered by

imagination in attack, then stalemate is the result. In the late 1950s an
early 1960s the Rugby League, faced with dwindling gates, attacked th
problem on three or four separate fronts at once.

First, in 1958, they attempted to open the game up by requiring th
acting scrum-half to pass the ball after a play-the-ball or else concede
scrum—hardly revolutionary, but a significant acknowledgment that
was passing, as well as running and tackling, that would make the gam
more attractive. Then, for the 1958-9 season, the Rugby League decide
to allow live B.B.C. coverage of Saturday afternoon League matches.
was a brave decision; the Football League had turned adamantly again
the live coverage of league Soccer matches, allowing, at this stage, only th
most cursory clips of recordings well after the matches were over; th
Rugby Union had established a pattern of allowing coverage of inte
national matches, but the Rugby Union were not concerned with th
profit that might or might not be made by the clubs' gate-money, and fe
they could amply compensate them through the contract fee; and th
Rugby League had the warning example of American Football befor
them, where unlimited coverage of professional games had halved atten
dances in Los Angeles. However, the Council decided that the contra
money, together with the diplomatic potential of television to bring th
game to people who had never seen it before, at least justified a year
experiment. By 1960 they were able to report that there had been n
significant drop in gates on the Saturdays when matches had been show
live, and they signed up for another thirteen live games for the followin
season.

This established a pattern that was both to change and to save Rugb
League. The amazing commercial success of Soccer—quite apart from i
long established popular appeal—which was just beginning to make i
impact in the early 1960s, the Betting and Gaming Act of 1961 and th
subsequent impact of concentrated horse-racing on both television chan
nels on early Saturday afternoons, the sudden resurgence of interest i
Rugby Union in the late 1960s, would all, it can be argued, have take
toll of Rugby League's already unsure appeal during the 1960s. With th
courage to accept its chance and to sell itself on television the game was a
least making a positive stand for survival.

The B.B.C. had discovered in Eddie Waring a commentator wedde
perfectly to the game he was commentating on—unsentimental, dr
amused, yet excited by what he saw going on beneath him. He woul
invite letters from viewers on such intricacies of the game as puzzled then
used them to broaden his commentaries into a sort of Rugby Leagu
lecture. Under his good-natured guidance, Britain and television dis

covered a new sport—a remote and unappreciated ritual played on muddy afternoons in Wigan had become a much loved and keenly followed ritual played on muddy afternoons in Wigan.

In the 1960–61 season the Third World Cup tournament was played in Britain, with all the games televised. The pro-TV and anti-TV factions each had a field day. The France v. New Zealand match was watched by a mere 3,000 in a downpour and only 10,700 saw New Zealand play Australia; television took much of the blame. Yet throughout the tournament, though the Rugby was disappointing, the matches were watched by millions of viewers who were never likely to stand on the terraces themselves. And in spite of less gates and poor weather, the television fees covered the tournament's losses.

There were signs, too, that there might be a major breakthrough abroad to make up for disappointment felt by the League when the Italian government finally refused to recognise the young Italian Rugby League. On their way back from Australia after the second World Cup in 1957, Great Britain and France played a couple of rather desultory exhibition matches in South Africa. The games were not particularly well received, but the League succeeded in signing a number of prominent South African players, with St Helen's carrying off the plum in the shape of Tom Van Vollenhoven, a blond winger who, along with Billy Boston, Vince Karalius and Neil Fox became one of the game's sure-fire television successes in the 1960s.

Then, in 1961, a syndicate of South African businessmen backed two separate Rugby League organisations; five Rugby Union giants (including Hennie van Zyl, Charlie Nimb and Martin Pelser who had toured Britain with the Springboks earlier that year) signed for the League game, and there were even unofficial hopes that the next Rugby League World Cup would welcome a fifth country to the competition. In fact, though the two Leagues soon became one, and though the game prospered in South Africa long enough to send a touring side to Australia and New Zealand and beat the latter in a test match, interest waned fast and there have been no real signs of a revival since.

Still the League at home were anxious for more competition and higher gates. In the 1961–2 season they decided to revive, after half a century of argument, the two-division system. It had proved a disaster in the three seasons between 1902–6, when clubs in the second division died for lack of spectators; this time the keen competition in the season before the split, particularly among clubs in the middle of the League determined to keep their money-spinning fixtures with the big-name clubs, put attendance figures up by twenty-five per cent. But that was the extent of its success. The experiment had been scheduled for three seasons. In January 1964, after Bradford Northern had announced that it was unable to go on and had to cancel the remainder of its fixtures, and after several other second division clubs had experienced severe financial difficulty, the experiment was abandoned.

With the reversion to a single, thirty-club League, they instituted a sixteen-club championship play-off at the end of the season in place of the four-club play-off of the past (on the principle of more knock-out games, more spectators), and even a competition for the bottom fourteen clubs, an otiose affair that was mercifully dropped after one season. And within a decade, for the start of the 1973 season, the League were preparing once again to try to make the two-division system work.

Televised Rugby League, for all its popularity, had emphasised time and again the stultifying tendencies of unlimited possession. Rugby League had deliberately rejected the Union's convention of releasing the ball once a fair tackle has been made, but by so doing had presented themselves with the problems faced by American Football in its formative days—namely, that a strong side leading on points was finding it reasonably easy to hang on to the ball for long periods, to close the game up, and to make life as frustrating for the spectators as for the opposition. The Americans had opened up their game by measuring territory won or lost and if ten yards was not gained in four attempts, possession was forfeited to the other side. In the 1960s, Rugby League brought in a series of similar rules. Distance was not a criterion, but length of possession was: a team was allowed to hang on to the ball for four tackles and four subsequent play-the-balls, and then had to either kick or score a try, or else concede a scrummage to the other side. The new legislation worked. The probing, lofted kicks characteristic of Rugby Union became more frequent as a last resort; players became less inclined to 'die' with the ball, more ready to throw it from hand to hand in the hope of finding a gap in the defence. Into the early 1970s the Rugby League were still experimenting with this rule, trying to achieve the desired balance between the old negative tactics and the provision of a fair opportunity for the side in possession to mount an effective attack; after persistent pressure from players, the possession limit was increased to six tackles for an experimental period.

They looked for spectators in other ways, too. The compulsiveness of television, the continuing success of the other football codes, and a general change in working-class attitudes which no longer included an automatic Saturday afternoon 'at the match' as part of the winter weekend programme, were making things difficult for a minority sport—even a minority sport as major as Rugby League. Teams started to play regular weekday evening fixtures under floodlights, and the B.B.C.'s annual Floodlit Trophy, screened regularly on a midweek evening, kept the game very much in the public eye. To compete further with more powerful Saturday rituals, in December 1967 the first Sunday matches were played in the Rugby League, with encouraging returns from the turnstiles; by the early 1970s, the League had virtually given up the battle for Saturday spectators—frequently the only Saturday game to be played was the one being televised live—the rest would be waiting for two o'clock on Sundays, for the millions to pour out of the Northern clubs and pubs and on to the Rugby League terraces; like American Football, and like French and Australian Rugby League, the British Rugby League has now begun to establish itself as a Sunday spectator sport.

These crowd-wooing attempts of the last ten years or so have not been strokes of desperation. Rugby League has not, since the war, had to stare extinction in the face as it occasionally seemed to in its early years. It has given itself time to look closely at new experiments, and has not been afraid to change or even discard any that did not seem to work—the quick abandonment of the two-divisions plan in the 1960s was one occasion when retreat was both honourable and sensible. But the game has not yet hit the jackpot; perhaps it should be content with what it has achieved in its considerable amateur following as well as on the professional side, trusting in its essential appeal, as a hard, uncompromising game, and not expecting miracles of spectator-attraction from new competitions and administrative changes.

In no country where Rugby League is played is it that country's major winter sport: in Britain and France professional Soccer and Rugby Union have many more adherents; in New Zealand it can never hope to compete with Rugby Union; in Australia, while making the headway in Queensland and New South Wales, it faces increasing competition from Australian Rules Football which already dominates Victoria, South Australia and Western Australia. The game's spirit and energy and adaptability have all enabled it to survive as an alternative to Rugby Union and will ensure that it does not die; but it would need inspired new legislation or a radical change in spectators' attitudes for it to recapture the massive following it commanded in the heady days after the Second World War.

10

outlook changeable

The World Game: the 1970s and beyond

The overriding trend of world football this century has been for the various major branches to drift steadily away from the common roots to which they all trace their origin. But in one or two areas they appear to have taken hints from each other, reacted similarly to problems common to all types of football, and actually drawn closer together in the promotion and conduct of their games.

All the most popular football games have, for example, developed miniature versions of themselves. The increase in leisure through the 20th century has tended paradoxically to make spectators less patient and long-suffering than they were before, and a failure to provide drama at regular intervals is quickly reflected in falling attendances. The long league competition, even the drawn-out knock-out tournament, tends to get less support in its early stages than it might have expected in the past; the final matches, on the other hand, are received with even greater crowds and even greater hysteria. The ideal answer, from the impresario's point of view, is a tournament which can be watched from first stage to final in a single day—and this is the principle by which seven-a-side Rugby and five- or six-a-side Soccer have become so successful.

The six-man American Football, on the other hand, has developed for economic reasons. It was originated in 1934 by the athletics coach at a high school in Nebraska to provide football at schools too small to run an 11-man team and a back-up team of substitute players, which would at the same time carry smaller risk of injury. But its popularity in the depression years owed as much to its financial saving as to anything else, and as a game requiring barely half the equipment of the regulation 11-man game, and only half the number of officials, it was adopted at many schools in the United States and Canada in the 1930s and 1940s.

It is essentially the same game as the parent Football, with a three-man scrimmage line, a quarterback, a half-back and a full-back on each side, and the one significant departure from the regulation rules is that every snap by the offence team must be followed by a forward or a backward pass—no rushing, therefore, is allowed by the quarterback, and no attacks launched by the quarterback handing the ball off, as so often in the full-sized game, to his rushing backs. In the 1950s there were variations using five-man and eight-man formations, but in general the miniature American Football has been a convenient method of giving young boys a taste of the college and professional games rather than as a lure for spectators.

The same would have been true in the early forms of reduced-team Soccer. Outdoor six-a-side or five-a-side Soccer has been played for a long time in schools and youth organisations where full-size teams and full-size pitches have been unavailable; both emerged logically from the parent game, and in the first instances had no variations in the rules apart from the necessity to waive the off-side law. But one of Soccer's qualities not shared by the other football games is its easy adaptability as an indoor game. While the Rugby games and American Football involve a lot of falling about, and Gaelic and Australian need plenty of space for the game to have any meaning at all, it only takes minor adjustments to the rules to make Soccer into an ideal gymnasium game.

The rules for five-a-side indoor football eliminate all kicking above shoulder height (which in turn, of course, cuts out all heading and all spectacular leaping by the goalkeeper). The goalkeeper is alone in a large semi-circle round his goal, and it is an offence for any player on either side to enter it; physical contact—shoulder-charging and the like—is forbidden. The lack of touch-lines means that the walls can be used as extra players to receive and return passes, and the game is a fast-fluctuating, non-stop exchange of touch-passing and sharp-shooting; its seven-minute halves are quite enough to leave the eight outfield players feeling as if they have played squash for half an hour, and scores at the end of a short, quarter-of-an-hour game are usually equivalent to those after a 90-minute, 11-a-side match. Indoor tournaments—with tiers of spectators and the pitch enclosed by a low, waist-high wall—are simple to organise and quickly completed. The London professional clubs have held a five-a-side competition towards the end of the season for the past twenty years, and the opportunity of seeing established Soccer stars playing three or four games in an evening has generally guaranteed a full house.

Rugby, like American Football and Soccer, has devised a scaled-down version for schoolboys, with eleven per team, reducing the size of the pitch, eliminating line-outs and emphasising the game's basics—running, passing and physical contact. But seven-a-side Rugby is the oldest of all these miniature games and, because it tampers only minimally with the laws of Rugby Union, is probably the most effective for both players and spectators. It was invented at Melrose, in the Border counties of Scotland, where the first seven-a-side tournament was held in 1883, only a few years after the foundation of the Rugby Union, and it has always found its keenest performers in the Borders. Sevens spread southwards after the First World War. First Carlisle staged a tournament in 1920, then Percy Park, in Northumberland, in 1921. The most prestigious of them all, having long ago ousted the Melrose Sevens as the year's premier competirtion, is the Middlesex Sevens, held since 1928 at Twickenham with a eputation for capacity crowds, prodigious beer-drinking and, stirring football.

Sevens laws differ from Rugby Union only in the length of the game (seven to ten minutes per half) and in necessary technicalities involving the three-man pack and line-out. But the tactics are very different. Possession of the ball is of paramount importance, for defence of a full-sized Rugby pitch by a seven-man team is very difficult. Tactical kicking, either to touch or into space, is therefore rare; teams in possession tend to hold on to the ball, passing languidly among themselves, always backing up a colleague like basketball players, waiting for a gap to appear in the defensive chain—perhaps through an opponent committing himself too early to a tackle—through which an attack can be launched; once a fast wing threequarter is on his way, there is little that can stop him.

Sevens has become a well-established end of season relaxation for Rugby League football, too, where tournaments are held every year at both Leeds and Wigan. Ever-eager to adopt a good crowd-pulling gimmick to its own use, the Rugby League was running an annual seven-a-side tournament at Bradford's Odsal Stadium in the 1930s (it was generally dominated by Huddersfield, led in those days by A. E. Fiddes, a former Hawick Rugby Union player who had imported all the tricks of Sevens from his days in the Borders).

Seven-a-side Rugby has tended to raise in the traditionalists the same uncharitable feelings that cricket traditionalists reserved for the increasing spate of one-day cricket competitions that arose in the 1960s. But Sevens is a complement to, rather than a substitute for, the regulation Rugby Union or Rugby League game, and once the serious business of the season is over it provides enjoyment for both players and spectators; so far it has met with considerably less enthusiasm abroad than it has in the Home Countries, but the climax to the Scottish Rugby Union's centenary celebrations in 1973—when Sevens teams from England, Scotland, Ireland and Wales, as well as sides composed of New Zealand, Fijian, South African, Australian and French players, contributed to a highly entertaining tournament—could become the model for many similar, equally attractive, events.

The controversy over substitution, a problem that has been faced by all the various football codes this century, is essentially a controversy over professionalism. In a purely amateur game—a game played solely for the fun of playing—substitution is counter-productive; there are few sadder sights on a wet winter Sunday morning than a fully kitted footballer sitting under a blanket in a public park, in the forlorn hope that one of his colleagues is going to get injured. But the alternative is also unsatisfactory: most amateur football is not played solely for fun; it is played with the object of winning points in a league, however humble, or ties in a knock-out tournament, however insignificant. And here the voluntary lack of substitutes might, from time to time, produce ludicrously unjust results. Each football code has rationalised its attitude to substitution in its own characteristic way, but clearly there will be further changes in the laws of many of the games, and the trend at present is towards a freer, rather than a more restricted, use of substitutes.

The game that has stood out longest, predictably, is Rugby Union Football. Rugby, the authorities have argued, is a game for the players themselves, not for the prestige that a club can gain by good results nor the enjoyment that spectators can derive from an evenly matched contest; and to sit players idly on the sidelines with the likelihood that they will not be called upon to replace an injured team-mate would be a denial of this principle. In the late 1960s the International Board somewhat grudgingly made a rule allowing replacements in international matches, or matches involving touring teams, on condition that a doctor was satisfied that the player leaving the field was genuinely injured and had no hope of returning fit to the field. But this still leaves a wide range of important matches liable to be rendered absurd by injury. The first Knock-Out Cup Final in English Rugby, a competition of enormous significance for the future popularity of the game, was plunged into the deepest anti-climax by the fact that Moseley were reduced to twelve men in the final stages of the game (one man sent off, two others injured); the second Knock-Out Cup Final suffered a similar fate in 1973 when Bristol's captain and hooker John Pullin was badly injured early in the game.

On a number of occasions in the past few years injuries have unbalanced that once most prestigious of occasions, the Oxford–Cambridge match at Twickenham. With the principle having been altered for international games, the Rugby Union was soon showing signs of capitulation to more general substitution for injured players, particularly in the increasing number of competitive matches, but nothing was more certain than the stiff opposition such concessions were bound to encounter.

The opposite extreme, of course, is American Football. It may be a cynical view, but the impression is that gridiron football has never really been an amateur game because no one has ever played it for pleasure; they have played it because they are good at it, because they are intensely loyal to the school or college or university or club to which they belong, and they have played it to win. Ever since Walter Camp began tinkering with the rules of Rugby, and certainly ever since it became legal to block or interfere with men other than the one carrying the ball, the injury rate has been high and substitutes patently essential. Old football players writing in, say, the 1930s, would recall with near disbelief that in their youth it had still been necessary to be hurt—or at least to feign injury—to be replaced. But teams had always carried a number of substitutes with them, and soon it became legal to replace players at will.

From the establishment of the Professional Leagues in the 1920s, substitutions became even more widespread. By 1926 a coach could name 18 players for any one game; by 1935 it was 24—more than double the size of a single team; and during the 1940s it fluctuated between 28 and 33. It is now even higher—the forty mark was reached by 1964—largely through the adoption of the free substitution rule in 1949. This was a revolutionary step for football: no longer was a team restricted to 11 men who might be replaced if they were hurt or ineffective, but were theoretically expected to work both on offence and defence; now came the era of the specialist. Men could leave the field and return at the whim of the coach. The two-squad system was developed as two quite separate teams in attack and defence. Specialist kickers would be retained merely to land field goals and extra points after a touchdown—they might be on the field of play no more than three minutes a game, but they were a vital part of the new football set-up. Other special squads would be coached in such specialised suicide missions as kick-off returns—fast, bull-like spearheads recalling the old days of the flying wedge, but more dedicated, trained to a higher exactness of team cohesion, knowing that the injuries received in forcing the ball an extra two yards were all in a good cause, and that there were other kick-return men waiting on the bench if they had not recovered by the next kick-off.

The American substitution system, though it has inevitably been copied in the colleges, can only be suitable for a professional sport; the expense, the degree of specialisation, the long periods of non-involvement can only endure where teams are dedicated to winning and to providing a spectacle, rather than giving an afternoon's exercise to the enthusiastic amateur. For that reason alone any extension of free substitution to other forms of football will be fiercely opposed; but substitution of one sort or another is already an important factor in all the other codes. Gaelic Football has apparently countenanced substitutes right from the formation of the Gaelic Athletic Association—another indication, perhaps, of the violence of the early encounters; one of the earliest copies of the rules drawn up by Maurice Davin and Michael Cusack says that 'Pushing or tripping from behind, holding from behind, or butting with the head shall be deemed foul, and the player so offending shall be ordered to stand aside, and may not afterwards take part in the match, nor can his side substitute another man.' The Gaelic game now allows up to three substitutes at any time in the match, and Australian Football, which has provided for substitution since 1930, counts its 19th and 20th men as such an integral part of the team that whether they step on to the field or not they are regarded, for the purposes of record, as having played.

Despite its breakaway from the Rugby Union and its professional attitude towards the laws of the game, the Rugby League allowed no substitutes until the 1964–5 season, and then stipulated that up to two injured players could be replaced in the first half. A year later, after complaints about abuses to the rule, injuries were no longer necessary to warrant replacement but still the substitution had to be made before the start of the second half. Now they can be made at any time in the match, so that tactical substitution is every bit as common as substitution for injury. And a further step towards free substitution has been introduced by which the man substituted can return to the field once his injury—or the state of the game—permits.

In Soccer, tactical substitution is probably even more frequent. Replacement of injured players came very late; the hangover of amateurism held a powerful influence over the Football Association and its many fellow bodies, and even the frequent, glaring evidence of matches being spoiled by injury had done little to persuade them to relent. In England, there had been a spate of F.A. Cup Finals in which the losing side had been handicapped by injury, either by playing part of the match with men missing, or struggling with a crippled player limping on the wing— Arsenal in 1952, Bolton Wanderers in 1953, Manchester City in 1955, Manchester United in 1957, Blackburn Rovers in 1960, all played on as heroes, but all lost the Cup in what had become unsatisfactory football matches.

As far back as 1908 England had allowed Wales to substitute an injured goalkeeper (injuries in this vital specialist position have always presented the most telling case for substitution) but this was a gentlemanly gesture rather than an earnest of intent, and it was 1970 before the British Home Internationals officially sanctioned substitutes. In friendly, non-competitive internationals substitutes were often allowed after agreement by both national associations, but not until Olympic Games of 1968 and the World Cup of 1970—both held in the heights of Mexico and prone, it was feared, to all sorts of respiratory difficulty—were substitutes allowed for major international competition.

In the British leagues the conservative attitudes did not waver until 1966, when it was agreed to allow one substitute if the referee was satisfied of a genuine injury to the departing player. That part of the rule proved unworkable, and substitution of one player at any time for any reason was soon adopted. In the senior leagues it is clearly a necessary precaution against injury, but the use of substitution for tactical reasons will present considerable problems to football's administrators in the future. In Europe, the mental and physical pressures on footballers are increasing every year with the demands for more matches, more competitions, more events to make better economic use of the stadiums. Already the more successful British clubs are playing between fifty and seventy matches a season, and their managers are obliged to think not of a first team and reserves, but a first team squad of fifteen or sixteen players out of which, each week, he selects an eleven plus a substitute.

For competitive international matches managers now name sixteen players—eleven to start the match, the rest substitutes of which two can actually be used as replacements. It can only be a matter of time before such a system is demanded for club matches (some European and South American club competitions already operate it); it will have the distinct advantage that there is always a substitute goalkeeper on hand, and will thus do away with the frequent and unsatisfactory drama provided by an inexperienced half-back struggling uneasily into a green jersey while the specialist at the job is carried off with concussion. But it will also lead to even greater fire-power for a strategically-minded manager, and the original purpose for substitution—insurance against accidental injury—will be lost in the computations of a team's tactical capability.

The American system of free substitution (which, incidentally, is also an integral part of America's other three major professional team games—baseball, basketball and ice-hockey) may still be a long way from the other football codes, but already specialisation is an important part of Rugby (a good hooker is essential to a team's effectiveness, and even international sides have been known to field place-kickers who had neither the speed nor the skill to merit selection otherwise). It is not inconceivable that League Soccer clubs will one day have a tall high-leaping header of the ball held in reserve and released onto the field only for free kicks and corners; and even sharp-shooting, dead-ball marksmen bred, trained, cossetted and specially booted just to take penalty kicks.

Whether or not any of the other football games, in their increasing popularity and competitiveness, opt for the American style of squad system, their short-term futures as part of a booming entertainment business are not threatened. All the games have room for expansion, either in popularity at home or in the attraction of new interest abroad, and most of the codes can measure a current popularity with healthy returns at the turnstiles.

It is a safe enough prediction that Soccer will remain the world's major spectator sport—certainly for the rest of this century, which it has already made its own, and probably well into the next. Of the world's Soccer-playing nations (at the last count 141 of them were affiliated to FIFA, and there are several others, China being the obvious example, where the game is widespread), the number that can still be described in a footballing sense as underdeveloped is diminishing fast. There was a slow start for Association Football in Asia, despite the fact that Japan had an Association by 1921 and Iran in 1922, but teams from the Far East have already made their impact in the World Cup—notably the explosive North Koreans in 1966 who humiliated the Italians in Middlesbrough and, even more dramatically, caused Portugal's supporters heart-failure in the quarter-finals before being eliminated; and matches in the Asian qualifying group for the World Cup are now no longer the ramshackle affairs they used to be; the prospect of China's possible entry into that football arena some-time in the future, and the inevitable improvement brought by the European immigrants to the industrial towns of Australia, will ensure that competition becomes even stiffer.

In Africa the potential is, if anything, even greater. The astonishing talents discovered in former colonies by France (mainly in the Arab north) and Portugal (in Mozambique and Angola) only hint at what exciting football skill exists unexploited in Black Africa, though the genius of the Negro players welded into Brazilian and Peruvian national teams give some idea of what intensive coaching and sympathetic management might achieve. Egypt and Morocco have both competed, without a great deal of success, in the World Cup Finals and the footballers of Zaire surprisingly qualified for the World Cup Finals of 1974. It cannot be long before a Black African football squad follows the lead of Kenya's athletics team to make a decisive impact on world competition.

Sadly, Africa's most exciting prospect for international football should be South Africa. Just as Brazil's dominance in the world game has been achieved by welding together the varied talents of the Negro and the Portuguese players, so South Africa could hope to blend the African, British and Dutch elements into a powerful unit. Coaching schemes for all racial groups in South Africa have attracted a number of British professionals for some time, and a successful National League (white, of course) has played semi-professional football since the late 1950s.

The intransigence of South Africa's apartheid policies makes the prospect of a multi-racial national team—developed, necessarily, from multi-racial league football—something of a pipe dream, but it is not quite so remote as it might have been ten years ago. The widespread rejection of South Africa by so many international sports bodies, sometimes voluntarily, sometimes by weight of public opinion, has already made the Republic's government waver towards compromise and occasionally to turn a blind eye towards violation of apartheid in sport; and if, in attempting to save their beloved Rugby from total isolation, the government is persuaded to lower some of the barriers to multi-racial sport, the fast-developing footballers can only benefit.

In Europe, the problem for the future would appear to be one of containment rather than expansion. The Soccer season in Britain, as well as in most European nations, is nine months long—and longer in a World Cup year. Yet still the major competitions are over-subscribed, and still there is talk of a super-league—a league of the outstanding European clubs, even of outstanding world clubs. The idea is not new, of course. Gabriel Hanot proposed a form of European League as early as 1934, confirming the French in the position of sport's principal innovators (without ever really excelling at any international team game, the French concern for sport has produced the driving force, often in the face of the most depressing apathy, for the launching of the modern Olympic Games, the World Cup, the European Cup, the Rugby League World Cup and the formation of FIFA).

A European League would have immediate crowd and television potential, but whether it would add much to the present round of European competitions is doubtful. Though the European Cup, Cup-winners Cup and U.E.F.A. Cup are dogged by a two-leg format that virtually guarantees that one match out of every two is going to be a dull, defensive struggle for one team and a battle against mounting frustration in attack for the other, they create great excitement in the latter stages and contribute a lot in the exchange of footballing ideas. The participants are, inevitably, the most successful clubs in the various national leagues, and any candidates for a European League would come from just the same pool of consistently high-placed teams; the case for the European super-league has yet to be made convincing.

The proposals for a World League are even less likely to meet with enthusiasm. The one current international football competition that can be counted an unmitigated failure is the grandiose-titled World Club Championship, a single home-and-away tie, first played in 1960, between the winner of the European Cup and the winner of the Copa de los Libertadores, the South American cup. The reputation for on-the-field violence in these matches is all too justified. Both Celtic and Manchester United, the only British team to have qualified, were involved in the ugliest of brawls in the South American leg of their matches; and from the two subsequent finals, both involving the Argentinian champions, Estudiantes de la Plata, their European opponents, A.C. Milan and Feyenoord of Rotterdam both returned home with badly injured players. The following year, Feyenoord's successors as European champions, Ajax of Amsterdam, refused to contest the World Club Championship, thus depriving it of such little prestige as it still held.

The conduct of players on the field is a continuing problem for Soccer in all parts of the world—not merely in the sort of clashes that make regular competition between European and South American players such an unappetising prospect. For a long time it was the habit of British footballers and British journalists to despise their overseas opponents merely for their different attitudes to the physical contact necessary in the game. The British, it was felt, were direct and fair; the Europeans played fancy football but lay down and cried when dispossessed by a hard, challenging tackle. The British, on the other hand, were infuriated by the body-checking and obstruction that seemed to their opponents a natural part of the defensive repertoire, while the Europeans would roar at the referee in disbelief should a Briton disturb the sanctity of the opposing goalkeeper with a (perfectly legal) shoulder charge.

The attitudes persist, and a long history of unsatisfactory international refereeing has done little to ease the mistrust on both sides. The South American tactics have added a third, almost incomprehensible, dimension —a policy of petty intimidation to destroy the composure of opponents. European teams in World Club Championships have been subjected to spitting, hair-pulling, painful elbow-jabs and shin-kicks which inflame rather than maim and, once self-control is lost, result in the sort of mayhem seen at the Racing Club v. Celtic tie when four Scotsmen and two Argentinians were sent off in the same game.

Soccer, like Rugby, is a physical contact sport with some specific rules and, more important, a whole Geneva Convention of its own about what is the done thing and what is not. Without in any way breaking the laws, Rugby and Soccer players are entitled to get away with, as P. G. Wodehouse has put it, 'a certain amount of assault and battery . . . which, if done elsewhere, would result in fourteen days without the option, coupled with some strong remarks from the bench'. But once the assault and battery goes beyond legitimate attack and defence, and becomes a cold, pragmatic method of softening up an opponent, when the criterion is not what has to be done to win the ball but how much one can get away with while winning it, both games must look to their future reputations. It is easy to punch another man in a set scrimmage without the referee seeing; it is almost as easy to knee the goalkeeper in the groin in a goalmouth scramble and avoid detection. The tragedy of both games is that, with the spread of competition, money and win-at-all-costs attitudes, some players have come to accept these methods as standard behaviour.

To counter them, it may well be necessary to increase the refereeing strength in both Soccer and Rugby. Soccer has already experimented tentatively with two referees per match, and the linesmen have considerable powers of intervention in cases of foul play. The Rugby referee, however, has had an increasingly unenviable job, particularly as his touch judges have no jurisdiction over what happens on the field of play. The laws of the game are extremely complex and, in many cases, their interpretation is left to the discretion of the overworked referee; bending these rules to their limit, while quite at variance with the spirit of the game, will inevitably accompany the present competitive attitudes. (Running interference on the American pattern, for example, has always been a non-starter in Rugby because the offside law prohibits anyone in front of the ball taking part in the play; however, a subtle form of running interference has been introduced almost unnoticed into the game by a variation of the dummy scissors movement between, say, scrum-half and fly-half, by which the dummy runs *in front of* the scrum-half instead of behind him, thus momentarily shielding him from the advancing defenders.) Firm control of Rugby did much to preserve its best qualities in the early days, but it will need more than a single referee required to look in three directions at once to eliminate all such pieces of rule-bending from the modern game.

In the other football games there is less danger of abuse. All are very hard and very fast, and have been characterised from the start by physical contact, which, by some quirk of human nature, has made them less prone to petty ill-temper and calculated niggling. American Football, where the action at the snap is so fast and unpredictable and where the laws are again so complex, has taken the opposite extreme from Rugby and saturated the field with officials each watching a separate aspect of play—a system which may cause overcrowding but which undoubtedly works.

In Australia and Ireland, and in the Rugby League game too, there is rarely lasting trouble between players and the rules are so liberal on the question of physical contact that petty abuses become irrelevant. Outbursts of temper are both understandable and inevitable, but they rarely cause concern unless, as in the Rugby League World Cup Final between Britain and Australia at Leeds in 1970, two teams start slugging out their frustrations in front of the television cameras; in which case it takes some soothing words from the authorities and some righteous comment on the sports pages before the matter is allowed to be forgotten.

'The face that the game presents to the public is determined by the conduct of the players, spectators and officials', writes the former County Down Gaelic Football captain, Joe Lennon, in his *Coaching Manual*. 'The mood of this face changes as regularly as the mood of any one of these three groups. In a moment it is artistic, thrilling and magnetic. A moment later it can show a very different face—the face of the Gael in anger, which, we must admit, is not very pleasant to behold.' Nor the face of the Yorkshire Rugby League player in anger, nor the Australian Footballer in anger; but anger is one thing, calculated cheating another, and the more violent games have been successful in keeping a check on the former (so successfully that Australian Football has never felt the need for an umpire to have sending-off powers) and virtually eliminating the latter.

After a number of unhappy years of uncertainty, Rugby Union appears to be entering another era of prosperity. The new laws limiting kicking to touch have added to the status of the runners and passers, and the new emphasis in the Home Countries on coaching and squad training, have gone a long way to closing the quality gap between British Rugby and that of New Zealand and South Africa. There is obvious room for expansion for the game throughout the world, and the list of hitherto 'minor' Rugby nations itching for an opportunity to tour in the British Isles and France is matched only by the number eager to welcome British touring teams to their pitches abroad. Australia, heavily outnumbered by adherents to Rugby League, Soccer and Australian Football, is still producing creditable Rugby Union teams, including a state team from Queensland good enough to beat the Lions touring party that was about to ride roughshod over the pride of New Zealand Rugby. But with increasing talk of a Rugby Union World Cup, the established nations will soon have to get used to the idea of playing international matches with such hitherto unconsidered nations as Argentina, Japan, Canada, and Romania—eventually, one would imagine, under a world body more representative than the present International Board. As with Soccer, the future of the game in South Africa rests in the hands of the Government and its future interpretation of its apartheid policy.

At the same time, the Home Unions will inevitably find difficulty in maintaining their aggressively amateur stand. Already many of the oldest values have been eroded, and regular competition is standard throughout the British Isles, though in many cases the Unions wash their hands of such tournaments by regarding them as 'unofficial'. The Unions have recently been considering commercial sponsorship of matches, tours, and so forth; the question of players' meagre expenses on overseas touring parties has never been satisfactorily tackled. Demands on the so-called amateur players in a Rugby season are enormous: travel, training, international and representative calls interfering with club programmes, coaching at club level—the more accomplished a senior Rugby player, the more of his life he is expected to give to the game. With the large contracts paid by television into the game, and the ever-increasing crowds at major matches, Rugby has become a dedicated professional sport in which the principal attractions, the players, are not paid.

The fact that the very best players are attracted to a handful of senior clubs (who willingly pay expenses to attract the players vast distances every weekend) is only another manifestation of the game's professional outlook in Britain, and apart from breaking with dearly held tradition the game itself would be affected very little by a system which paid the players for their entertainment value. The one main difference would be that the game was better: there would be more time for practice, particularly for teams selected for representative matches; improved coaching in schools and clubs would do the game immeasurable good; and, quite conceivably, increased promotion of the game leading to bigger crowds and greater receipts would indirectly benefit the smaller clubs unwilling to pay their players.

Professional Rugby Union would, of course, put an added strain on Rugby League. One vital benefit to the Union clubs would be an almost complete end to the slow drift of talented amateurs to Yorkshire and Lancashire seeking reward for their talents, and without them Rugby League would lose an important ingredient from its present blend of hardness, determination and flair. The other side to the argument, that more players would be willing to have a go at Rugby League if they knew they were not thereby automatically barred from the Union, may have some weight, but there are not many players brought up in Rugby Union in Britain or France who have changed codes because they prefer the thirteen-a-side game—the financial lure has merely proved stronger than their instinctive loyalties to the game they were taught in their youth.

In 1972 a team of consultants retained by the Rugby League looked pessimistically at the falling club gates—down by a half between 1961 and 1971, a fall of well over a million spectators per season—and predicted the death of the game by the late 1970s unless drastic steps were taken with the organisation. In some cases high-powered businessmen have adopted the ailing finances of the clubs (expenditure of some £400,000 on a sports complex at Warrington Rugby League Club in the early 1970s was showing encouraging returns at the turnstiles within two years), but only a few of the more attractive clubs can expect this. The latter stages of each cup tournament are reasonably well attended, though the proliferation of competitions all involving the same few clubs seems to have encountered the law of diminishing returns, and the habit of playing matches on Friday evening or Sunday afternoon, to counter the attractions of League Soccer, has met with only moderate success.

However, Rugby League's ability to escape imminent disaster has been demonstrated before, and their enterprise has repeatedly put that of the home Rugby Unions to shame. It could be that while Rugby Union reluctantly faces the approach of professionalism, Rugby League will be looking towards a healthy amateur involvement in what should not be automatically regarded as a professional game. Several universities are infuriating the more traditional Rugby Union clubs by producing equally keen Rugby League teams; there is a flourishing amateur Rugby League competition in London and the Home Counties, well away from the League's traditional home, and attracting more than just Northern exiles to make up the teams. Whether the game will make any further progress abroad, however, is doubtful. Failure in Italy and South Africa, polite but fast-waning interest in the 1950s from one or two American Football teams, are not encouraging to further experiments.

The future health of Rugby League, both here and abroad, depends very much on the attitude of the Rugby Union. If the amateur game remains doggedly and unequivocally amateur, the professional game could spread even further, with increased support from frustrated Union men in search of a living. But if, as seems probable, the Rugby Union comes to some sort of compromise with professionalism, half Rugby League's *raison d'être* will have gone. The other half, a vibrant, hard, spectacular game demanding courage, speed and resilience from its players, will take a lot of killing, but with one of its traditional sources of players dried up, and with an increasing lack of support from the Northern working man, it could not prosper for long outside its traditional stronghold.

The prospects for Gaelic Football, on the other hand, must have improved vastly by the Gaelic Athletic Association's removal of the Ban on foreign games in 1971. At a time when no game can afford to be introspective, it has at last opened its doors to all Irish sportsmen as opposed to those few willing to isolate themselves in nationalistic purdah, rejecting other men's games as inferior and the people who played them as heretics. Gaelic Football, whatever the attitude of the G.A.A. may have been in the past, is not an age-old rite bedded in the mists of Ancient Irish history; it is the descendant, much tampered with, of the same sort of uninhibited village brawls that fathered Rugby Union and American Football and Soccer. As such it is a very good game that has weathered well through the doctrinal quarrels of its founders, and may well attract much of its future talent from Irishmen previously put off by the game's political exclusiveness.

Working alongside Rugby Union and Soccer, it is possible that Gaelic Football's intrinsic excitement may capture the urban Irish in the same way that Australian Football has won new fans from traditional Rugby strongholds; if it could achieve that, and at the same time make further progress among Irish communities abroad with the intensification of its already popular tours, it could begin to win important converts in places that up to now have never heard the word 'Gaelic'.

Its recent links with Australian Football could also have some significance for the future of both games—players and spectators in both camps would relish the chance of international competition and a series of, say, Gaelic Football test matches in Ireland and matches under Australian Rules in Melbourne and Perth would add a dimension to both games that neither could have dreamed of ten years ago. But whatever the possible outcome (and for there to be any sort of contest the G.A.A. would have to swallow its pride and sanction some form of part-time professionalism for players), it is clear that Australian Football is in no way dependent on outside help at present. There are considerable difficulties to expanding the game outside Australia and its immediate sphere of influence; the size of ground required is quite alien to any but the cricket-playing nations (baseball parks could conceivably be used, Gaelic Football grounds would be very restricting), but that is a minor consideration compared with the very nature of the game itself, which might well prove too much of an acquired taste for people less tolerant than the English-speaking nations of other people's pastimes.

Australian Football has one great psychological difference from all the other football codes—its great climaxes are not provided by the act of scoring. In Soccer and in Gaelic Football, the be-all and end-all of the game is the ball entering the goal-net; in the Rugby games, in American and Canadian Football, it is the touchdown or the try, the triumphant dash for the line. In Australian Football, just occasionally, an amazing goal from sixty yards might bring a crowd to its feet, but in general the great moments of drama are provided by the tremendous leaps to make a mark, the 'screamers' taken at impossible heights against impossible odds; once a mark is made within, say, forty yards of the target, the catcher gets his free kick, and a goal or a behind is almost inevitable, almost an anti-climax. Scores are very high, goals and points easy to come by; they are not exciting in themselves. It is not hard to appreciate the supreme skills of the full-forwards nor to roar with the crowd at their feats, but watching Australian Football requires a readjustment to the normal reactions of a football spectator, and potential audiences for Australian Football in Europe or Asia might not be willing to make that effort just to appreciate a strange new game.

However, fears that the game might be submerged in a tide of Soccer-playing migrants now seem absurdly alarmist. It still maintains a reasonably good-natured rivalry with the Rugby codes in New South Wales and Queensland (Rugby men call Australian Football 'aerial ping-pong'; Australian Rules men call Rugby—both codes—'open air wrestling'), and neither expects to concede much ground to the other; but if the pessimists are right, that even with its heritage of sporting fanaticism Australia and its tiny population are not able to support four flourishing football codes, it will not be Australian Football that goes to the wall—any game that can provoke an active Anti-Football Campaign dedicated to persuading the citizens of Melbourne that they are spending too much time, energy and emotion on Australian Rules Football, must be in a very buoyant condition.

Which leaves only American Football and its Canadian half-brother. It is strange to realise that the professional game, now as firmly established on America's autumn scene as election campaigns and Thanksgiving, was barely viable twenty-five years ago and was played in front of crowds that would make English second division Soccer teams blush for shame. It has swelled not as an afternoon sport but as a successful branch of show business. Even the 'amateur' game, in the universities and colleges, is played with the razzmatazz, the big squads and the all-demanding dedication of the pro game which so many college players see as their logical employer after graduation.

It will never be a social pastime for ageing romantics with footballing fantasies, nor for executives trying to keep in trim during their spare time, nor even for the fit and keen, thirty-year-old who was 'quite good at college, trying to keep in touch with the game in one of the lower teams'. It no longer has the aura of manly character-building that it once claimed, the kind that caused Dwight Eisenhower to say, and doubtless thousands of other Americans to nod in approval, that 'football develops a great leadership and a great team spirit. I liked it and I often have said that I cannot recall during World War II of ever having to relieve an ex-football player for lack of aggressive leadership, in whatever level of command.'

It is now, apart from anything else, an extremely expensive game to play; enormous squads serviced by teams of coaches, medical staff, trainers, etc.; long distances to travel, even to the nearest away fixture; elaborate uniforms (the full protective and decorative rig-out for a typical pro lineman costs in the region of £120). And the fact that this talent is used for only a dozen or so games spanning only three or four months of the year means that a lot of valuable property is lying idle and unproductive for long periods at a time, while there is every reason to suppose that fans would welcome a longer season.

Expansion of American Football—despite a cheeky remark from a Russian official that the game might be used in training Soviet ice-hockey players—will probably be seen only in America. There is plenty of room for it, and it should not be difficult to translate the present spectator boom into bigger leagues, more professional teams, more top-class stadiums within reach of more fans. Meanwhile, the gigantic television contracts signed with the National Football League and the new World Football League by the major networks should ensure that the professional game is kept in touch with its fanatical public, and guarantee its continued reign as America's chief autumn preoccupation.

The only obvious danger to the overwhelming popularity of football—in whatever guise—throughout the world is that the vital part played by television over the last twenty years or so might eventually backfire. Football's excitement increases in direct proportion to the excitement of the crowds watching it; a clumsy, nervous Cup Final bayed at by 100,000 partisan fans will always be more exciting than the most skilfully accomplished football played in a half-empty stadium. This excitement can, of course, be transmitted by television to the twenty million viewers at home—but only so long as the 100,000 fans do not themselves decide that they could also share the excitement at home.

The tremendous upsurge in football of all codes—particularly among young boys and girls who twenty-five years ago would probably never have seen a football match of quality—is due almost entirely to television; but at the first sign of a drop in attendance figures, every football code—

Rugby League and Rugby Union, Gaelic and Australian, American and Association—will forget their dependence on the television contract fees and begin (indeed, have already begun in some cases) to begrudge at first live coverage of the games, and later even recordings of them.

It is then that football's future will be decided, for no matter how popular the games are now, and no matter how healthy their communal future appears to be, without television to provide the unrelenting service of preview, commentary, recording, analysis, discussion and back to the next preview, football will lose the popular loyalty which, in a comparatively affluent, mobile and leisure-conscious society, is more fickle than ever before.

If television time is reduced, interest among the young will decline, and the stadium terraces, far from picking up the followers that television has let down, will find themselves with too little appeal even for their traditional supporters. It is a danger that football faced from the moment it enlisted—again in its various world-wide forms—the potent help of television in proclaiming its excitement to whole populations of new enthusiasts. Football would have made dull progress through the 1950s and 1960s without television, and television would have lost the confidence of half the world if it had reflected life for twenty-five years without its full share of football. It may yet prove that the world isn't big enough for both of them—certainly not for both of them on their present scale.

Even if football should be the loser—and there can be no full-time score until well into the next century—it will not fade away. Football is both a sport for spectators and a sport for participants; when crowds began watching it a hundred years ago, they were watching enthusiastic participants who played because they wanted to and because they had invented and developed a game—in one form or another—that other people wanted to play as much as they did. If people paid money to watch them they were gratified, but they would have played just as readily in a public park with no spectators at all.

If, in a hundred years' time, the spectators have all moved on, and television and its electronic descendants have harnessed other crazes and other religions to their bandwagons, the players will still be there—the kickers and catchers, dribblers and passers, runners and tacklers. People will still want to play some sort of football, just as for the last two thousand years someone, somewhere, has always wanted to play football. Whether or not anyone wants to watch will be irrelevant.

bibliography

Andrew, Bruce, *Australian FootballHandbook* (Australian Football Council)
Arlott, John, *Concerning Soccer* (Longmans, Green, 1952)
The Book of Football part-publication (Marshall Cavendish)
Cottrell, John, *A Century of Great Soccer Drama* (Hart-Davis, 1970)
Danzig, Allison, *Oh, How They Played the Game* (Macmillan, New York, 1971)
Davies, W. J. A., *Rugby Football* (Webster, 1924)
Lord Desborough of Taplow, *Fifty Years of Sport* (Walter Southerwood, 1913)
Frewin, Leslie (ed.), *The Saturday Men* (Frewin, 1967)
G.A.A. Annual (Gaelic Athletic Association)
The Game part-publication (Marshall Cavendish)
Gaulton, A. N., *The Encyclopaedia of Rugby League* (Hale, 1968)
Glanville, Brian, *History of the World Cup* (Times Newspapers, 1973)
    Soccer, A Panorama (Eyre & Spottiswoode, 1969)
Green, Geoffrey, *The History of the Football Association* (Football Association/
    Naldrett Press, 1953)
James, Brian, *England v. Scotland* (Pelham Books, 1969)
Lennon, Joe, *Coaching Gaelic Football for Champions* (Lennon, Co. Down, 1964)
Macdonald, John, *Britain versus Europe* (Pelham Books, 1968)
Macklin, Keith, *History of Rugby League Football* (Stanley Paul, 1962)
Marples, Morris, *A History of Football* (Secker & Warburg, 1954)
Meggyesy, Dave, *Out of Their League* (Paperback Library, New York, 1971)
Michael, Paul, *Professional Football's Greatest Games* (Prentice-Hall, New
    Jersey, 1969)
National Football League, *The First Fifty Years* (Ridge Press/Benjamin, New
    York, 1969)
Pawson, Tony, *100 Years of the F.A. Cup* (Heinemann/Pan Books, 1972)
Pelmear, Kenneth (ed.), *Rugby Football, An Anthology* (Allen & Unwin, 1958)
Plimpton, George, *Paper Lion* (Deutsch, 1968)
Purnell's Encyclopaedia of Association Football (Purnell, 1972)
Rafferty, John, *One Hundred Years of Scottish Football* (Pan Books, 1973)
Rathet, Mike, *Pro Football* (Henry Regnery, Chicago, 1972)
Report of the Commission of the G.A.A. (Gaelic Athletic Association, Dublin,
    1971)
Reyburn, Wallace, *A History of Rugby* (Arthur Barker, 1971)
Rothman's Football Yearbook
Rothman's Rugby Yearbook
Sewell, E. H. D., *Rugger: The Man's Game* (Hollis & Carter, 1950)
Shearman, Montague, *Athletics and Football* (Badminton Library, 1889)
Signy, Dennis, *A Pictorial History of Soccer* (Hamlyn, 1968)

Sixty Glorious Years (Gaelic Athletic Association, Dublin, 1946)

Smith, Raymond, *The Football Immortals* (Creative Press, Dublin, 1971)

Smith, Robert, *Illustrated History of Pro Football* (Madison Square Press, New York, 1970)

The Sports Illustrated Book of Football (Lippincott, New York, 1960)

Titley, U. A. and McWhirter, Ross, *Centenary History of the Rugby Football Union* (R.F.U., 1970)

Treat, Roger, *The Official Encyclopaedia of Football* (A. S. Barnes, New York, 10th, revised, edition, 1972)

Young, Percy M., *A History of British Football* (Stanley Paul, 1968)

The extract from *Days without Sunset* by Denzil Batchelor is reproduced by permission of Eyre and Spottiswoode.

appendix

The following pages contain a few basic details about the essential elements of the six major varieties of football. Measurements shown on the diagrams are in each case the maximum allowed in the laws of the game.

American Pro Football

Ball Elliptical   *Teams* Eleven per side
Substitution Virtually unlimited; any number of players on either side may be replaced after every play. Squads may number as many as forty per team
Scoring Touchdown, crossing the opponents' goal line with the ball, or catching a forward pass in the opponents' end-zone—six points

Extra point, conversion of touchdown from a snap on the two-yard line in front of the goalposts—one point

Field goal, kicked at any time from a snap by the team in possession—three points

Safety, causing the ball to go dead behind your own goal-line—two points to your opponents
Duration of game One hour of actual playing time, in four quarters of fifteen minutes each. Teams change ends after each quarter, and leave the field at half-time
Officials Referee, umpire, linesman (plus assistants), field judge, back judge

American College Football

Rules differ from Pro Football in a number of details:
Field The goal is wider—two posts 23 ft 4 ins apart with a crossbar 10 ft from the ground
Substitution Many major colleges have the facilities to support unlimited substitutions, but squads tend to be smaller and emphasis on specialisation less extreme
Scoring After a touchdown, as an alternative to the kicked 'extra point', college teams can attempt to run the ball across their opponents' line from a 3-yard snap. This is worth two points
Goal (Professional) Posts 18 ft 6 ins apart extending from crossbar 10 ft high. Crossbar supported by a single post set 6 ft behind the line
Goal (College) Tall posts 23 ft 4 ins apart, set on end line; crossbar 10 ft high

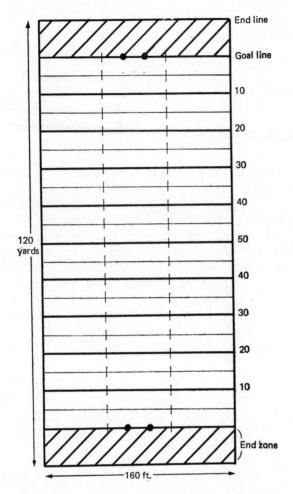

End line

Goal line

10

20

30

40

50

40

30

20

10

End zone

120 yards

160 ft.

Up to the end of the 1973 season the Pro Football goal stood on the Goal line. As part of a radical set of rule changes in the summer of 1974, the National Football League moved it back 10 yards to stand, like the College goal, on the End line.

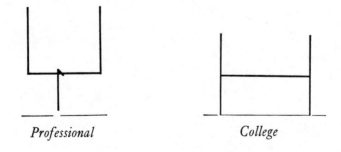

Professional   *College*

Association Football

Ball Spherical   *Teams* Eleven per side

Substitution Varies in different countries and for different types of competition. Usual allowance is one or two nominated substitutes per team, who may be used at any time of the match for any reason, with the permission of the referee. Any player who is replaced may not return. In some competitions, five substitutes per team may be nominated, of which two may be used

Scoring A goal equals one point. In certain knock-out competitions, to break a deadlock, a result may be achieved by staging a succession of penalty kicks. Occasionally, for the same reason, goals scored by a visiting team outweigh an equal number scored by a home team

Duration of game Ninety minutes, in two halves of forty-five minutes each. The teams change ends at half-time when, in senior football, they may leave the field for up to ten minutes. Time may be added by the referee to each half to make up any lost through injury, etc.

Officials Referee, two linesmen

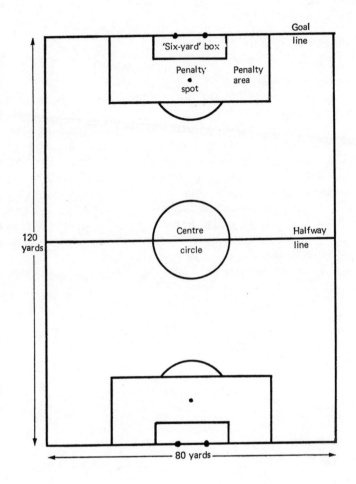

Goal Posts 8 ft high supporting a crossbar 8 yards across; net below crossbar and between posts

Australian Football

Ball Elliptical   *Teams* Eighteen per side

Substitution Two nominated substitutes—19th and 20th men—per team. They may be used at any time during the game. A player who is replaced may not return to the field

Scoring Goal, kicked between the two centre posts (goal posts) without touching the posts or a defending player on the way—six points

Behind, kicked over the line between the goalposts and the side posts (behind posts), or kicked over any part of the goal line by way of a defending player or a goal post—one point

Duration of game One hundred minutes, in four quarters of 25 minutes each. The teams change ends after each quarter, leave the field at half-time, and may take a break of up to five minutes, without leaving the field, between the third and fourth quarters

Officials Field umpire, two boundary umpires, two goal umpires

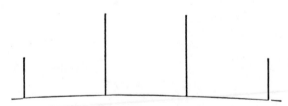

Goal Two posts at least 20 ft high, 7 yards apart (goal posts); flanking these, 7 yards from each, a post at least 10 ft high (behind posts)

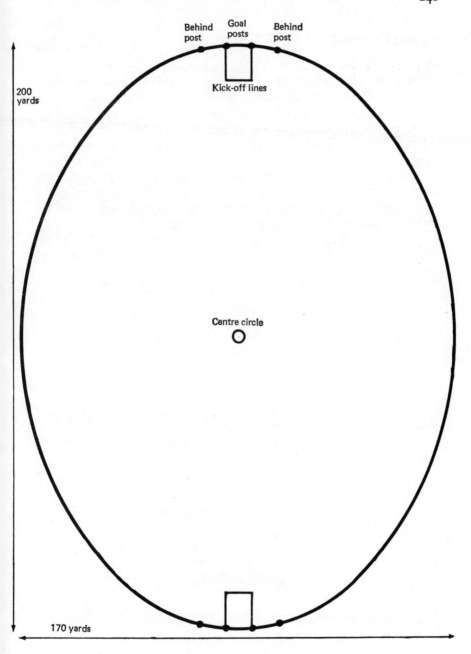

Behind post   Goal posts   Behind post

Kick-off lines

200 yards

Centre circle

170 yards

Gaelic Football

Ball Spherical   *Teams* Fifteen per side
Substitution In case of injury, three men per team may be replaced by substitutes. Once replaced they may not return to the field
Scoring Goal, kicked or fisted between the goal posts and under the crossbar—three points

Point, kicked or fisted between the goal posts above the crossbar—one point
Duration of game In most cases sixty minutes in two halves of thirty minutes each. The teams change ends at half-time. In the later stages of certain major competitions, two forty-minute halves are played
Officials Referee, two linesmen, four goal judges

Goal Tall posts 7 yards apart; crossbar 8 ft high. Net below crossbar and between posts

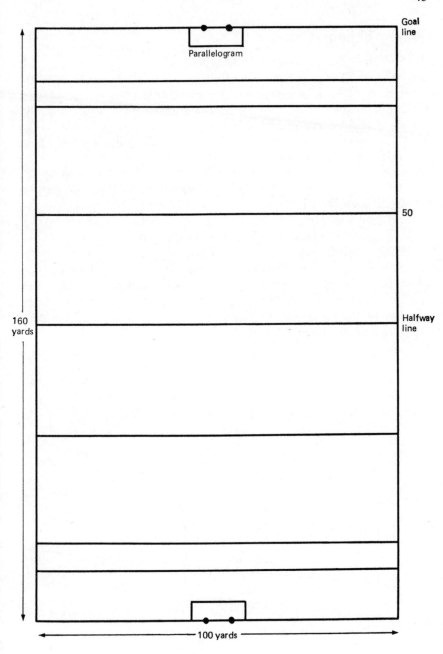

Goal
line

Parallelogram

50

Halfway
line

160
yards

100 yards

Rugby Union

Ball Elliptical   *Teams* Fifteen per side
Substitution Varies in different countries. In matches involving international or regional representation, up to two replacements are allowed from five nominated reserves *provided that* a doctor is satisfied that the substituted player is unfit to continue with the game. In Britain substitution has been prohibited in club and county matches, but a relaxation in the rules seems likely soon
Scoring
  Try, grounding the ball with the hand behind the opponents' goal line
  —four points
  Conversion of a try, by place-kicking a goal—two points
  Drop goal, drop-kicked from open play—three points
  Penalty goal, from place-kick—three points
Duration of game Eighty minutes, in two halves of forty minutes each. The teams change ends at half-time, which is no more than a token break and for which the teams do not leave the field. The referee may add on time for stoppages or time-wasting
Officials Referee, two touch judges

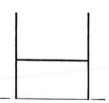

Goal Tall posts 18 ft 6 ins apart; crossbar 10 ft high

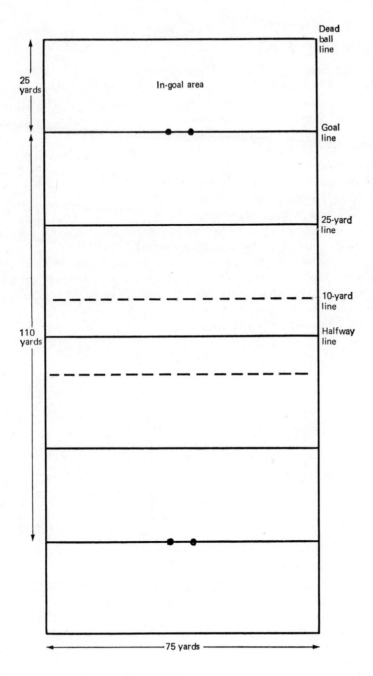

Rugby League

Ball Elliptical   *Teams* Thirteen per side

Substitution In professional games in Britain any two players may be substituted at any time during the game. An injured player who has been substituted may return to the field, but he cannot thereafter be substituted again. Rules vary in different countries

Scoring Varies in detail from country to country. In Britain:

Try—three points

Conversion of a try—two points

Drop goal—two points

Penalty goal—two points

(In certain matches against overseas opposition the drop goal has been reduced in value, by agreement, to one point)

Duration of game Eighty minutes, in two halves of forty minutes each. The teams change ends at half-time, when they leave the field for up to ten minutes. The referee may add on time lost through stoppages for injury, etc.

Officials Referee, two touch judges

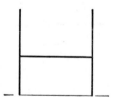

Goal Tall posts 18 ft 6 ins apart; crossbar 10 ft high

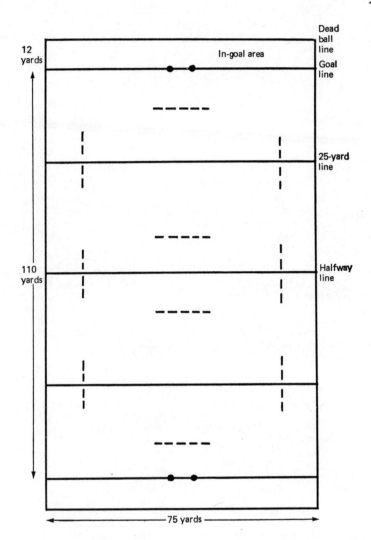

12 yards

In-goal area

Dead ball line

Goal line

25-yard line

110 yards

Halfway line

75 yards

index

The initials F.C. after a name denote an Association Football Club; R.L.F.C. denotes Rugby League Football Club, and R.U.F.C. Rugby Union Football Club. Australian Football clubs are named in full, and Gaelic Football teams are listed under their respective county or province. American and Canadian Football teams almost invariably qualify the name of the club's home city with a distinctive team name, e.g. Massillon Tigers, Chicago Bears. Figures in italics denote illustrations.

Irish Football Association, 41, 78
Irish F.A. Challenge Cup, 78
Irish Rugby Union, 78
Italy, international Rugby Union, 208;
 international Soccer, 109, 117, 119–
 120, 121, 124, 223, *Pl. 35, Pl. 37*;
 Rugby League, 210, 213

Jack, David, 115
James, Alex, 115, *Pl. 38*
James, Carwyn, xiii, 205
James, David and Evan, 152
Japan, international Rugby Union,
 207–8, 209, 227, *Pl. 55*
Japanese Football Association, 223
Jeanette American Football club,
 Pennsylvania, 166
Jessop, Gilbert, 138
John, Barry, xv, 205
Johnson, Alex, 115
Jones, Lewis, 204, *Pl. 22*
Joyce, James, 79
Juventus F.C. *see* Turin

Karalius, Vince, 213
Kelleher, Kevin, 142
Kennedy, Walter, 76
Kennington Oval, London, 25, 26, 31,
 34, 37–8
Kerry, Gaelic Football, xiii, 78, 83–4,
 85, 90, 93, 94, 95, 100, *Pl. 26, Pl. 49*
Kershaw, C. A., 141
Kettering F.C., 21
Kilburn No Names F.C., 16
Kildare, Gaelic Football, 83–4, 94
Kilmarnock F.C., 30
Kinnaird, Hon. Arthur Fitzgerald (later
 Lord), 23, 25, 26, 28, 30, 32, 34, 108
Kocsis, Sandor, 126
Kubala, Ladislao, 187
Kyle, Jack, 201

Lafayette College, Pennsylvania, 167
Lambeau, Earl 'Curly', 171–2
Lambert, Jack, 115
Lancashire Football Association, 33
Laois, Gaelic Football, *Pl. 26*
Larard, Alf, 137
Latin Cup, 181
Latrobe American Football club,
 Pennsylvania, 166, 167
Law, Denis, 185
Lawton, Tommy, 123, 124, 185
Layden, Elmer, 161–2
Lee, Dick, *Pl. 17*
Leeds R.L.F.C., 218
Leeds City F.C., 113
Leeds United F.C., 15, 30, 184, 186,
 196, *Pl. 58, Pl. 59*
Lehigh University, Pennsylvania, 69

Leinster, Gaelic Football province, 83,
 94, 95
Lennon, Joe, 227
Liddell, Billy, 125
Lillywhite, John, 19
Lindsay, G. C., 51
Liverpool F.C., xiii, xv, 117, 186
Liverpool City R.L.F.C., 136
Llandovery School, 46
Llanelli R.U.F.C., xiii, 46, *Pl. 22*
Locomatavia R.U.F.C., Bucharest, 208
Lombardi, Vince, xiii, 195
London Highfield R.L.F.C., 148
London-Irish, Gaelic Football, 83
Loretto School, 44, 50, 51
Los Angeles Rams, 190, 191, 193
Los Angeles Tigers, *Pl. 44*
Louth, Gaelic Football, 84, 85
Love, James, 32
Luckman, Sid, 179, *Pl. 47*
Lynch, Jack, 101

McCracken, Bill, 112, 113
McGill University, Montreal, 62, 197
McGregor, William, 36–7
McIntyre, Hugh, 32
Maclagan, W. E., 56
McLaughlin, J. H., 40
Mack, Connie, 167
Mackay, Dave, *Pl. 59*
McNeil, Harry, 29
Madden, John, 117
Madrid: Atletico F.C., 185; Real F.C.,
 182, 183
Magarey Medal, 91
Maidenhead F.C., 27
Malvern College, 9, 50, 51
Manchester City F.C., 104, 184, 186,
 188, 221, *Pl. 38, Pl. 41*
Manchester United F.C., 104–5, 108,
 117, 127, 183, 184, 186, 221, 225
Manningham R.L.F.C., 131
Mannion, Wilf, 124, 185
Marindin, Major Francis, 24, 29, 39
Marlborough College, 9, 50, 51
Marylebone Cricket Club, 34, 55
Massillon Tigers, 166, 167, 168, 170
Matthews, (Sir) Stanley, 2, 124, 126,
 184, *Pl. 56*
Maxwell, Bob, 155
Maynard, Don, xv, 195
Mayo, Gaelic Football, 99
Meads, Colin, 142
Mears, H. A., 104
Meath, Gaelic Football, 99, 100, *Pl. 27*
Meisl, Hugo, 109, 118, 119, 122
Melbourne Cricket Ground, 90, 97,
 Pl. 8c, Pl. 9, Pl. 51, Pl. 52, Pl. 53
Melbourne Grammar School, 87–8
Melrose R.U.F.C., 218